TEACHING
in the LIFE *of the*
CHURCH

A Multiple Case Study of Nonformal
Christian Education in Cambodia

DARIN R. CLEMENTS

Book 10 of the APTS Press Monograph Series

WIPF & STOCK · Eugene, Oregon

TEACHING IN THE LIFE OF THE CHURCH
A Multiple Case Study of Nonformal Christian Education in Cambodia

Copyright © 2024 Asia Pacific Theological Seminary Press /
Darin R. Clements

No part of this book is to be reproduced, stored in retrieval systems or transmitted in any form or by any means—electronic, mechanical, photocopy, recording, or otherwise without the permission of the publisher except for brief quotations in printed reviews.

Published in the Philippines by

Asia Pacific Theological Seminary Press
444 Ambuklao Rd
2600 Baguio City
www.apts.edu
aptspress@apts.edu

Wipf and Stock Publishers
199 W 8th Ave, Suite 3
Eugene, OR 97401

Teaching in the Life of the Church
A Multiple Case Study of Nonformal Christian Education in Cambodia
By Clements, Darin R.
Copyright © 2024 APTS Press All rights reserved.
Softcover ISBN-13: 979-8-3852-3036-5
Hardcover ISBN-13: 979-8-3852-3037-2
eBook ISBN-13: 979-8-3852-3038-9
Publication date 8/9/2024
Previously published by APTS Press, 2024

TABLE OF CONTENTS

Chapter 1   1
Introduction to the Research

Chapter 2   23
Literature Review and Conceptual Framework: Educational Contexts of Non-Formal Christian Education

Chapter 3   43
Literature Review and Conceptual Framework: External and Internal Roles of Non-Formal CE

Chapter 4   63
Literature Review and Conceptual Framework: Organizational Approaches of Non-Formal CE and Teachers of Non-Formal CE

Chapter 5   83
Research Methodology

Chapter 6   107
Presentation of the Cases: The Provincial Cases

Chapter 7   123
Presentation of the Cases: The Capital City Cases

Chapter 8   139
Cross-Case Analysis and Findings: Organizational Models and Roles

Chapter 9   159
Cross-Case Analysis and Findings: Non-Formal CE Teachers

Chapter 10   187
Cross-Case Analysis and Findings: Non-Formal CE Teachers (cont.)—Perspectives of the Educational Context and Presentation of Findings

Chapter 11   213
A Model of Approaches to Non-Formal CE Among AGC Churches

Chapter 12 *Conclusion and Recommendations*	225
References Cited	237
Appendix A	245
Appendix B	249
Appendix C	253
Appendix D	257
Appendix E	261

ACKNOWLEDGEMENTS

I would like to thank Dave Johnson, Director of APTS Press, for his encouragement and friendship throughout the process of publishing my dissertation. I am grateful to Frank McNelis, Larry Brooks, and the rest of the APTS editing team for their outstanding editing work. I responded to every email from them as quickly as I could. I hope they found the work enjoyable and fulfilling.

I am deeply grateful to Joseph Saggio, my dissertation supervisor. His friendship, collegiality, and guidance made the process of research and writing an outstanding experience on which to build for years to come. Along with Dr. Joe, I am grateful for my committee members–Weldyn Houger, Barbara Houger, and Alan Johnson. They have been an invaluable part of my journey as a missionary and educator for many years. Completing my dissertation with them was a privilege and a joy.

I owe a great debt of gratitude to my Cambodian colleagues for granting me the privilege of learning from their churches. They warmly welcomed me into their church families, shared their stories, and patiently answered my questions. I am also grateful to the teachers and leaders who welcomed me into their classes and shared their perspectives and experiences with me.

Most especially, I would like to thank my beloved wife, Dianna. She gave me the space to complete this research, listened to me think out loud, read every page of text (twice!), and, most importantly, believed in me when I felt overwhelmed in the dissertation process. We truly shared this journey as co-ministers should.

PREFACE

Clements Dissertation
Teaching in the Life of the Church:
A Multiple-Case Study of Nonformal Christian Education in Cambodia

Not all dissertations need to be published. I did not plan to publish my dissertation when I graduated from Asia Pacific Theological Seminary with a Ph.D. in 2019. I was happy to put what I had learned to work through teaching, supporting the development of schools that are part of the Asia Pacific Theological Association (APTA), and publishing a few journal articles. Dave Johnson, Director of APTS Press, persuaded me otherwise. As the first Ph.D. from APTS (which includes a standing review for publication), I yielded.

Beyond this personal reason, I chose to publish my dissertation for two reasons. First, though quite narrow in scope (as good qualitative research should be), this research makes a modest contribution to the growing scholarship on Christianity in Cambodia. Second, this research makes an empirical contribution to the field of nonformal Christian Education from an Asian context in which Christians are a tiny minority. As my literature review indicates, the field of nonformal CE is dominated by a North American point of view (which ironically is facing a general breakdown of historical CE institutions like Sunday school). While much of the literature is useful in the Majority World, it does not take into account the education levels, educational contexts, and social dynamics of places like Cambodia. For example, the findings from my cases indicate that nonformal CE in Cambodia has more in common with the Sunday school movement in the 19th century than with the functions, organizational structures, and teaching approaches discussed in current literature. As I have presented these ideas in class, feedback from students has consistently confirmed that my findings resonate with contexts across Asia Pacific.

I published this book with three types of readers in mind. First, readers interested in Christianity in Cambodia will get a snapshot of how some Pentecostals in Phnom Penh and in provincial contexts are carrying out the vital work of teaching in their churches. Readers will note that nonformal CE is an essential element of church life in these cases, not a specialized ministry department. Second, readers who are reflecting on nonformal CE in Majority World contexts may find points of connection with the literature review, case descriptions, findings, and the resulting descriptive model. And finally, novice researchers can benefit from the methodological detail I have included, the descriptions of the cases, and the protocols in the appendices. In addition to being necessary to evaluate the validity of the research, I hope that this material will provide useful examples of research design, data collection methods, and data analysis. APTS Press does not normally include such material in its published dissertations, but there is a need for qualitative research to be better understood and rigorously applied in postgraduate theological education.

All doctoral research is a journey. Doctoral research that involves matters of theology and church life should also be a transformative spiritual journey. My own journey involved precious time spent with pastors, elders, and teachers as they welcomed me into their lives and permitted me to learn from them. I was deeply touched by their warm hospitality and amazed by what they generously shared. I was further surprised when the process of analyzing data and writing the final chapters led to times of worship and prayer as I experienced the Holy Spirit's presence in the research process. I emerged from this undertaking with more than an academic credential. I gained a clearer sense of calling, a fresh set of tools with which to serve, and a deeper respect for the complexities of local church ministry, especially in places where Christianity has a minority status. It is my prayer that the Holy Spirit will give readers insights and encouragement through these chapters, especially readers who are on journeys similar to my own.

PUBLISHER'S PREFACE

We are pleased to offer this tenth title in our APTS Press Monograph Series. This is the publication of the author's Ph.D. dissertation done through the Asia Pacific Theological Seminary in Baguio City, Philippines. The purpose of this series is to give our readers broader access to good scholarship that would otherwise be unavailable outside of the academic community. This is part of our ongoing commitment to discipleship through publishing. The other nine titles in this series are:

Theology in Context: A Case Study in the Philippines by Dave Johnson,

Leave a Legacy: Increasing Missionary Longevity by Russ Turney,

Understanding the Iglesia ni Cristo by Anne Harper,

A Theology of Hope: Contextual Perspectives in Korean Pentecostalism by Sang Yun Lee,

Business In Islam: Contextualizing Mission in Muslim-Majority Nations by Robert J. Stefan,

A Multi-Media Literacy Project: Toward Biblical Literacy in Bangladesh by Teresa Chai,

Third Wave Pentecostalism in the Philippines: Understanding Toronto Blessing Revivalism's Signs and Wonders Theology in the Philippines by Lora Angeline Embudo Timenia,

Reformation from Below: Looking at Münster Anabaptism Anew Through Korean Minjung Theology by Youjin Chung, and

The Korean Healing Movement by Jun Kim

All are available at www.aptspress.org. If you have any questions, you can reach us through our website. We would be happy to hear from you.

God bless you as you read this book.

THE PUBLISHER

CHAPTER 1

Introduction to the Research

The story of the growth of the Church in Cambodia is remarkable in the history of the Church[1] worldwide. From the arrival of Gaspar de Cruz, a Dominician priest, in the 16th century[2] to the beginning of Evangelical missions in the 20th century, Christianity struggled to take root in the nation and grew only slowly. Then, between 1970 and 1975, the Church experienced an explosion of growth (up to as many as ten thousand people) as the besieged, pro-Western Lon Nol government granted missionaries the freedom to evangelize.[3] After the fall of the capital city, Phnom Penh, in April 1975, the Church was decimated by the Khmer Rouge (1975-1979) and further suppressed under Vietnamese occupation (1979-1989). In 1989 only an estimated two hundred Christians remained.[4] However, by 2016, the total number of professing Christians had reached about five hundred thousand people or 3.2 percent of the population.[5] (For more details, see "Background and Context" later in this chapter.) Table 1.1 gives an idea of how the Christian population that year fit into the general religious context of Cambodia.

---

[1]The term "Church" (capital "C") is used throughout to refer to Christianity in a corporate sense, while the term "church" is used to refer to local congregations.

[2]Catholic Cambodia, "Church's History," http://catholiccambodia.org/eng/community-history (accessed December 4, 2014).

[3]Steven Hyde, "A Missiological and Critical Study of Cambodia's Historical, Cultural, and Sociopolitical Characteristics to Identify the Factors of Rapid Church Growth and Propose Its Future Prognosis" (PhD diss., Bethany International University, Singapore, China, 2015), 46.

[4]Ibid., xxxii-xxxiii.

[5]Joshua Project, "Cambodia," http://joshuaproject.net/countries/CB (accessed January 7, 2017).

Table 1.1. Religions in Cambodia as of 2016[6]

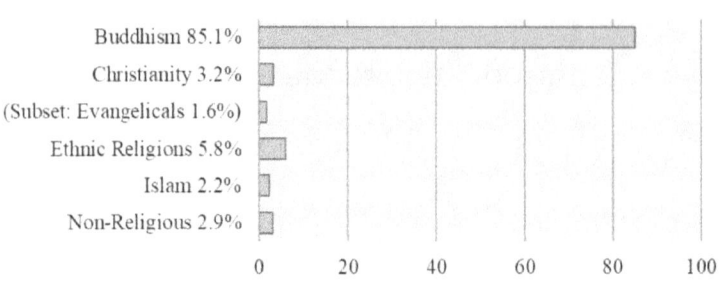

Estimated Population: 15,787,000

The remarkable growth that has been experienced across the spectrum of denominations, fellowships, and traditions is testimony to the sacrifice of missionaries from many countries, sustained efforts to be culturally relevant,[7] and the Cambodian Church's passion to share the Good News and plant churches. At the same time, however, church leaders from across organizational lines have been publicly raising the alarm about the lack of development in local church discipleship programs. As a result, although the Church has grown numerically, it generally lacks depth in biblical literacy.

Cambodia has also made remarkable progress in recent years as a nation. The population grew from 8.6 million in 1989 to 15.7 million in 2016.[8] As to the economy, the "GDP grew at an annual rate of over 8

---

[6]Adapted from ibid. "Christianity" refers to "Professing Christian," which is "the broadest possible classification of Christian." Evangelicals are a subset of Christianity based on their theological commitments rather than denominational affiliation. (See the "Definitions" page of Joshua Project website for more details.)

[7]Many church leaders and congregations have shown great care in developing a Cambodian expression of Christianity. However, cases as to a lack of sensitivity to culture abound. See the following for critical views of missionary activities: Brian Maher and Seila Uon, *Cry of the Gecko: History of the Christian Mission in Cambodia* (Centralia, WA: Gorhan Printing, 2012); François Ponchaud, *The Cathedral in the Rice Paddy: The 450-Year-Long History of the Church in Cambodia,* 2nd ed. (Phnom Penh, Cambodia: Catholic Catechetical Center Cambodia, 2012); Darin R. Clements, "The Church Reborn Out of the Killings Fields: A Preliminary Sketch of the Pentecostal/Charismatic Movement in Cambodia" (paper presented at the Theological Symposium of the Asia Pacific Theological Association, Yangon, Myanmar, July 26-27, 2016).

[8]"Cambodia Population," Country Meters, http://meters.info/en/Cambodia (accessed December 13, 2016).

percent between 2000 and 2010 and by at least 7 percent since 2011."[9] Furthermore, expansion of the education system has been one of the key items in the National Strategic Development Plan, resulting in impressive increases in primary- and secondary-school enrollments. Universal access to primary school is truly within Cambodia's grasp, although teacher quality remains a concern.[10]

Considering these development indicators and the general growth and organizational development of the Cambodian Church since 1989, it would seem reasonable to expect to find fellowships and local churches developing useful approaches to education in order to assimilate new believers. However, development of Christian Education (CE) in local churches is conspicuously missing in the picture of the Church. Research into those churches that have developed useful approaches for instructing their adherents in the faith could yield a fresh lens for understanding non-formal CE in other developing nations.

This chapter introduces a multiple case study of non-formal CE among Assemblies of God of Cambodia (AGC) churches. Section 1 provides a statement of the problem, statement of the purpose of this research, and statement of the central question. Section 2 deals with the background and context via an overview of Cambodian church history, a brief description of the development of the AGC and the researcher's relationship with the AGC. Sections 3, 4, and 5 address the delimitations of the research, limitations to the research, and definitions and abbreviations of key terms. Sections 6 and 7 discuss the significance of the study for CE research and present the research design. Finally, section 8 recaps the chapter's content and provides an overview of the book.

---

[9]Central Intelligence Agency, "Cambodia," The World Factbook, https://www.cia.gov/library/publications/the-world-factbook/geos/cb.html (accessed December 13, 2016).

[10]"Net primary enrollments increased from 83.8 percent in 1992 to 96.4 percent in 2012, and net secondary enrollments from 16.6 percent in 2000 to 35.1 percent in 2012." Prateek Tandon and Tsuyoshi Fukao, "Educating the Next Generation: Improving Teacher Quality in Cambodia," in *Directions in Development: Human Development* (Washington, DC: World Bank, 2015), 1, http://dx.doi.10.1596/978-1-4648-0417-5 (accessed June 9, 2015).

Statement of the Problem

The phenomenon of recent church growth in Cambodia without concurrent development in discipleship programs or non-formal CE[11] raises many questions, especially considering the rapid development of the nation's education system since 1993[12] and a virtual national obsession with formal education as a means of social mobility and family security. While literature on CE is abundant, most of it originates from and addresses socioeconomic situations dissimilar to those found in Cambodia.[13] This research sought to address these two gaps by describing, exploring, analyzing, and understanding the non-formal CE approaches of four AGC churches from two different socioeconomic situations.

Statement of Purpose

The purpose of this multiple case study is to describe, explore, and compare approaches to non-formal CE among AGC churches across socioeconomic situations.

Central Question

The central question addressed by this multiple case study is, What approaches to non-formal CE have been developed by AGC churches? Following a research design suggested by John Creswell,[14] the approaches

---

[11]"Non-formal CE" refers to CE that is intentionally structured but lacks formal assessments and accreditation. The classic example would be Sunday school. See "Delimitations" and "Definitions" for more details.

[12]The current constitution was promulgated in 1993, providing opportunity for massive foreign assistance in educational development.

[13]One useful book is Judith Lingenfelter and Sherwood G. Lingenfelter, *Teaching Cross-Culturally: An Incarnational Model for Learning and Teaching* (Grand Rapids: Baker Academic, 2003). Other possibilities include Heeja Kim, "Korean Christian Education: Past, Present, and Future," in "International Perspectives on Christian Education," supplemental issue, *Christian Education Journal* 10, S3 (Fall 2013): S222, http://journals.biola.edu/ns/ cej (accessed June 25, 2015); and Tan Giok Lie, "The Context and Challenges of the Church's Educational Ministry in Indonesia," in "International Perspectives on Christian Education," supplemental issue, *Christian Education Journal* 10, S3 (Fall 2013): S235, http://journals.biola.edu/ns/cej (accessed June 25, 2015).

[14]John W. Creswell, *Educational Research: Planning, Conducting, and Evaluating Quantitative and Qualitative Research*, 4th ed. (Boston: Pearson Education, 2014), 134-135.

to non-formal CE among the AGC churches in this study were described and explored in depth through these six procedural sub-questions:

1. How are approaches to non-formal CE organized in each of the cases? What is the rationale for each organizational approach?
2. How did the current approaches to non-formal CE in each of the cases originate and develop over time?
3. How are teachers recruited, developed, and resourced in each case? What ideas about teaching and learning influence this process?
4. What are the perceived contributions of the approaches to non-formal CE to the health and mission of each case?
5. How do approaches to non-formal CE among the cases reflect the Cambodian educational context?
6. How do approaches to non-formal CE among the cases compare across socioeconomic situations?

Background and Context[15]

Although the Church in Cambodia is almost entirely first generation and currently one of the fastest growing in the world,[16] its history dates back well before its rebirth in the early 1990s. This section begins by presenting selected key events in Cambodian church history up to 1993, the year in which the current national constitution granted freedom of religion to the citizens and made legal recognition of churches possible (see sub-section titled, "Rebirth of the Cambodian Church"). With that broader context in view, this present section will describe development of the AGC from 1990 to 2016 as the context for research into non-formal CE among its churches. Lastly, in order to place myself within the research context, I have included a discussion of my own involvement with the AGC since 1997 and some of the experiences that inspired the questions driving my research.

---

[15]The historical content of this sub-section was adapted from Clements, "The Church Reborn."

[16]Russ Mitchell, "The Top 20 Countries Where Christianity Is Growing the Fastest," Disciple All Nations, August 25, 2013, https://discipleallnations.wordpress.com/2013/08/25/the-top-20-countries-where-christianity-is-growing-the-fastest (accessed January 27, 2017). Mitchell makes his assertions using data from "Christianity in Its Global Context, 1970-2020," Center for the Study of Global Christianity, Gordon-Conwell Theological Seminary, South Hamilton, MA: June 2013, www.globalchristianity.org/globalcontext.

The Catholic Church in Cambodia

The first recorded presence of Christianity in Cambodia was the arrival of Gaspar de Cruz, a Dominician priest, at the court of King Ang Chan in the royal city of Longvek in 1555.[17] Throughout the three hundred years leading up to establishment of the French protectorate (1863-1953), Catholic communities were comprised primarily of Portuguese and Vietnamese.[18] The French protectorate brought an influx of missionaries and provided political stability that would allow for visible development of the Church, including construction of buildings to manifest its presence and work.[19] Independence from France in 1953 caused the Catholic Church to shift its orientation toward the Cambodian people "who were assuming increasing levels of responsibility."[20] The first Cambodian priest, Simon Chhem Yen, was ordained on November 7, 1957,[21] and the first Cambodian bishop, Joseph Chhmar Salas, was ordained on April 14, 1975, only hours before Phnom Penh fell to the communists.[22]

When Cambodia reopened to the outside world in the early 1990s, the Catholic Church began to rebuild its communities, beginning with identifying and gathering survivors. Its second priority was to build a "Church with a Cambodian face," instead of simply rebuilding the physical and organizational structures of the past.[23] Creating a 'Cambodian face' meant finding common ground with Buddhism and spreading the faith through a "catechumenical approach."[24] By 2011, the Catholic Church had grown to 10,000 Cambodians and 20,000 Vietnamese. Of the seventy-six priests serving the Church, five were Cambodians.[25]

---

[17]Catholic Cambodia, "Church's History;" Steven Hyde, "History of the Church in Cambodia."
[18]Ponchaud, *The Cathedral in the Rice Paddy*, 36, 51.
[19]Ibid., 121.
[20]Ibid., 149.
[21]Ibid., 145.
[22]Ibid., 201.
[23]Ibid., 279.
[24]Ibid., 283-284. The Catholic Church's 'catechumenical approach' will be discussed further in the literature review in Chapter 3.
[25]Ibid., 291.

Evangelical Missions, 1923-1989

The first Evangelical missionaries arrived in 1923 under auspices of the Christian and Missionary Alliance.[26] David Ellison focused on establishing a Bible school, while Arthur Hammond worked on a full translation of the Bible into the Khmer language,[27] using the American Standard Version (ASV) as a guide.[28] The completed text was finally printed in London in 1954. The United Bible Societies (UBS) began working on a new translation in the early 1970s, but their offices in Cambodia were closed from 1975 to 1992 during the Khmer Rouge regime and the Vietnamese occupation (see below). The Khmer Standard Version (KHSV) was eventually published by UBS in 1997 and again in 2005.[29] Although there have been a few independent efforts at Bible translation in recent years, the KHSV and the 'Hammond Bible' (or 'Red Bible, as it is affectionately called due to the red edges of its pages) are the most widely used versions. AGC churches utilize both, although the KHSV is more common.

From the first Catholic presence in 1555 to the overthrow of Prince Sihanouk in 1970, the total number of Evangelical Cambodian Christians never exceeded several hundred. A few thousand people became believers during the years leading up to the fall of Phnom Penh in 1975; but the church was almost entirely wiped out as the Khmer Rouge brutally reset the nation's development to 'year zero,' in accordance with their plan to create a Maoist-style utopia. The regime's policies and direct actions resulted in the deaths of between one and two million people, many of whom were executed in the now famous 'killing fields' located all over the country.

The church that survived was severely repressed under the Vietnamese, who swept the Khmer Rouge out of power in 1979 and occupied the nation until 1989. Many Cambodians fled the country in the face of this turmoil and were gathered in refugee camps along the Thai border. These camps became the womb from which the Cambodian Church would be reborn.[30] While many new Christians made their way

---

[26]Maher, *Cry of the Gecko*, 17.
[27]The word "Khmer" is the English designation for the Cambodian language.
[28]Dave Manfred, email message to author, January 23, 2015.
[29]Bible Society in Cambodia, "About Us," http://biblecambodia.org/about-us/. See also http://biblecambodia.org/khov-history.html.
[30]Don Cormack, *Killing Fields, Living Fields: An Unfinished Portrait of the Cambodian Church—the Church that Would Not Die* (Crowborough, UK: OMF International, 1997), 451.

to a third country, a dedicated cohort (including significant leaders like Barnabas Mam) prepared to return to rebuild their nation. Pastor Barnabas reports that there were approximately two hundred Christians of all groups left in Cambodia when Vietnamese troops withdrew in 1989 under pressure from the United Nations.[31]

Rebirth of the Church in Cambodia, 1993

Steven Hyde views the formation of a new government and ratification of a new constitution, backed by the patronage of the United Nations in 1993 as the year of the rebirth of the Cambodian Church and the most important condition for its growth since then. "From this point until the present, there has been historically unprecedented freedom of worship in Cambodia and unparalleled growth of the Church. Previous to 1993, there were more Khmer Christian churches outside of Cambodia's borders than in the country, but this would soon change."[32]

I have personally witnessed this unprecedented freedom and growth since 1997 as the government has generally given grace to the Church in light of its constitutional right to exist and the legal ambiguity[33] governing its existence. At the same time, the Church in Cambodia has taken its cultural expressions seriously, has tried to respect and work with the government, and has benefited greatly from waves of missionary activity originating from many other countries.

Table 1.2 provides an overview of the key events in Cambodian church history up to 1993 that have been described in this chapter. Table 1.3 provides a visual representation of the total current Christian population in Cambodia according to affiliation and notes that about 50 percent of the current Christian population is Evangelical in its theological orientation.

---

[31] Barnabas Mam, *Church Behind the Wire* (Chicago: Moody Publishers, 2012), 346.
[32] Hyde, "A Missiological and Critical Study," 79.
[33] The laws pertaining to churches are not comprehensive and subject to change. In many cases, quality of the relationship between church leaders and government officials determines how strictly the laws are followed.

Table 1.2. Key events in Cambodian church history up to 1993[34]

1555	First recorded Catholic presence, Dominican priest Gaspar de Cruz.
1863-1953	French protectorate.
1923	First Evangelical missionaries, Christian and Missionary Alliance.
1954	Publication of the full Bible in the Khmer language.
1970	Overthrow of Prince Sihanouk by General Lon Nol. (Evangelical Christians numbered less than 1,000.)
Early 1970s	Influx of Western Evangelical and Charismatic missionaries. (Number of professing Christians swelled to between 5,000 and 10,000.)
1975-1979	Khmer Rouge regime—eradication of all religion.
1979-1989	Occupation by Vietnam—suppression of the Church
Late 1970s to early 1990s	Growth of the Church in the refugee camps along the Thai border.
1989	About 200 Christians remained in Cambodia.
1993	Promulgation of a new constitution backed by the United Nations, and freedom of religion granted to Cambodian citizens.

---

[34]Sources: Catholic Cambodia, "Church's History"; David A. Chandler, *A History of Cambodia*, 4th ed. Southeast Asian edition (Chiang Mai, Thailand: Silkworm Books, 2008); Maher, *Cry of the Gecko*, 17; Cormack, *Killing Fields*; Bible Society in Cambodia, "About Us"; Mam, *Behind the Wire*, 346; Hyde, "A Missiological and Critical Study," 79.

Table 1.3. Estimated Christian population in Cambodia[35]

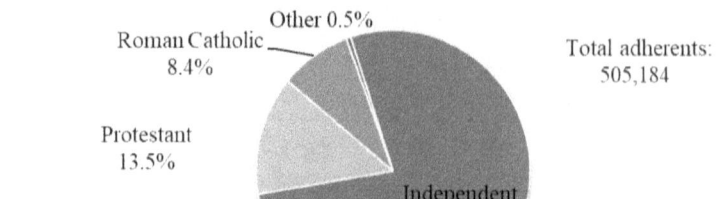

Roman Catholic 8.4%
Other 0.5%
Protestant 13.5%
Independent 76.6%
Total adherents: 505,184

Note: Evangelicals make up about 50% of the total adherents. See Table 1.5.

Development of the Assemblies of God of Cambodia

The first resident Assemblies of God (AG) missionaries, Randy and Carolyn Dorsey (USA), arrived in Cambodia in June 1990 under protocols with the Cambodian government to establish two children's homes, open a medical clinic, and teach English.[36] In the following years, additional AG missionaries came from France, the Philippines, Australia, and Malaysia. The Assemblies of God Missionary Fellowship (AGMF), at various times in its history, has included as many as fourteen nations representing North America, Central America, Northern Europe, and across Asia.

Cambodia Bible Institute (CBI) was founded by the AGMF in 1994 as a one-year ministerial training program, with Steve Sullivan (USA) as director, Fred Capapas (Philippines) as dean of students, and Nora Catipon (Philippines) as business administrator/registrar. CBI continues to function as a joint venture between the AGMF and the AGC and now offers vocational ministry training up to the bachelor's-degree level in Khmer and lay ministry training in Khmer and Vietnamese at the certificate level. By 2015, roughly half of CBI's 300 graduates were from AGC churches.

---

[35] Joshua Project, "Cambodia." Statistics for Evangelicals are based on theological orientation rather than denominational affiliation.

[36] Carolyn Dorsey, "Information Regarding the Founding of the Assemblies of God Work in Cambodia" (Springfield, MO, May 2005).

The AGC was formally organized in 1997 with twelve recognized pastors and twelve churches.[37] A five-member national committee was elected, with Kheok Srin as the first chairman. In 2010, it further organized into six districts, each led by a locally elected committee. In 2013, the AGC reported having churches in all but four provinces out of a total twenty-four cities and provinces. By 2016, it numbered 202 churches,[38] fifty-nine formally recognized pastors, 183 'leaders,' and 13,360 'members' (5,944 adults and 7,416 children).[39]

Table 1.4 provides a summary of key events in AGC's history; and Table 1.5 graphically shows the statistical relationship between the AGC and the larger Evangelical community.

Table 1.4. Key events in AGC history[40]

1990	Arrival of Randy and Carolyn Dorsey, first Assemblies of God Missionaries (USA).
Early 1990s	The Assemblies of God Missionary Fellowship included the USA, France, the Philippines, Australia, and Malaysia.
1994	Establishment of Cambodia Bible Institute.
1997	Establishment of the General Council of the AGC and the first AGC National Committee with Pastor Kheok Srin as chairman.
2000	The AGC had about twenty congregations with an estimated 1,000 constituents.
2010	The AGC organizes into six districts.
2016	The AGC numbers 202 congregations, fifty-nine recognized pastors, 183 leaders, and 13,360 members (5,944 adults and 7,416 children).

---

[37]Report of the AGC National Executive Committee, Phnom Penh, Cambodia, 2012.
[38]Includes all levels of development.
[39]AGC internal documents. At the time of writing, constitutional amendments were in progress to formally recognize and classify local churches. The terms 'leader' and 'member' are not defined in the constitution.
[40]Sources: Dorsey, "Founding;" AGC National Executive Committee.

Table 1.5. The AGC and Evangelical Christianity in Cambodia[41]

Total adherents: 252,592

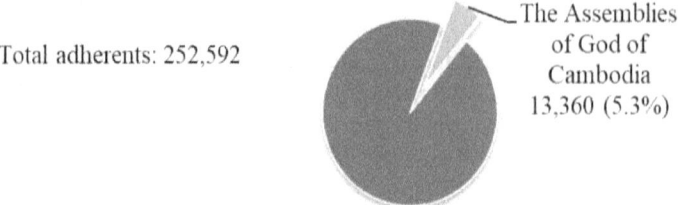

The Assemblies of God of Cambodia 13,360 (5.3%)

The Researcher's Relationship with the AGC

My wife, Dianna, and I arrived in Cambodia as short-term personnel with Assemblies of God World Missions (USA) in January 1997 to work with church planters Rick and Lurece Shell in Siem Reap province. The Shells had been planting churches in the Philippines several years before redeploying to Cambodia in 1990. Dianna and I taught English classes as part of their evangelism strategy until factional fighting between the two dominant political parties necessitated our evacuation just six months after arriving. During that short time, however, we saw firsthand that people were hungry for education. More than 200 applied for our first English classes as a result of only word-of-mouth advertising and without any information about our program. That hunger for education, which could lead to an improved standard of living, continues to intensify to this day, quality notwithstanding. This popular interest in education raises a question about the Church. Considering its growth plus the national trends in education, why has CE development lagged so significantly in church life?

We returned to Cambodia as career missionaries with AGWM in July 1999. After several months of language and culture study, I became the director of Sihanoukville Children's Home in the port city of Sihanoukville, serving with my wife in that ministry from 2000 to 2002. Since the orphanage was running smoothly, we were asked to give special attention to its spiritual aspects. We did our best to engage this challenge as pastors, not chaplains. Being a teacher by nature, I gravitated toward an educational approach.

---

[41] Joshua Project, "Cambodia," and AGC unpublished internal documents. Statistics for Evangelicals are based on theological orientation rather than denominational affiliation.

The responses of the staff members taught me much about teaching and learning in Cambodia. Although many were not Christians, all of them seemed interested in spiritual things. When I offered voluntary Bible studies for those who wanted to know more about Christianity, I was surprised to have nearly 100 percent participation.[42] The natural hunger they had toward the Bible convinced me that a desire to read and understand the Scriptures could be taken as one sign of genuine conversion. The hunger for biblical knowledge that I witnessed once again raised questions as to why growth of the Church in Cambodia has not been accompanied by growth in non-formal CE.

Serving at Cambodia Bible Institute since 2002 has given me a special perspective regarding the Church's growth. I taught my first class that year as part of the Church Planters Training Program, which ran from 2002 to 2007. I later served as dean of the students for one year and business manager for three years under the directorship of Fred Capapas (Philippines). When we returned to Cambodia after our furlough, I was academic dean from 2009 to 2013 under Kelly Robinette (USA). I served as the director from 2015 to 2019.

I have participated in the changes CBI has undergone from being a church planters training school to being a broad-spectrum vocational ministry training school. These changes have always been motivated by a desire to track with the development of the AGC. The first generations of students were generally older than I, and many had already been serving in local church ministry for some time before having the opportunity to study at CBI. Those first-generation believers knew their Bibles well and brought real-world questions to the classroom.

We watched the economic changes come quickly as student after student acquired cell phones. Sadly, we also watched as these new students' Bible knowledge became weaker despite increasing levels of study in the local school system. While very few of the early generations of students had completed high school, by contrast, 76 percent of students in the vocational ministry training levels at CBI in 2016-2017 were high school graduates.[43] Notably, almost half had been sent to CBI by Cambodian pastors.

---

[42]The argument could be made that the staff may have felt coerced to participate as part of their employment. Realizing this possibility, we took steps to ensure that employees did not feel pressure to participate. We were also aware that Buddhist staff members would consider themselves Christians while they worked at the orphanage.

[43]In Cambodia, students must complete high school and then pass comprehensive national exams in order to graduate. Students who fail are not considered graduates.

Every year I asked my students how many of them were *second generation* Christians. I clarified my question by asking how many grew up in a Christian family as opposed to converting to Christianity. Only two students have ever raised their hands in response to this question. However, while the Cambodian Church is still almost entirely made up of first-generation Christians, the ministry generation we were beginning to see at CBI was now between the first and second generations. Even though they were first generation believers, most of our students were coming into church ministry in the context of partially formed systems and young denominations. Despite the advantages over students of just ten years ago, the level of biblical knowledge of these students was noticeably weaker. These observations led me to ask them how many AGC churches had CE programs. The almost complete lack of CE programs amongst our churches created the impetus for this research.

Delimitations of the Research

Two important delimitations of this study are presupposed by the central question of this research: What approaches to non-formal CE have been developed by AGC churches? The first delimitation was its exclusive focus on AGC churches. This delimitation was important for the following reasons. (a) I had a long-standing relationship with the AGC, which provided natural access to the four cases (at the same time, staying within the AGC focused my time and energy on the important stakeholders of the findings). And (b) delimiting to the AGC bounded my research to a single tradition and ensured better comparability between cases and across socioeconomic differences.

The second delimitation was its focus on non-formal CE, that was considered part of normal church life by the cases. This research did not examine Christian day schools and education programs that functioned as parachurch organizations (i.e., separate funding, separate administrations, and paid staffs). Educational efforts such as English classes and preschools were included when they met the criteria of non-formal CE (see "Definitions" below) and were carried out as part of a congregation's regular activities.

Limitations of the Research

This research had to take four limitations into consideration. The first one was the developmental stage of the AGC (see "Background and Context" above). Formally organized teaching ministries were rare in AGC churches because the ministry of teaching was still emerging as a defined role in local church life. Additionally, the terminology describing church ministries of all types had not yet become standardized throughout the fellowship.

The second limitation involved taking special care in triangulating data. In Cambodia, as in many Asian contexts, face-saving tactics are often employed to avoid shame or to put another person at ease. Such measures are generally viewed as a matter of politeness rather than deception. With regard to church activities, answering interview questions straightforwardly may not be as comfortable as speaking in terms of what should happen, what a person intended to do, or what a person would do if conditions permitted. The design of this research attempted to mitigate this effect through a significant amount of onsite exposure to each case, collecting multiple types of data from a variety of sources, and member-checking.[44]

The third limitation was the narrow transferability of the findings of this qualitative research, as evidenced by use of four purposely chosen cases. Case study research is bounded to a particular situation, "a contemporary phenomenon within a real-life context."[45] The goal is not generalizability but transferability (i.e., "the ability to apply findings in similar contexts and settings").[46] This research was not intended to address CE in all conceivable contexts but to aid in understanding non-formal CE among the AGC and to be transferrable to the wider Christian community in Cambodia and similar socioeconomic contexts outside of Cambodia.

The fourth limitation was my role as a long-term missionary and Bible school leader in Cambodia (see "Background and Context" above). My experience as a missionary with the AGC was special in that I formed much of my understanding of local church ministry and many vital ministerial relationships over the course of our service in Cambodia from 1997 to 2019.[47] In a very real sense, I grew up in ministry along with the current generation of AGC pastors and national leaders.[48] Thus,

---

[44]Creswell, *Educational Research*, 259; Robert K. Yin, *Case Study Research: Design and Methods*, 4th ed., in *Applied Social Science Research Methods*, vol. 5, ed. Leonard Bickman and Debra J. Rog (Los Angeles: SAGE Publications, 2009), 182.

[45]Yin, *Case Study Research,* 2.

[46]Linda Dale Bloomberg and Marie Volpe, *Completing Your Qualitative Dissertation: A Road Map from Beginning to End*, 2nd ed. (Los Angeles: SAGE Publications, 2012), 9.

[47]I was twenty-three years old when we first arrived in Cambodia.

[48]Additionally, one of my most important mentors in Bible school ministry was a missionary from the Philippines.

my long-term service with the AGC meant access to cases, cultural awareness, Khmer language skills, and opportunities for genuine reciprocity.[49] However, I had to be careful to avoid unintentional coercion due to my status as a teacher, to handle information with discretion, and to uphold the principles of informed consent in a culturally sensitive manner. At the same time, I also had to be rigorous in data analysis in order to offset potential biases due to personal familiarity with the cases and participants.

Definitions and Abbreviations of Key Terms

The following definitions were used in the implementation of this study:

> *The Assemblies of God of Cambodia* (AGC) refers to the General Council of the Assemblies of God of Cambodia, a Pentecostal fellowship formally organized in 1997 (see "Background and Context" above). The AGC is a member of the World Assemblies of God Fellowship (WAGF), which is not a legislative organ but "a cooperative body of worldwide Assemblies of God national councils of equal standing" committed to "the furtherance of the Gospel to the ends of the earth."[50]

Christian education (CE) refers to Bible-based teaching carried out by a local church for the purpose of communicating the message of salvation through Jesus Christ to nonbelievers (Acts 1:8), nurturing believers to maturity in their faith (Matthew 28:18-20), and equipping believers in Jesus Christ for ministry (Ephesians 4:11-13). (See "Delimitations" above for restrictions in the scope of how the term CE is employed in this study.)

Non-formal education refers to "deliberate educational strategies based on meeting people's needs outside of the formal school model."[51] Generally speaking, non-formal education differs from informal (e.g.,

---

[49]On reciprocity, see Margaret D. LeCompte and Jean J. Schensul, *Designing and Conducting Ethnographic Research: An Introduction*, 2nd ed., in *Ethnographer's Toolkit*, book 1, ed. Jean J. Schensul and Margaret D. LeCompte. (Lanham, MD: AltaMira Press, 2010), 313-315.

[50]"Fellowship," World Assemblies of God Fellowship, http://worldagfellowship.org/fellowship (accessed January 2, 2017).

[51]Gary C. Newton, "Nonformal Education," in *Evangelical Dictionary of Christian Education*, ed. Michael J. Anthony (Grand Rapids: Baker Academic, 2001), 506.

learning the family business) in that it is more structured and intentional. Non-formal education differs from formal education in that it typically does not involve formal evaluations that culminate in the conferral of accredited diplomas or degrees.

Non-formal CE refers to Bible-based education in a local church context that is under the administration of church leadership, is structured or semi-structured, and has Christian discipleship and service as its goals. Therefore, non-formal CE does not include church-based or church-related education that has parachurch features, such as a separate administration, separate funding, and (typically) paid staff.

Socioeconomic situations/contexts refer to social settings characterized and limited by societal and economic dynamics. People in Cambodia naturally differentiate between the capital city (*reachthhiani*) and the provinces (*kaet*). This study followed these commonsense classifications as well.

Significance of the Research

This study's findings and the resulting descriptive model are significant in two ways—transferability and the literature gap. First, the significance lies not in the research's *generalizability*, which relies on a representative sample, but on its *transferability*, which "refers to the fit or match between the research context and other contexts as judged by the reader."[52] The goal here was to particularize the research and bring out the 'Khmerness' of the four cases in order to make a contribution to thinking about CE from a Cambodian context. The findings and resulting descriptive model should prove transferable to three contexts.

The first and most closely matched context for transferability is the AGC, the research's primary stakeholder. The AGC does not currently gather statistical information beyond the number of churches, pastors, leaders, and constituents (adults and children).[53] Thus, the study's findings could be an asset to the strategic planning of AGC's National Executive Committee. Additionally, the descriptive model presented in Chapter 11 can help the AGC strengthen CE across the fellowship by providing a framework for evaluation and development.

---

[52] Bloomberg and Volpe, *Completing Your Qualitative Dissertation*, 113.
[53] Statistical data are currently collected on an irregular and inconsistent basis. Moreover, standards and categories for recognizing local churches are unclear. As a result, the exact number of AGC churches is uncertain at this time. Constitutional changes are in the planning stage that will make collecting reliable information more feasible.

Another context for transferability is the wider Christian community in Cambodia. Steven Hyde, who has studied the Church's growth, says that the low level of CE development among AGC churches would likely be typical across all churches. Specifically, 55 percent of the churches in his sample had a single worship service per week as their only means of spiritual formation and biblical education.[54] The general view is that less than one in ten churches have developed consistent approaches to non-formal CE.[55] The research findings presented here offer some baselines for thinking about the churches that are doing CE. Additionally, the descriptive model in Chapter 11 offers a framework for evaluating or studying CE in order to create approaches that are more effective or more natural for local churches across traditions.

Lastly, the findings of this study are transferrable to non-formal CE development in similar socioeconomic situations and educational environments. The conditions affecting the development of CE in Cambodia are not entirely unique. Unlike the West, where overall education levels are good and Sunday School was once a powerful force for spiritual formation and community education, the churches in socioeconomic and educational contexts similar to Cambodia encounter obstacles at a fundamental level when they begin to engage in non-formal CE. Thus, we need to understand these dynamics and the values that drive them so we can develop effective approaches to non-formal CE for contexts that lack the economic and educational progress that has contributed to CE development in the West. The descriptive model constructed from the findings presented in Chapter 11 provides a framework for studying these dynamics.

The second area of this study's significance has to do with the literature gap. Literature about Christianity in Cambodia is still in its early stages and much of what has been written is popular in nature. CE at the local-church level has received little attention even in literature that analyzes factors affecting church growth or describes ministerial training (or the lack thereof). No research has been conducted on non-formal CE among AGC churches.

The literature also lacks lenses for thinking about CE in contexts like Cambodia. A lot of good literature on CE has been produced by

---

[54] Hyde, "A Missiological and Critical Study," 106. Another 34 percent of churches in the sample did meet for worship multiple times per week.

[55] Steven Hyde, conversation with the author, Phnom Penh, Cambodia, September 25, 2015. This generalization has also been expressed by other church and mission leaders.

the West and is utilized in much of the rest of the world. Generally speaking, it strives to work with current educational philosophy and aims at universal principles. The problem for contexts like Cambodia is that these principles were primarily developed in and for Western socioeconomic situations with high levels of literacy, strong national education systems, relatively healthy economies, and good resources for curriculum and teacher training.

The findings of this research were used to create a descriptive model of AGC non-formal CE that makes possible a two-way critique. In the first instance, non-formal CE in Cambodia needs to be critiqued in view of principles that have proven to be universal over time and across contexts. In the second instance, the findings offer a critique of prevailing models at points in which they do not fit the socioeconomic or cultural dynamics of contexts like Cambodia. Just as there has been a call for contextual theologizing, so there may also be a need for a more intentionally and deeply contextualized approach to thinking about CE, one that is more holistic than simply using local artwork and stories. The descriptive model constructed from this research provides a framework that can be used to discover dynamics that affect the development of effective, contextualized CE in socioeconomic situations similar to those in Cambodia.

Design of the Research

The design of this research followed the multiple case study approach of Robert Yin. According to him, "Case studies are the preferred method when (a) 'how' or 'why' questions are being posed, (b) the investigator has little control over events, and (c) the focus is on a contemporary phenomenon within a real-life context."[56] The research design began with a central question directed toward a set of four cases. Each case was then described, explored in depth, and analyzed through six procedural sub-questions over a series of phases.[57] Data were collected using ethnographic methods in order to have both emic and etic perspectives of AGC approaches to non-formal CE.[58] Table 1.6 provides an overview of the design following the procedural sub-questions. Chapter 5 gives a full presentation of instrumentation development, data collection methods, and data sources.

---

[56] Yin, *Case Study Research*, 2.
[57] John Creswell, *Educational Research*, 134-135.
[58] Ibid., 470-471.

Table 1.6. Research design overview

	Central question: What approaches to non-formal CE have been developed by AGC churches?
Case selection, informed consent	
Data collection	Sub-question 1: How are approaches to non-formal CE organized in each case? What is the rationale for each organizational approach?
	Sub-question 2: How did the current approaches to non-formal CE among the cases originate and then develop over time?
	Sub-question 3: How are teachers recruited, developed, and resourced in each case? What ideas about teaching and learning influence this process?
	Sub-question 4: What are the perceived contributions of the approaches to non-formal CE to the health and mission of each case?
Focus groups (member checking, additional perspectives)	Sub-question 5: How do approaches to non-formal CE among the cases reflect the educational context?
Cross-case analysis	Sub-question 6: How do approaches to non-formal CE among the cases compare across socioeconomic situations?

The first phase of the research involved selecting four cases (local AGC churches) for study and securing the informed consent of each church's leadership. The four cases were comprised of two cases each from two socioeconomic situations—the capital city and provincial locations. The number of cases was chosen to strengthen transferability, while providing sufficient time for in-depth study of each one. The differences between individual churches and differences in findings across socioeconomic situations provided what Yin calls 'theoretical replication' (i.e., "contrasting results for anticipatable reasons").[59] The key criteria for selection of cases were accessibility, representation of the

---

[59] Yin, *Case Study Research*, 54.

socioeconomic contexts, and a reasonably developed approach to non-formal CE.

The second phase involved collecting data relevant to sub-questions 1 through 4 from multiple sources to ensure triangulation.[60] Working through an ethnographic lens, data was collected from documents, interviews, formal surveys, and participant observation.[61] Two of the three types of interviews described by Yin were employed—in-depth interviews, focused interviews, and formal surveys.[62] This phase utilized in-depth interviews with church leaders to gather background information about the church, congregation statistics, personal information about the pastor, and insight into the philosophy of the church. Additional in-depth interviews focused on aspects of their approach to non-formal CE, such as organizational structures, class arrangements, and teacher selection and training. Focused interviews were conducted with key individuals as needed to confirm, narrow, or flesh out themes and questions that emerged from in-depth interviews and observations.

The second phase employed a case study protocol to ensure reliability of the findings and to create "replication logic" across the cases.[63] I began with a well-developed but tentative protocol that was refined in response to emerging data in an iterative fashion. The resulting protocol, fully described in Chapter 5, reflects the approach to all four cases and provides a strong basis for the cross-case analysis that was conducted in the next phase.

After conducting in-case analysis of the data, the third phase of research employed focused groups to corroborate findings, further explore perspectives about teacher-student roles, and collect data about their views of the educational context. Peter Knight notes that focus groups can be a valuable way for researchers to check their findings against the perceptions of participants and to "both provide chances for them to ask for explanations of unexpected findings and to clarify details."[64] In order to gain a range of perspectives, each focus group included a selection of participants with varying relationships to the case's non-formal CE, those participants being the pastor, church leaders (teaching or non-teaching), and teachers who were not leaders.

---

[60]Ibid., 114.
[61]Margaret D. LeCompte and Jean J. Schensul, *Ethnographic Research*, 70, 175-179.
[62]Yin, *Case Study Research*, 107-108.
[63]Ibid., 54, 79.
[64]Peter T. Knight, *Small-Scale Research* (London: SAGE, 2002), 70.

The fourth phase involved cross-case analysis to address sub-question 6 regarding how approaches to non-formal CE compared across socioeconomic situations. This phase looked at the data in aggregate and across cases. Some data clearly showed differences between socioeconomic situations (e.g., teacher demographics), while other data led to an overall picture of how the cases approach non-formal CE. Chapters 8 through 10 present a detailed cross-case analysis and the findings that emerged from that analysis.

Chapter Summary and Book Overview

Chapter 1 of this dissertation is an introduction to a multiple case study of non-formal CE approaches among AGC churches. The purpose of this qualitative research was to create a descriptive model for understanding non-formal CE among AGC churches by exploring the components and values driving it in four cases that have engaged in sustained efforts at non-formal CE and have reached a relatively strong level of CE development. The central question asked what approaches to non-formal CE have been developed by AGC churches.

No research has been conducted on CE among AGC churches, and the literature on CE in Cambodia and similar socioeconomic contexts is limited. Therefore, it was necessary to conduct a broad literature review in Chapters 2 through 4. This review was used to construct a conceptual framework for collecting and organizing data, which is presented at the end of Chapter 4.

Chapters 5 through 11 address the research project itself. Chapter 5 describes the research methodology in detail. Chapters 6 and 7 present each of the cases with specific reference to the first three sub-questions. Chapters 8 through 10 present a cross-case analysis of the data from the cases and discuss a series of findings that were used to construct a descriptive model. Chapter 11 presents a descriptive model of AGC non-formal CE constructed from the findings set forth in Chapter 10. Lastly, Chapter 12 summarizes the findings of the research, considers useful applications of the findings, and suggests lines of inquiry for further research.

CHAPTER 2
Literature Review and Conceptual Framework: Educational Contexts of Non-Formal Christian Education

Introduction

Chapters 2 through 4 review the literature that was used to develop the conceptual framework for this multiple case study of approaches to non-formal CE among AGC churches. The framework for exploring non-formal CE in contexts like Cambodia can be pictured as an inverted pyramid, with four levels representing the aspects that are increasingly particularized to a given congregation. Figure 2.1 is a basic diagram of the framework. A detailed diagram of it is presented at the conclusion of this three-chapter literature review.

Figure 2.1. Basic conceptual framework for exploring non-formal CE among AGC churches

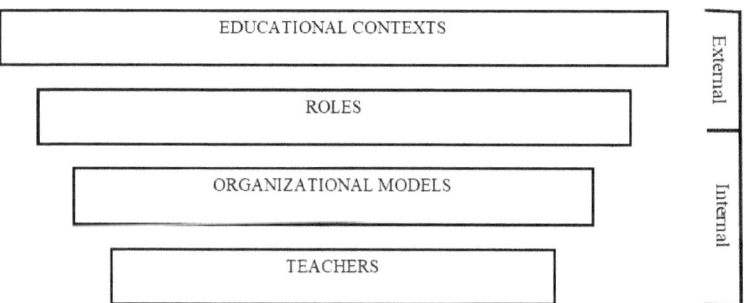

I have constructed this conceptual framework for exploring non-formal CE from the literature discussed in these chapters. It is not an adaptation of an existing framework, but rather a composite of probes for exploring conditions and values affecting non-formal CE. I originally conceived of this framework as two-dimensional concentric circles. However, as I began to develop each level, I found the model to be inadequate. So I turned it on its side, pulled the center down like a cone and expanded it into the detailed framework presented at the end of Chapter 4 as Figure 4.6. This change allowed for each level to explore its part of the framework in different ways.

This conceptual framework is not intended to explore all the conditions that could affect non-formal CE, but I do believe it does explore the conditions and values relevant in Cambodia at this time and at this stage of research. Each of the four levels also point to additional lines of inquiry for research in Cambodia or contexts like those found in Cambodia.

Chapter 2 begins the literature review with a discussion of the historical antecedents to this research. The rest of the chapter through Chapter 4 then work through the four levels of the conceptual framework. Chapter 2 addresses the first level—the educational context of non-formal CE. This level represents external realities that can influence a church's approach to non-formal CE both from social science and from formal education like the national education system. Chapter 3 addresses the second level—the roles of non-formal CE, including those that are external (e.g., engaging the society around the congregation) and internal (e.g., conversion, discipleship, spiritual formation). Chapter 4 addresses the framework's third and fourth levels; the third is organizational approaches to non-formal CE, of which there are three basic models, and the fourth looks at the teachers of non-formal CE. Chapter 4 concludes with an overview of the fully developed conceptual framework for exploring approaches to non-formal CE among AGC churches. This framework informs the research methodology, which is detailed in Chapter 5.

Historical Antecedents to the Research

Research into Christianity in Cambodia is in its very early stages. As a starting point, a few significant sources have endeavored to trace Cambodian church history and development. Steven Hyde's research provides one of the broadest explorations of that history to date, including Catholic Church history, Evangelical missions, and an analysis of factors in church growth.[65] Providing the Catholic perspective, François Ponchaud has carefully documented its history from the arrival of Gaspar de Cruz in 1555 to the present.[66] Brian Maher made one of the

---

[65]Hyde, "A Missiological and Critical Study;" Stephen Hyde, *Portrait of the Body of Christ in Cambodia* (Pehn, Cambodia: Words of Life Ministries, 2012); Hyde, "History of the Church in Cambodia."

[66]Ponchaud, *The Cathedral in the Rice Paddy*.

first large-scale efforts at creating a comprehensive timeline of church history, which he subsequently made available online.[67] Working from that timeline, Maher collaborated with Uon Seila[68] to describe and critique Evangelical missions in Cambodia, beginning with arrival of the first Evangelical missionaries (Christian and Missionary Alliance) in 1923.[69]

However, the classic work on church history in Cambodia is Don Cormack's *Killing Fields, Living Fields: An Unfinished Portrait of the Cambodian Church—the Church that Would Not Die*.[70] In contrast to the other works, Cormack presents Cambodian church history in narrative form and includes many personal accounts from the first generations of Evangelical Christians.

Three works have addressed the emergence of the Pentecostal/Charismatic movement in Cambodia. These studies constitute early efforts to formally describe a movement that has not yet been documented or analyzed. First, a master's thesis by Joshua Lovelace analyzed the first twenty-five years of the Assemblies of God of Cambodia (1990-2015). He described four periods of development in the history of the AGC and provided a detailed timeline and record of important actors in the AGC.[71] The second and third works look at the Pentecostal/Charismatic movement as a whole. Darin R. Clements sketched out key events, groups, and individuals in a conference paper.[72] Then he and Ken Huff described major outreach events, international ecumenical cooperation, ministerial training, church planting, and community development

---

[67]Brian Maher, "Cambodian Church History," in *Cambodian Christian*, http://www.cambodian christian.com/church_history (accessed April 30, 2014).

[68]Seila Uon, "Seila Uon's Story," *Mission in Cambodia*, https://www.youtube.com/watch?v=T92qw_LWU04 (accessed August 7, 2017). Seila Uon is a Pentecostal pastor who was part of the generation of church leaders that emerged in the early 1990s in Cambodia.

[69]Maher and Uon, *Cry of the Gecko*.

[70]Don Cormack, *Killing Fields, Living Fields: An Unfinished Portrait of the Cambodian Church—the Church that Would Not Die* (Crowborough, UK: OMF International, 1997).

[71]Joshua J. Lovelace, *From Seedtime to Harvest: The History of the Assemblies of God of Cambodia,* in *Pentecost Around the World Book 5* (Baguio City, Philippines: Asia Pacific Theological Seminary Press, 2019).

[72]Darin R. Clements, "The Church Reborn Out of the Killings Fields: A Preliminary Sketch of the Pentecostal/Charismatic Movement in Cambodia" (Paper presented at the Theological Symposium, Asia Pacific Theological Association, Yangon, Myanmar, July 26-27, 2016).

efforts across the spectrum of the Pentecostal/Charismatic movement in a chapter contribution to a book on Pentecostalism in Asia Pacific.[73]

Conceptual Framework—Level one:
Educational Contexts of Non-Formal CE

The first level of the conceptual framework is the educational context in which a local congregation is situated. This aspect is external to a church and not under its control. However, the educational context can influence a congregation's approach to non-formal CE in various ways, including providing a philosophical framework for teaching and learning, engendering expectations about teacher-student relationships, providing formal education to available teachers,[74] and creating an impetus for developing educational programs to meet social needs.

The first sub-section below considers the historical development of non-formal CE (e.g., Sunday school) in the educational contexts of England and the United States. The second sub-section explores the relationship between modern non-formal CE and social science. The third sub-section presents research on educational development in Cambodia in order to better understand the external conditions that can influence non-formal CE in the research context. Each sub-section ends with a summary.

Historical Development of Non-Formal CE in England and America

Social problems and lack of education provided the original impetus for the Sunday School Movement that dramatically impacted societies in England and the United States in the 19th century. Historical development of non-formal CE in these two countries is germane to this research because it took place in a time of emerging national education systems and social reforms. Unlike many countries in the West today where social institutions are well established and basic education is essentially universal, non-formal CE in contexts like those in Cambodia is developing against a backdrop of poor educational systems and pressing social issues.

---

[73]Darin R. Clements, Ken Huff, and Nyotxay, "The Development of Pentecostalism in Cambodia and Laos," in *Asia Pacific Pentecostalism*, ed. Denise A. Austin, Jacqueline Grey, and Paul Lewis (Lieden, The Netherlands: Brill, 2019), 129-149.

[74]See the section "Teachers of Non-formal CE" in Chapters 9 and 10.

Early Sunday Schools in England

The story of the Sunday school begins with Robert Raikes Jr., a newspaperman in Gloucester, England, who, in 1757, attempted to use his publication to initiate a range of social reforms. One of the many issues that worried Raikes was lack of education for working children. In the wake of the Industrial Revolution, poor children often worked long hours, six days a week. Raikes and many others were concerned about the social impacts of unsupervised children literally running wild on Sundays, their only day off from work. Many were destined to find themselves in the penal system as adults, an institution that Raikes had unsuccessfully sought to reform. After years of effort through philanthropic enterprises with only modest results, in 1780, Raikes opened the first Sunday school (for both boys and girls) in the kitchen of a woman named Meredith on Sooty Alley.[75]

Those initial Sunday schools were primarily concerned with teaching reading and writing. With the Bible as textbook, the larger goal was social transformation through education and evangelism that would lead to conversion and an accompanying transformation of morals and manners. The results were dramatic. As crime dropped noticeably, the movement gained national and international attention. However, not everyone supported Sunday schools. Despite the high ideals of the Enlightenment, many in the privileged classes (and even some of the clergy) opposed them on the grounds that educating the poor masses threatened social order.[76]

Nevertheless, the Sunday School Movement grew to the point that enrollment was approximately 400,000 by the time of Raikes' death in 1811 and 1,250,000 at the 50th anniversary of its founding.[77] Anthony and Benson note, "For many of these students, the Sunday school was the only means of educational input in their lives."[78] Among the list of

---

[75]Michael J. Anthony and Warren S. Benson, *Exploring the History and Philosophy of Christian Education: Principles for the 21st Century* (Grand Rapids: Kregel, 2003), 260-262; Gary C. Newton, "Sunday School, Early Origins," in *Evangelical Dictionary of Christian Education,* ed. Michael J. Anthony (Grand Rapids: Baker Academic, 2001), 672.

[76]Anthony and Benson, *Exploring the History,* 264-265; John L. Elias, *A History of Christian Education: Protestant, Catholic, and Orthodox Perspectives* (Malabar, FL: Krieger, 2002), 149, quoted in Anthony and Benson, *Exploring the History,* 260, note 2.

[77]James E. Reed and Ronnie Prevost, *A History of Christian Education* (Nashville: Broadman and Holman, 1993), 259.

[78]Anthony and Benson, *Exploring the History,* 265.

contributions in England, Wesley Willis credits Sunday school with fostering basic public education for all classes of society, helping to prioritize the need for social reforms in the thinking of the middle and upper classes, and encouraging adult education.[79]

Early Sunday Schools in America

While Sunday schools in England addressed a gap in an already existing school system, Sunday schools in America were one of the first institutions to emerge during the early decades of its national existence. After a number of 'prototype' Sunday schools and experiments,[80] the first of what became a movement of Sunday schools was launched in Philadelphia, Pennsylvania, prompted by a visit in 1811 from the British Presbyterian minister Robert May, who compared America's efforts with English Sunday schools.[81] Anne Boylan argues that "Sunday school first became an American institution because it promised to fulfill the broad millennial expectations of Evangelical reformers."[82] To these organizers, Sunday school would do more than educate the masses; it would promote a specifically Evangelical understanding of the Bible with the primary goal of the "personal experience of regeneration" of students and the ultimate goal of an Evangelical Protestant nation.[83]

Sunday schools emerged and worked in complement with common schools in America in the 19th century. While initially providing basic education, Boylan observes that "American Sunday schools divested themselves of that responsibility as much as possible by cultivating their early partnership with common schools."[84] This separation by basic education during weekdays and moral education on Sundays was largely completed by the 1830s.[85] However, in locations and segments of society where common schools did not yet exist, Sunday schools often provided basic education until public education was established.[86] In this way,

---

[79] Wesley R. Willis, *200 Years—and Still Counting! Past, Present, and Future of the Sunday School* (Wheaton, IL: SP Publications, 1979), 33-34.

[80] Anne Boylan, *Sunday School: The Formation of an American Institution, 1790-1880* (New Haven, CT: Yale University Press, 1988), 7. According to Boylan, the first such prototype was created by the First Day Society in Philadelphia, Pennsylvania in 1791.

[81] Ibid., 13.
[82] Ibid., 4.
[83] Ibid., 9-10.
[84] Ibid., 22.
[85] Ibid., 24.
[86] Ibid., 29.

Boylan concludes, "Sunday school enabled Americans to reject denominational schooling and class-oriented public education in favor of the ideal—if not the reality—of free public schooling for all."[87]

Historical Development of Non-Formal Christian Education—Summary

The educational context for the emergence of the Sunday School Movement in England was social reform and expansion of the national educational system to include all classes. In the United States, by contrast, Sunday schools were an early national institution that complemented the emerging common-school system and a key component in the expansion of Evangelical Protestantism. These conditions no longer drive non-formal CE in many places in the West because social institutions are well established and basic education is universally available.[88] In contexts like those found in Cambodia, social issues and gaps in the educational system can still create a space for development of non-formal CE. One clear difference, however, is that contexts like Cambodia lack the historically Christian societies that provided the environment for expansion of Sunday schools in England and America.

Non-Formal CE and the Social Sciences

Another aspect of the educational context that affects non-formal CE is the social sciences. Due to a long history of lay participation,[89] the social sciences may appear to have a minimal influence on non-formal CE. As Elmer Towns (also known as "Mister Sunday School") famously writes to Sunday school teachers, "Without a lot of education, church officer experience, or public recognition, you can influence a life for Christ."[90] Such a statement appears to be far removed from the ideal of the professional 'reflective teachers' in a formal educational system that

---

[87]Ibid., 59.

[88]I am generalizing here. There are both urban and rural communities in America, for example, where social issues and education gaps could be addressed effectively through non-formal CE.

[89]Anthony and Benson, *Exploring the History*, 263; Boylan, *Sunday School*, 101-132.

[90]Elmer Towns, *What Every Sunday School Teacher Should Know: 24 Secrets that Can Help You Change Lives* (Ventura, CA: Gospel Light, 2001), 17.

continues to hone their skills through in-class observation informed by evidence-based theories.[91]

This sub-section on non-formal CE and the social sciences both challenges the perception of a lack of reference to social science and weighs the difficulties of reciprocal interaction between CE and the social sciences. The insights discussed here were critical to development of this research as social science.

Non-Formal CE's Use of Educational Theory from a Distance

Despite the tradition of relying on lay teachers,[92] non-formal CE has made great use of educational theory developed by social science. For example, Johann Pestalozzi's theories about the nature of children were adapted and disseminated through Sunday school conventions in America as early as the 1820s.[93] Later, John Milton Gregory's *The Seven Laws of Teaching* (1886) built on Pestalozzi's concepts in an effort to strengthen both public and Christian education in the state of Illinois.[94] In the late 20th century, Howard Hendricks recast Gregory's seven laws specifically for Sunday school teachers in his book, *Teaching to Change Lives: Seven Proven Ways to Make Your Teaching Come Alive*.[95] To Hendricks, "a passion to communicate" is more critical to effective Sunday school teaching than methodology.[96] Lastly, Verda Rubottom's *First Steps for Effective Teaching: A Guide for Christian Educators* is a more recent publication in the tradition of Towns and Hendricks.[97]

The books by Towns, Hendricks, and Rubottom all work from current, evidence-based educational theories. At the same time, they reflect strong commitment to the importance of lay teachers through their relative brevity, use of non-technical jargon, practical focus, and a priority on the spiritual formation of teachers. These books are mentioned here

---

[91] Jack Snowman, Rick McCown, and Robert Biehler, *Psychology Applied to Teaching*, 12th ed. (Boston: Houghton Mifflin, 2009), 15.

[92] England's first Sunday schools in the 1790s employed professional teachers. Boylan, *Sunday School*, 101.

[93] Ibid., 124.

[94] John Milton Gregory, *The Seven Laws of Teaching* (Boston: Congregational Sunday-School and Publishing Society, 1886), 44, 50-51 (repr., San Bernardino, CA: ReadaClassic.com, December 12, 2015).

[95] Howard Hendricks, *Teaching to Change Lives: Seven Proven Ways to Make Your Teaching Come Alive* (Colorado Springs: Multnomah Books, 1987).

[96] Ibid., 15.

[97] Verda Rubottom, *First Steps for Effective Teaching: A Guide for Christian Educators* (N.p.: Xulon Press, 2012).

because they exemplify accessible non-formal CE teacher development material that brings teachers into engagement with social science from a distance.

Wilhoit: Non-Formal CE's Relationship with Social Science

In contrast, Jim Wilhoit argues that, despite CE's dependence on social science, evidence- based theories have had only minimal influence on its development and practice, saying that "Educational ideologies, theology, and common sense shape and inform Christian education far more than do rigorous empirical findings."[98] In his view, the flaw is at the grass roots where teachers uncritically labor to make their classes engaging for their students. Thus, he argues, the primary role of CE leaders is to "shape the values of the people who make up the Christian-education team."[99]

So, what is the nature of the relationship between CE and social science? Wilhoit describes several obstacles that stand in the way of a proper integration between the two.[100] First, the high cost of research prevents a lot of meaningful research into CE at the outset. Second, there is a built-in suspicion of social science because of its lack of interest in or outright rejection of spiritual realities; thus, it is not viewed as capable of measuring the objectives of CE (e.g., spiritual growth). Third, social science as a discipline requires long periods of time to validate, test, and refine its theories and models; CE tends to be out of sync or completely disconnected from that process. Lastly, social science is not a unified discipline in which "experimental findings tend to converge and are basically harmonious;"[101] rather, its research often leads to more questions. Especially with this last obstacle in mind, Wilhoit urges Christian educators to "abandon the proof-text approach"[102] in their engagement with social science.

Wilhoit's solution to this conundrum is for Christian educators to humble themselves and fully engage social science on its own terms. Such an approach requires formulating empirically verifiable theories, reading the key educational theorists instead of relying on secondary sources,

---

[98] Jim Wilhoit, *Christian Education and the Search for Meaning*, 2nd ed. (Grand Rapids: Baker Book House, 1991), 116.
[99] Ibid., 9-12.
[100] Ibid., 117-120.
[101] Ibid., 120.
[102] Ibid., 121.

recognizing that social science does indeed discover and describe 'truth' about human beings created in God's image, and becoming reflective practitioners that test social science's findings in the classroom.[103]

Yount and LeFever: Non-Formal CE Engages the Social Sciences

Despite many changes in non-formal CE in the West since the publication of Wilhoit's book in 1991, the obstacles to interaction with social science he described remain firmly in place. The distance between social science and local, non-professional CE practitioners is still substantial; and there seems to be little interest on the part of busy volunteer teachers in bridging that distance. Instead of trying to bring the two sides into conversation with each other, some CE writers have accepted a one-sided relationship in which social science has more to offer CE than CE has to offer social science. In other words, CE leaders and teachers can be reflective practitioners that legitimately take advantage of the findings of social science without engaging in the lengthy, expensive process of doing empirical research in return.

William Yount and Marlene LeFever are two examples of Christian educators who seek to take full advantage of the social sciences. First, Yount evaluates key schools of learning theory in terms of what they have to offer Christian educators. His work brings a Christian perspective to the insights of behavioral learning theory (Ivan Pavlov, E. L. Thorndike, B. F. Skinner), cognitive learning theory (Gestalt psychology, Jean Piaget, Jerome Bruner), and humanistic learning theory (Abraham Maslow, Carl Rogers, Arthur Combs).[104] He views these foundational theories as being "maps and compasses to aid the inexperienced teacher-traveler in charting the course to learning success."[105]

Yount offers his 'Disciplers' Model' as a framework for engaging the social sciences. Table 2.1 presents the seven components of his framework, six of which have counterparts in educational psychology. The 'Holy Spirit as Teacher' component has no counterpart[106] because naturalistic science assumes that "God exists only in the minds of religious

---

[103]Ibid., 122-129.
[104]William Yount, "Learning Theory for Christian Teachers," in *Introducing Christian Education: Foundations for the Twenty-First Century*, ed. Michael J. Anthony (Grand Rapids: Baker Academic, 2001), 101-110.
[105]Ibid., 101.
[106]William R. Yount, *Created to Learn: A Christian Teacher's Introduction to Educational Psychology* (Nashville: B&H Academic, 2010), 29.

believers, who are, in fact, deluded."[107] Therefore, while validating and using the findings of social science in his honest study of human learning and development, Yount accepts that faith and naturalistic science are irreconcilable as "forever enemies."[108]

Table 2.1. The Disciplers' Model and educational psychology[109]

The **Bible**, God's Eternal Word	**Content Mastery** The structure of the subject matter
The **Needs** of Learners	**Individual Differences** The personal needs of learners
Helping Learners **Think**	**Cognitive Development** How learners process information and think
Helping Learners **Value**	**Affective Development** (Humanistic theories) How learners develop values and attitudes
Helping Leaners **Relate**	**Social Context, Group Dynamics** How social interaction deepens learning
Helping Learners **Grow** in the Lord	**Maturation** How learners grow and change
The **Holy Spirit** as Teacher	— There is no spiritual counterpart

Second, Marlene LeFever's book, *Learning Styles: Reaching Everyone God Gave You*, works from Bernice McCarthy's hemispheric model of learning theory (left brain, right brain)[110] to present four learning styles as a paradigm for teaching Sunday school. The four that she draws from McCarthy are 'Imaginative Learners,' 'Analytic Learners,' 'Common Sense Learners,' and 'Dynamic Learners.'[111] Table 2.2 lists these four learning styles, along with the key questions that engage students with each learning preference.

---

[107]Ibid., 49.
[108]Ibid., 51.
[109]Ibid., 29.
[110]Marlene LeFever, *Learning Styles: Reaching Everyone God Gave You* (Colorado Springs: David C. Cook, 2004), 211-216.
[111]Ibid., 25.

Table 2.2. McCarthy's four learning styles[112]

Learning Styles	Key Questions
Imaginative	Why do I need to know this? (meaning)
Analytic	What do I need to know? (content)
Common Sense	How does this work? (experiment)
Dynamic	What can this become? (creative application)

Since students are more likely to disengage rather than adjust to a teacher's approach, teachers are responsible to adjust to the students and engage their preferred learning styles.[113] LeFever's model for teaching involves naturally progressing through the four learning styles in each lesson in such a way that all the students will be engaged in their own learning style at some point, thus freeing "them up to participate in activities that will not be in their strength areas."[114] Although McCarthy does not make reference to these learning styles, Lawrence O. Richards' time-honored Hook, Book, Look, Took (HBLT) approach[115] fits LeFever's teaching model very closely. Table 2.3 demonstrates how her model based on McCarthy's learning styles compares to Richards' HBLT lesson structure.

Table 2.3. McCarthy's four learning styles compared with the HBLT lesson structure[116]

Learning Styles	Key Questions	HBLT Lesson Steps	Goals
Imaginative	Why do I need to know this? (meaning)	Hook	• Gains attention • Surfaces a need

---

[112]Ibid.

[113]Ibid., 39n1.

[114]Ibid., 25-27.

[115]Lawrence O. Richards and Gary J. Bredfeldt, *Creative Bible Teaching*, rev. and exp. (Chicago: Moody Press, 1998), 154-161.

[116]LeFever, *Learning Styles*, 25; Richards and Bredfeldt, *Creative*, 160, figure 13.

Analytic	What do I need to know? (content)	Book	• Communicates the general and transferable principle from the passage
Common Sense	How does this work? (experiment)	Look	• Relates truth to life • Motivates the students to actions
Dynamic	What can this become? (creative application)	Took	• Identifies out-of-class application of truth to life

Non-Formal CE and the Social Sciences—Summary

The relationship between non-formal CE and social science is complicated and unidirectional. It is complicated because non-formal CE benefits from the findings of social science despite the latter's secular and naturalistic worldview. It is unidirectional because, while many good texts have been prepared for Sunday school teachers from the findings of social science, CE has generally not provided reciprocal value. While authors like Wilhoit have urged that CE should strive to engage the social sciences on equal terms, authors like LeFever and Yount have demonstrated that non-formal CE can take full advantage of the social sciences' findings without responding in kind. Following this line of thinking, the social sciences can provide a very useful set of tools for exploring non-formal CE in contexts like Cambodia.

Non-Formal CE and the Cambodian Educational Context

Approaches to non-formal CE always interact with the larger educational context, whether critically or uncritically. The educational context determines the education level of available teachers, understandings about the nature of teacher-student relations, educational philosophies, parental expectations, and ideas about the roles of education in general. This sub-section reviews the findings from research on education in Cambodia that can provide insights into non-formal CE in local churches in the country.

The sub-section covers three aspects of educational development. The first presents research covering historical developments from pre-colonial times to 1996. The second looks at two significant World Bank reports on educational development from 2008 and 2015. The third considers how the Cambodian state has used education to legitimize its power.

Historical Development of Education in Cambodia

Historically, Cambodia has not been successful at developing educational infrastructure. Sideth Dy's analysis of its experience with basic education demonstrates that education focused on traditional culture and basic literacy for specific categories of people for hundreds of years. Some progress was made near the end of French colonial rule (1863-1953) and during the reform efforts of the 1950s and 1960s under Prince Sihanouk. However, during the 1970s and 1980s, Cambodia experienced civil war, virtual abolition of educational institutions by the Khmer Rouge (1975-1979), and socialist-oriented education under Vietnamese occupation (1979-1989). It has only been since the international involvement of the 1990s that notable, long-term development in primary and secondary education has occurred.[117]

Supote Prasertsri published a report in 1996 on the progress of the nation's Education For All (EFA) program goals for year 2000. He set the stage for the challenges they were facing with these words:

> Unlike previous conflicts, it was the educated people—especially teachers—who were the targets of the destruction in this war [1970-1979]. Unfortunately, the goal of this destruction was largely achieved. Because of the great loss of trained teachers, the task of rebuilding the education system has faced one of the most difficult circumstances in this century.[118]

Prasertsri reported that the progress of rebuilding education infrastructure had faced heavy constraints over the previous sixteen

---

[117]Sideth S. Dy, "Strategies and Policies for Basic Education in Cambodia: Historical Perspectives," *International Education Journal* 5, no. 1 (2004): 90-97, http://www.iefcomparative.org (accessed April 30, 2015).

[118]Supote Prasertsri, *Rebirth of the Learning Tradition: A Case Study on the Achievements of Education for All in Cambodia* (Paris: United Nations Educational, Scientific, and Cultural Organization, 1996), 5, ERIC, a/n ED433269 (accessed June 9, 2015).

years.[119] Those constraints included the following: (1) Due to a lack of classrooms, three hundred thousand children ages six to ten (out of approximately two million) still did not have access to basic education; (2) teacher salaries were as low as $30 per month in urban areas and $20 per month in rural areas;[120] and (3) regarding the teachers, "Almost one-third of primary school teachers have themselves not completed lower secondary education."[121] Nevertheless, Prasertsri concluded that the EFA goals for year 2000 would likely be met, assuming political stability, progress on education legislation, and good coordination among various aid agencies.[122] The following sub-section demonstrates just how far Cambodia has come in educational development.

Current Developments in Education in Cambodia

Two major World Bank research reports (2008 and 2015) demonstrate that, since the Prasertsri report in 1996, Cambodia has made major strides in developing its national education system. Benveniste, Marshall, and Araujo in 2008 chronicled the significant progress made in primary education (grades one through six). For instance, in 2004, net primary enrollment rate had reached 76 percent with particularly strong gains among the poor, and the gross enrollment rate was 127 percent due to enrollment of over-age children. Secondary education, however, lagged behind; despite a goal of 51 percent by 2005, enrollment in 2004 was at 16.4 percent for lower secondary (grades seven through nine)

---

[119]David M. Ayres, *Anatomy of a Crisis: Education, Development, and the State in Cambodia, 1953-1998*, Southeast Asia edition (Chiang Mai, Thailand: Silkworm Books, 2003), 135-136. According to Ayres, this time period includes 10 years of socialist-oriented education under Vietnamese occupation in the 1980s.

[120]Prateek Tandon and Tsuyoshi Fukao, *Educating the Next Generation: Improving Teacher Quality in Cambodia*, in *Directions in Development: Human Development* (Washington, D.C.: World Bank, 2015), 3, http://dx.doi.10.1596/978-1-4648-0417-5 (accessed June 9, 2015). These salaries put teachers with families below the poverty line unless they had additional sources of income. Despite dramatic economic growth and increases in teacher salaries by 2015, married teachers with two children were still below the poverty line and far behind comparable professions.

[121]Prasertsri, *Rebirth*, 9. Lower secondary education refers to grades seven through nine. Luis Benveniste, Jeffery Marshall, and M. Caridad Araujo, *Teaching in Cambodia* (Washington, DC: World Bank, 2008), 3n1, datatopics.worldbank.org/hnp/files/edstats/KHMwp08.pdf (accessed October 29, 2015).

[122]Prasertsri, *Rebirth*, 26.

and 8.5 percent for upper secondary (grades 10 through 12). Tertiary enrollment stood at 1.4 percent of adults ages 19 to 22.[123]

In view of the progress in primary education and the challenges facing the growth of secondary education, Benveniste, Marshall, and Araujo focused the majority of their report on improving teacher quality, saying, "Almost two-thirds of secondary teachers have completed at least grade 12, while 18 percent had some post-secondary education."[124] However, while most of the teachers had completed pre-service training, the authors discovered that training to be of low quality, which affected mastery of content and pedagogical practices.[125] They also found, from their in-class observations of lower secondary teachers, that . . .

> Only half of lower secondary school teachers had lesson plans readily available on the day of an unannounced visit. Class time is mostly exclusively [sic] devoted to instruction or recitation. The time spent in applied individual or group work is low. Overall, classes tend to be highly structured with limited opportunities for interaction or creative thinking. Teachers tend to dominate the time-on-task through frontal instruction or asking questions.[126]

The World Bank report by Tandon and Fukao published in 2015 builds on the one by Benveniste, Marshall, and Araujoort in 2008. Tandon and Fukao found strong gains in both elementary education enrollment (from 83.8 percent in 1992 to 96.4 percent in 2012) and secondary education enrollment (from 16.6 percent in 2000 to 35.1 percent in 2012). However, only 67 percent of the 24,000 children in grades one through six who took the Early Grade Reading Assessment in 2010 could read. In fact, of those who would technically be defined as literate due to their education level, 47 percent could not comprehend the content.[127]

Tandon and Fukao focused on teacher quality as being the most important determinant in quality of education overall and, therefore, critical to national development across sectors. Their report provides

---

[123]Benveniste, Marshall, and Araujo, *Teaching in Cambodia*, 3. These numbers are about double the percentages of 1997, with 7.6 percent enrolled in lower secondary and 4.5 percent in upper secondary.
[124]Ibid., iii.
[125]Ibid., vi.
[126]Ibid., vii.
[127]Tandon and Fukao, *Educating the Next Generation*, 1.

evidence concerning attraction to teaching as a profession, how well teachers are trained, and how well they perform. Despite the traditional respect afforded teachers, pay was near the poverty line and the caliber of trainees represented the lowest scoring levels of the grade 12 comprehensive exams.

Once in the training program, candidate teachers were faced with trainers whose content mastery was often lower than that of a ninth-grade student. The approach in Teacher Training Centers typically involved dictating lessons, little questioning, and few applied activities. Despite adoption of teacher standards at the ministry level, most trainers either had not heard about them or did not use them in their classrooms.[128]

These two reports provide a window into the educational context in which non-formal CE in Cambodia must develop. My initial conclusion from this review of the literature was that non-formal CE programs would be strongly influenced by the national education system because CE teachers, students, and church leadership have all been shaped by it. However, the findings in Chapter 10 present a different result.

The basic assumption of the national educational system's influence on non-formal CE teachers fits with the research of Barbara Houger. She studied influences that shape pedagogical approaches of East Asian Assemblies of God Bible school instructors. Her study focused on the interaction among these four categories of influence—(1) ancient East Asian philosophies practiced in the region today; (2) contrasting cultural dimensions, values, and thought patterns experienced between the East and the West; (3) recent pedagogy and present reforms in East Asia planned for globalization and economic growth; and (4) Western pedagogy implemented in East Asia through colonization, invitation, and continued involvement, especially in higher education.[129]

In addition to the four points in her initial framework, Houger's research discovered two additional "lived educational experiences" that interviewees considered to be even more influential to their own educational approaches. First, their pedagogy was significantly impacted by the relational model of their own Bible school teachers; and second, the Bible school atmosphere they experienced was significant for their own spiritual growth and their understanding of the communal experience of Bible school education.[130]

---

[128]Ibid., 2-6.
[129]Barbara Rose Houger, "Instructors' Pedagogies as the Frame of Influence for East Asian Assemblies of God Bible Schools" (PhD diss., Biola University, 2011), 15.
[130]Ibid., 236.

Another condition not considered here is the impact of training provided to local churches to support non-formal CE development. Such training is often given either without reference to the national education system or as a complement to it. For example, AGC teacher training workshops concentrate on basic, student-focused skills for volunteer teachers who are often very young. Following are the topics covered in those the seminars—(1) How to Use Curriculum, (2) Classroom Management, (3) Leading a Child to Christ, (4) Effective Use of Games, Visuals, and Object Lessons, (5) How to Hold a Class in the Palm of Your Hand (i.e., delivering lessons with confidence), and (6) Walk Through the Bible (i.e., helping teachers remember major biblical characters and events from Creation to Revelation using one-word titles and hand signs).[131]

Ayres: The State's Use of Education in Cambodia

Education always has a purpose. In his classic book, *Basic Principles of Curriculum and Instruction*, Ralph Tyler begins with the statement that schools are to be "the agency for helping young people to deal effectively with the critical problems of contemporary life" and to transmit values from one generation to the next.[132] Those values may be democratic, socialist, or authoritarian. In order to be considered effective to a given society, educational systems and institutions must be aligned with the larger social values through behavioral norms (institutional culture), learning objectives, and the pedagogy employed.

Non-formal CE is also a means of transmitting values. This subsection considers the roles of non-formal CE in terms of how it can be used to instill values in adherents (internal) and to project values to the larger society (external). To understand some of the possible dynamics of communicating values through non-formal CE in the context of local Cambodian churches, we will consider David Ayres' analysis, in his book, *Anatomy of a Crisis: Education, Development, and the State in Cambodia, 1953-1998*, of how the Cambodian government has used development of its education sector to foster a set of social and political values. His book is a critical text for understanding Cambodian society, its government, and education system. Ayres strongly debunks the notion that "the Khmer Rouge was some extreme anomaly whose legacy is

---

[131]Diana Clements, email message to author, June 29, 2017.
[132]Ralph Tyler, *Basic Principles of Curriculum and Instruction* (Chicago: University of Chicago, 1949), 5.

the major impediment to development in contemporary Cambodia."¹³³ Rather, he assets, "The crisis was, and continues to be, a product of the disparity between the education system and the economic, political, and cultural environments that it has been intended to serve."¹³⁴

That disparity, Ayres concludes, is a formal education system that works toward the competing goals of "making Cambodia look modern and, at the same time, sustaining the key tenets of traditional polity, where leadership is associated with power and where the nature of the state is perceived to be a function of that power."¹³⁵ Or to state the matter another way, power traditionally flows in one direction in Cambodia. "While those at the top governed, those at the bottom existed to be governed."¹³⁶

The modern-looking Cambodia that Ayres analyzed is one in which educational development and reforms are driven by the World Bank and International Monetary Fund, both entities whose loans to developing countries push "market-oriented reform through a policy of leverage."¹³⁷ This strategy is part of the so-called New World Order that . . .

> . . . symbolizes a global conquest by the free market paradigm, [which is characterized by] increased skepticism in regard to the capacity of the state to serve as an engineer of both social change and economic growth, and an increased belief in the supremacy of the free market.¹³⁸

In other words, Ayres argues, the government of Cambodia is using free-market oriented agencies like the World Bank to develop educational infrastructure as one means by which it is consolidating and legitimizing itself with traditional notions of absolute power.

Ayres' analysis of the disparity between the government's notion of power and the worldview embedded in its formal education system raises the following questions as to the possible uses of non-formal CE in Cambodia:

1. Are the traditional notions of power described by Ayres evident in local churches?

---

¹³³Ayres, *Anatomy*, 6.
¹³⁴Ibid., 3.
¹³⁵Ibid.
¹³⁶Ibid., 11.
¹³⁷Ayres, *Anatomy*, 163. The World Bank study by Benveniste, Marshall, and Araujo referenced above is a case in point.
¹³⁸Ibid., 162.

2. Do local churches use non-formal CE to legitimize their power structures?
3. If so, are those power structures influenced by biblical ideals, or is there disparity between the biblical ideals taught and the power structures of that congregation?
4. Unlike the government's need for a formal education system, do some local churches neglect non-formal CE because it is unnecessary to the maintenance of their power structures?

Non-Formal CE and the Cambodian Educational Context—Summary

Understanding the development of the national education system of Cambodia is critical to thinking about its impact on development of approaches to non-formal CE by AGC churches. Historically, Cambodia has not been very successful at providing a good education infrastructure and the necessary teacher resources. While much progress has been made since the involvement of major international organizations in the 1990s, teacher quality is a persistent issue. Moreover, the question of formal education in Cambodia may have as much (or more) to do with political power than with social development. These issues are critical to thinking about the development of non-formal CE because they affect such things as the availability and quality of teachers, teaching-learning styles, and even potential use of education in the church.

CHAPTER 3

Literature Review and Conceptual Framework: External and Internal Roles of Non-Formal CE

Conceptual Framework—Level 2: The Roles of Non-formal CE

The second level of this framework for exploring the development of approaches to non-formal CE among AGC churches covers the roles of non-formal CE. The roles under consideration here are divided into the general categories of external and internal. External roles engage the society around the congregation, such as educational needs and social issues; whereas internal roles focus on values and needs within the congregation itself. In keeping with the trajectory of this literature review (i.e., from external to the congregation to specific to the congregation), the external roles will be considered first, even though the internally-focused roles tend to dominate non-formal CE activities.

These categories represent two ends of a spectrum rather than two distinct functions. Figure 3.1 presents a spectrum of non-formal CE roles in local churches. While many CE programs clearly focus on either internal or external needs, some programs cannot be so clearly defined or include elements of both sides of the spectrum. Evangelism is one element of non-formal CE programs that could fit the spectrum at several junctures. In this discussion, it is considered an internal role for two reasons—(1) the external roles considered here are primarily designed to address needs in the community, regardless of whether members are added to the congregation; and (2) one of the primary roles of internally focused non-formal CE is to confirm the personal faith (i.e., conversion) of the congregants.

Figure 3.1. Spectrum of non-formal CE roles in local churches

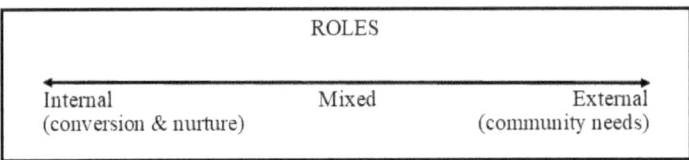

External Roles of Non-Formal CE

Non-formal CE has the potential to benefit the communities in which congregations are located. That potential is determined by the needs in society, the desire of churches to address those needs, church resources, and the church's understanding of their place in society. This subsection reviews examples of the ways in which churches have served the needs of their communities through CE. In the first example, the early Sunday school movements in England and America addressed critical gaps in public education. The second example considers implications for non-formal CE from the work of Paulo Freire in literacy and social empowerment, that is followed by Cheryl Bridges Johns' critique of his ideas from a Pentecostal point of view. The third example, again from a Pentecostal perspective, presents ways in which non-formal CE is addressing poverty in the Philippines. The fourth example is from Miller and Yamamori's landmark study of Pentecostal social engagement. The fifth example suggests additional external roles of non-formal CE from civic engagement in Korea and Indonesia.

Early Sunday School Movements and Gaps in Public Education

While Chapter 2 already discussed early development of Sunday schools in England and America in relation to the larger educational context, those points are revisited here to consider how churches engaged the needs of their societies through CE. These examples can provide insights into potential external roles of non-formal CE in contexts like those found in Cambodia, where segments of society struggle with exploitation and lack of basic education.

Wesley Willis chronicles the experiences and motivations of Gloucester newspaperman Robert Raikes, who became the father of the Sunday school movement in England. Raikes saw that the lower classes were living in a spiritual vacuum, even during a time of spiritual and social renewal through the preaching of men like John Wesley and

George Whitefield. Willis describes the situation with which Raikes was familiar thusly:

> Life in the wildly growing cities was generally godless and inhumane, with terrible physical conditions, exploitation of the lower classes, abuse of children, and other intolerable social inequities. By combining an educational mission with a spiritual mission, the Sunday school provided an important answer to these problems.[139]

Willis explains that Raikes did not originally intend for Sunday school to be an agency of the church. Rather, "He saw it as a means to reach the dregs of English society, to rescue the unfortunate castoffs of a calloused society."[140] Although the Bible was the key text and basis for the morals taught, the primary goal was to teach literacy, because Raikes understood ignorance to be at the root of the social problems he witnessed around him.[141] A great supporter of Sunday schools, John Wesley was personally responsible for bringing them into the Methodist structure for the purpose of evangelism and spiritual instruction.[142]

As the potential for social reform became evident, the privileged classes soon got involved as teachers and financial backers. Referring to statements by Ellwood Clubberly, Willis says that the Sunday school movement accomplished what an act of Parliament could not. "[It] awakened in the lower classes a desire for educational reform, but also stimulated the upper and middle classes to recognize their responsibility to bring about educational and social reform."[143]

Sunday schools in America differed from those in England in at least three key ways. First, unlike the active support of the privileged classes in England for social reform, Anne Boylan describes Sunday schools in America as part of "the new middle-class vision of an expanding free-labor economy and a democratic state."[144]

Second, instead of addressing gaps in an existing education system, Sunday schools in America grew in a complementary relationship with a newly developing education system. As America expanded westward during the first part of the 19th century, Sunday schools were seen as a

---

[139] Willis, *200 Years—and Still Counting!*, 27.
[140] Ibid., 20.
[141] Ibid.
[142] Ibid., 32.
[143] Ibid., 34-35.
[144] Boylan, *Sunday School*, 3.

legitimate means of basic education until tax-supported common schools could be established.[145] Additionally, with the abolition of slavery in the 1860s, Sunday schools were utilized as an initial means of meeting "an overwhelming demand for education from the newly freed black people."[146]

Third, unlike England's Sunday school movement, which started outside the church and was later assimilated into it, America's Sunday schools were part of an Evangelical Protestant vision of America. To that end, missionaries were sent out by agencies like the American Sunday School Union and the American Home Missionary Society to start Sunday schools in "places destitute of religious institutions."[147] They often became the primary religious gatherings in such places and frequently led to the establishment of permanent congregations.[148] As time progressed, Sunday schools increasingly relinquished the role of providing basic education but retained the role of providing moral education. Although Boylan argues that the role of Sunday schools in basic literacy must not be overstated, she concludes that they did effectively complement the growing common-school system and provided one of the most basic functions of any educational system—cultural transmission.[149]

Paulo Freire: Literacy and Empowerment Through CE

Paulo Freire (1921-1997) was a Brazilian-born educator who made important contributions to understanding the power of politics and class in education. Growing up during the Great Depression, his family fell from a comfortable middle-class status into abject poverty when he was just eight years old. At age eleven, he began to formulate his ideas about the power of literacy to overcome poverty and class oppression.[150] After earning a PhD in 1959, he worked in the Brazilian government's welfare and education agencies, including the National Plan of Adult Literacy. Freire's ideas about awakening the poor and oppressed led to his imprisonment and expulsion in 1964. After working in Chile, teaching at Harvard, and serving with the World Council of Churches for

---

[145]Ibid., 24, 53.
[146]Ibid., 29.
[147]Ibid., 34.
[148]Ibid., 33-34.
[149]Ibid., 33.
[150]Vernon L. Blackwood, "Freire, Paulo," *Evangelical Dictionary of Christian Education,* ed. Michael J. Anthony (Grand Rapids: Baker Academic, 2001), 303.

a time, he returned to Brazil where he became a professor at the Catholic University of Sao Paulo in 1981.[151]

In *Pedagogy of the Oppressed*,[152] one of his most influential texts, Freire attacked what he called "banking education," which he defined as an approach to education that de-humanizes students by turning them into "'containers,' into 'receptacles' to be 'filled' by the teacher."[153] He explained, "In the banking concept of education, knowledge is a gift bestowed by those who consider themselves knowledgeable upon those who [sic] they consider to know nothing."[154] In practical terms, banking education kills students' ability to think critically and reinforces their social roles as "adaptable, manageable beings"[155] who have been domesticated to the status quo.

Three terms are paramount in Freire's works—dialogue, praxis, and "conscientization." The first term, *dialogue*, emphasizes the intelligence of students and the cooperative role between students and teachers in the process of learning and developing critical thinking. Simple transference of knowledge is tantamount to propaganda, not education,[156] Freire's own words are irreplaceable on this point:

> Through dialogue, the teacher-of-the-students and the students-of-the-teacher cease to exist and a new term emerges: teacher-student with students-teachers. The teacher is no longer merely the-one-who-teaches, but one who is himself taught in dialogue with the students, who in turn while being taught also teach. They become jointly responsible for a process in which all grow.[157]

The second term, *praxis*, is the ability of humans to understand and transform their situations.[158] Freire certainly had revolutionary ideas in mind with this concept, his basic educational implication being that all human beings must be treated with dignity, as possessing inherent intelligence regardless of their class or background. Indeed, he urges that

---

[151]Reed and Prevost, *A History*, 354-355.
[152]Paulo Freire, *Pedagogy of the Oppressed*, 30th anniversary ed., trans. Myra Bergman Ramos (New York, NY: Continuum, 2005).
[153]Ibid., 72.
[154]Ibid.
[155]Ibid., 73.
[156]Ibid., 68.
[157]Ibid., 80.
[158]Ibid., 125.

praxis is essential: "For apart from inquiry, apart from praxis, individuals cannot be truly human."[159]

The third term is the Brazilian word *conscientizacao* (or *conscientization* in English). Freire explained that, unlike English, Portuguese does not separate the ideas of conscience and consciousness into distinct categories.[160] He thus infused the word with additional meaning to refer to the awakening of persons to the real situations around them. The translator of *Pedagogy of the Oppressed* defines the term *conscientization* as "learning to perceive social, political, and economic contradictions, and to take action against the oppressive elements of reality."[161] The word became so strongly vested with revolutionary meaning by some groups that he ceased using it in 1974.[162]

In conclusion, Freire was deeply informed by his Catholic faith and saw the Church as uniquely positioned to be holistic and to liberate oppressed people by speaking with a prophetic voice.[163] His work is famously credited with providing the framework for Liberation Theology.[164] Even so, his emphasis on student-centered education, literacy as foundational to social reform, and transformation of individuals and societies through education have implications for external roles of nonformal CE in socioeconomic situations like those found in Cambodia.

Cheryl Bridges Johns: Critique of Paulo Freire

Cheryl Bridges Johns has considered Freire's concepts from a Pentecostal perspective, especially in Chile and Brazil where he had personally worked and made a significant impact.[165] In her view, Freire's core concepts of dialogue, praxis, and conscientization resonate with Pentecostals. Her model of a Pentecostal catechesis places teachers and students in dialogue with each other, teachers being "facilitators of God's actions and presence in the teaching-learning process" who do not "attempt to rule over students but rather to facilitate a divine-human

---

[159]Ibid., 72.
[160]William B. Kennedy, "Conversation with Paulo Freire," *Religious Education* 79, no. 4 (Fall 1984): 514, EBSCOhost, ATLA Religion Database (accessed September 7, 2016).
[161]Translators note, Freire, *Pedagogy of the Oppressed*, 35n1.
[162]Kennedy, "Conversation," 514.
[163]Blackwood, "Freire, Paulo," 303-304.
[164]Ibid., 304; Reed and Prevost, *A History*, 355.
[165]Cheryl Bridges Johns, *Pentecostal Formation: A Pedagogy among the Oppressed* (Eugene, OR: Wipf and Stock, 1998).

encounter."¹⁶⁶ This encounter is the essence of Pentecostal hermeneutics, which "involves a dialectic between present experience and biblical witness."¹⁶⁷

However, Johns notes two points of divergence between Pentecostalism and Freire. First, being people deeply committed to the Scriptures, Pentecostals have failed to engage the "interface between the text of Scripture and the textual landscape of their socio-political reality."¹⁶⁸ This observation agrees with Miller and Yamamori, who conclude that, despite emerging as a powerful movement of social transformation, Pentecostals are not typically organized to bring about social justice through structural reforms and governmental policies.¹⁶⁹ Second, Johns critiques Freire as denying "the validity of the oppressed's experience" by not giving credence to their own understanding of reality, specifically their understanding of God's role in history.¹⁷⁰ Therefore, she concludes that a Pentecostal catechesis is the work of the local church as a teaching community in which all expressions of church life (non-formal CE included) bring everyday experience into dialogue with God's revelation (Scriptures) under the energizing and guiding work of the Holy Spirit.¹⁷¹

Joel Tejedo: Pentecostal Social Engagement Through Education

Joel Tejedo is a Filipino seminary professor and researcher who looks at how Pentecostal churches address poverty in cities and villages. He argues that Pentecostals are drawn to address social issues by their theology. Based on God's holistic involvement in creation, "We can understand that our response to the needs within society should likewise be holistic."¹⁷² Furthermore, both the Old and New Testaments evidence a strong theme of social and economic justice through the Spirit-empowered acts of leaders, Spirit-inspired voices of the prophets, and concern of the early church for the poor.¹⁷³

---

¹⁶⁶Ibid., 124.
¹⁶⁷Ibid., 100.
¹⁶⁸Ibid., 35.
¹⁶⁹Donald E. Miller and Tetsunao Yamamori, *Global Pentecostalism: The New Face of Christian Social Engagement* (Berkeley, CA: University of California Press, 2007), 4.
¹⁷⁰Johns, *Pentecostal Formation*, 59-60.
¹⁷¹Ibid., 86, 121, 124.
¹⁷²Joel A. Tejedo, *The Church in the Public Square: Engaging Our Christian Witness in the Community* (Baguio City, Philippines: Sambayanihan Publishers, 2016), 2.
¹⁷³Ibid., 3-10.

Despite its reputation of having a "preoccupation with otherworldly eschatology and one-way ticket evangelistic effort[s]," Tejedo's research in the Philippines has shown that "Pentecostal civic engagement has been increasingly recognized as one of the resource capitals that empowers the lives of the poor."[174] When asked to agree/disagree with statements regarding local church action to combat poverty, respondents identified conversion as the top priority and education as the second.[175] The education in view here includes addressing gaps in the formal educational system. As an example, one ministry Tejedo cited teaches science, mathematics, character building, and value formation as part of its Saturday feeding program for children, while the adults receive livelihood and economic training.[176] With education as one of the primary activities, the goal of this Pentecostal, holistic approach to poverty is to see individuals transformed into "spiritually, socially, and economically responsible citizens in the community."[177]

Miller and Yamamori: Progressive Pentecostals and Social Engagement

Joel Tejedo's research dovetails with the conclusions of Donald Miller and Tetsunao Yamamori in their landmark phenomenological study of global Pentecostalism as an emerging force in social engagement. They use the term Progressive Pentecostals to describe "Christians who claim to be inspired by the Holy Spirit and the life of Jesus and seek to holistically address the spiritual, physical, and social needs of people in their community."[178] Following the example of Jesus, who fed the five thousand (Matthew 14:15-21), touched lepers (Matthew 8:1-4), and offered living water to the socially marginalized (John 4:7-29), Progressive Pentecostals feel called by the Holy Spirit to bring transformation to their communities through service that transcends boundaries of race and religious affiliation.

Educational programs surfaced as an important component in Pentecostal social engagement. Some of Miller and Yamamori's examples include a racially integrated preschool system in Johannesburg,

---

[174]Ibid., 13.
[175]Ibid., 28.
[176]Ibid., 34.
[177]Ibid., 35.
[178]Miller and Yamamori, *Global Pentecostalism*, 2. Miller and Yamamori exclude groups that only engage the society around them in order to seek conversions or to propagate a "health and wealth" message.

South Africa;[179] an educational program for "dump children" in Cairo, Egypt, through short camps and an extensive follow-up program;[180] an outstanding tutoring program in Singapore that fits the competitive educational ethos of that country;[181] and church-run elementary and secondary schools in Kampala, Uganda, that offer a Christian alternative to the overfull classrooms of the government system.[182]

Kim and Lie on Civic Engagement in Korea and Indonesia

Two journal articles point to the civic potential of non-formal CE. In the first article, Heeja Kim examines CE's historical role in Korean nationalism. Korea has the unique distinction of being the only Asian nation colonized by a non-Western power. Christianity put down deep roots during Japanese colonization and then played a strong role in the development of nationalism. When Korea's Declaration of Independence was signed in 1919, many of the signers had been educated in mission schools. Fifteen of the thirty-three signers were Christians, a remarkable representation out of a population that was one percent Christian.[183] Although Kim's article refers to formal CE programs, non-formal CE programs can have a similar impact in contexts like Cambodia by addressing shortcomings in the national education system.

The second article speaks of civic engagement as a role of CE in Indonesia, where Christians face discrimination and persecution for their faith. Tan Giok Lie cites several politicians and government officials who were urging churches to teach their people how to engage in the political process so that Christian voices can be properly represented in the formulation of public policy.[184] The idea presented here is that of the Christian community being invited to participate in the public forum *as Christians*. Non-formal CE can be a means by which Christian communities learn how to participate in that forum productively. This

---

[179] Ibid., 75-79.
[180] Ibid., 80-83.
[181] Ibid., 93.
[182] Ibid., 96.
[183] Heeja Kim, "Korean Christian Education: Past, Present, and Future," in "International Perspectives on Christian Education," supplemental issue, *Christian Education Journal* 10, S3 (Fall 2013): S222, http://journals.biola.edu/ns/cej (accessed June 25, 2015).
[184] Tan Giok Lie, "The Context and Challenges of the Church's Educational Ministry in Indonesia," in "International Perspectives on Christian Education," supplemental issue, *Christian Education Journal* 10, S3 (Fall 2013): S235, http://journals.biola.edu/ns/cej (accessed June 25, 2015).

idea rings true in contexts like Cambodia, where civic engagement is not restricted by political doctrines of separation between church and state.

External Roles of Non-Formal CE—Summary

This section reviewed several examples of ways in which non-formal CE has fulfilled roles that were external to local churches. The early Sunday school movement in England started as a means to address gaps in the national educational system and bring about social reform.[185] In 19th century America, Sunday schools complemented the growing educational system by providing basic education in locations where it was not yet available.[186] In the work of Paulo Freire, CE became a powerful tool for social empowerment through literacy and creating a critical awareness of social injustice.[187] Speaking from a Pentecostal point of view, Joel Tejedo sees non-formal CE as one of the most important tools a local church can use in combatting poverty by supplementary basic education and livelihood training.[188] Lastly, examples from Korea[189] and Indonesia[190] demonstrate that CE can be a means by which Christians can impact civil society. These examples demonstrate that non-formal CE has the potential to effectively address educational and social needs in the communities surrounding local churches.

Internal Roles of Non-Formal CE

The second level of this conceptual framework—roles of non-formal CE—also includes the roles that are internal to a local church. This section first reviews internal roles of non-formal CE from various Evangelical points of view. It next considers the long-standing tension between conversion and nurture in non-formal CE. It then presents key themes from Horace Bushnell's book, *Christian Nurture*,[191] one of the most influential texts in the development of CE from the 19th century to

---

[185]Willis, *200 Years*.

[186]Boylan, *Sunday School*.

[187]Freire, *Pedagogy of the Oppressed*; Blackwood, "Freire, Paulo," 303; Reed and Prevost, *A History*, 354-355; Kennedy, "Conversation," 514.

[188]Tejedo, *The Church in the Public Square*.

[189]Kim, "Korean Christian Education."

[190]Lie, "The Context and Challenges."

[191]Horace Bushnell, *Christian Nurture* (New York: Scribner, Armstrong & Co., 1876), Christian Classics Ethereal Library, https://www.ccel.org/ccel/bushnell/nurture.html (accessed January 28, 2017).

the present. And lastly, it looks at how the Catholic Church in Cambodia has made the catechism its primary tool of conversion.

Evangelical Perspectives on Internal Roles of Non-Formal CE

The internal roles of non-formal CE can be described in a variety of ways, depending on the perspective of the authors and/or the tradition. This sub-section surveys representative Evangelical points of view in order to provide orientation for a conceptual framework for studying non-formal CE in contexts like those found in Cambodia.

Williams: An Evangelical Orientation

Dennis Williams begins his discussion of CE by distinguishing it from the pluralistic connotations of the term "religious education" as defined by the Religious Education Association. He uses the term CE to designate a specifically Evangelical orientation in which the Bible is the foundation and authority of what is taught and the source for expected outcomes.[192] Williams identifies these four primary purposes of Evangelical CE:

> [1] to bring people to a saving faith in Jesus Christ, [2] to train them in a life of discipleship, [3] to equip them for Christian service in the world today, and [4] to develop in believers a biblical worldview that will assist them in making significant decisions from a Christian perspective. . . . so that they can impact society with the message of the gospel.[193]

Wilhoit: Transformative CE

Jim Wilhoit issued this dire warning in 1991—"Christian education is in crisis. It is not healthy and vital; as a discipline, it is bankrupt."[194] The problem was not a lack of activity, but rather a lack of both purpose and critical application of social science. Table 3.1 compares three common approaches to CE that Wilhoit considers inadequate, all of which have roots in educational psychology.[195] Transformational CE is

---

[192]Dennis Williams, "Christian Education," in *Evangelical Dictionary of Christian Education,* ed. Michael J. Anthony (Grand Rapids: Baker Academic, 2001), 132-133.
[193]Ibid., 133.
[194]Wilhoit, *Christian Education,* 9.
[195]Ibid., 73-103.

his alternative to these approaches and proposed solution to the crisis he described above. Transformational CE has these three goals— "(1) the equipping of believer-priests for service and worship; (2) the cultivation of a servant's heart and skills; and (3) the establishment of a teaching environment that is open to the working of God's renewing grace."[196]

Table 3.1. Four contemporary approaches to CE[197]

Approach	Originator/ Proponent	Teacher's Role	Aim
Romantic	Jean Jacques Rousseau (1712-1778)	Gardener	Personal growth and self-fulfillment
Transmissive	Mortimer Adler, et al.	Technician	Efficient transmission of valued knowledge and skills
Developmental	John Dewey (1859-1952)	Coordinator	Equipping the learner with useful mental tools
Transformative	Jim Wilhoit, et al.	Guide	Transforming the learner

Richards and Bredfeldt: Teaching for Life Change

In their seminal book, *Creative Bible Teaching*, Lawrence Richards and Gary Bredfeldt flesh out transformative CE in practical terms. The simply stated goal of "teaching for life change" requires teachers to address two questions—"What do I want the student to learn? and How do I want the student to change?"[198] In this biblically-based, student-centered approach, "Creative Bible teachers focus on helping learners bridge the gap between the world of the Bible and the world of the student."[199] Again, the goal is life change through engagement with the Bible, not just transmission of knowledge. This life change happens

---

[196]Ibid., 108.
[197]Ibid., 74-102, 114.
[198]Richards and Bredfeldt, *Creative Bible Teaching*, 131.
[199]Ibid., 132.

when teachers help learners engage the Bible in all three of Bloom's domains of learning—cognitive (head), affective (heart), and behavioral (hands).[200]

Estep, Anthony, and Allison: Theologically Driven CE

James Estep, Michael Anthony, and Gregg Allison argue that Evangelical CE is primarily a theological enterprise, saying, "Christian education is *Christian* because what we believe theologically should inform and influence not only the content of education in the church but also the overall approach to education in the church."[201] Along with the authors cited above, their approach views CE as having a transformative role in the lives of congregants. The difference with this approach is that it is driven by systematic theology. CE driven by theology evinces the following characteristics—(1) has "a theologically informed constructive use of social science theories," (2) "has a theologically informed purpose," (3) "features a theologically informed selection of content," and 4) "evidences a theologically informed design."[202] The theologically informed purpose in point number 2 is further described as being "for the glory of God, maturity in the Christian faith, and the advancement of the kingdom."[203] CE in this approach primarily "serves the pastoral function of nurturing faith within the community of the church."[204]

Dettoni: Shifting from CE to Spiritual Formation

John Dettoni represents a fresh way of thinking about the nature and role of CE. He and the other authors of *The Christian Educator's Handbook on Spiritual Formation* advocate a return to the historical idea of Christian nurture and discipleship as the central mission of the church, as opposed to simply having an education department within a fragmented array of church ministries.[205] Spiritual formation

---

[200] Ibid., 135-138.

[201] James R. Estep Jr., Michael J. Anthony, and Gregg R. Allison, *A Theology for Christian Education* (Nashville: B & H Publishing, 2008), 2.

[202] James R. Estep, "What Makes Education Christian?" in *A Theology for Christian Education*, James R. Estep, Michael J. Anthony, and Gregg R. Allison (Nashville: B & H Publishing, 2008), 38.

[203] Ibid.

[204] Ibid., 40.

[205] John M. Dettoni, "What Is Spiritual Formation?" in *The Christian Educator's Handbook on Spiritual Formation*, eds. Kenneth O. Gangel and James C. Wilhoit (Grand Rapids: Baker Books, 1994), 11-14.

is, therefore, a meld of traditional notions of nurture and discipleship. Dettoni emphasizes three key words in this conception of spiritual formation—formation, discipleship, and maturity. *Formation* refers to the transformation that should take place in people's lives as they grow in biblical knowledge. *Discipleship* implies a life of intentionally following Jesus. *Maturity* describes the goal of transformation—i.e., "to become mature, complete, and perfect like Jesus Christ."[206] Thus, in the spiritual formation understanding, the purpose of CE is to nurture believers to be mature followers of Jesus Christ through a total church approach, of which education is a pervasive element.

Conversion Versus Nurture

Any consideration of the internal roles of non-formal CE must take into account childhood faith. Two distinct strains of thought emerged in the American Sunday school experience that remain issues in the hearts of many non-formal CE teachers to this day—(1) Are children born into Christian families in need of a radical conversion experience? and (2) Must small children convert in the same way as adults despite their lack of capacity to comprehend Christian teaching and its implications? While Evangelicals saw conversion as paramount during the early decades of Sunday schools in America, mainline denominations decried such treatment of children as (in the words of Horace Bushnell) "a virtual abuse and cruelty."[207]

As America's Sunday school movement progressed through its first decades and common schools took over basic education, the role of Sunday schools shifted decidedly toward "preparation for conversion," with the focus being on "emotional and spiritual rather than purely intellectual processes."[208] The emphasis on conversion came directly from the doctrine of depravity. Since, as Evangelicals understood it, children were still more emotional than intellectual in their reasoning, the lessons, books, and approach needed to speak to them about their spiritual condition through emotional and spiritual experiences. For this reason, many stories in the Sunday school publications of that time could be considered "religious terrorism" by today's sensibilities. They

---

[206]Ibid., 15-16.
[207]Bushnell, *Christian Nurture*, 41.
[208]Boylan, *Sunday School*, 138.

included depictions of horrifying consequences for mundane sins and "stories emphasizing the nearness of death."[209]

This emphasis on conversion included keeping teacher-student ratios small (1:6-10), thus "annihilate[ing] the boundaries between intellectual knowledge and emotional understanding of Protestant doctrine, turning Sunday school into an incubator of conversion."[210] The revivalistic approach to conversion with its dramatic experiences began to mellow during the last half of the 19th century, and Bushnell's concepts of "Christian nurture" began to have increasing influence on Christian thinking about childhood.[211] (See next sub-section for a discussion of his ideas.)

The tension between conversion and nurture no longer creates the conflicts in America that it once did. Indeed, the Evangelical points of view described in the previous sub-section embrace both conversion and nurture. Williams placed bringing people to a saving faith in Jesus Christ[212] first in his list of purposes. Elmer Towns, in his book, *What Every Sunday School Teacher Should Know*, includes "knowing the spiritual condition of each student" (i.e., salvation) in his inventory of what teachers should know about their students.[213] However, he devotes twenty-two out of twenty-four chapters to nurture/teaching; only the last two deal with leading a child to Christ and friendship evangelism.[214]

The emphasis on nurture can also be seen in Estep, Anthony, Allison, and Dettoni through their intentional use of the language of nurture (including the term itself) in their understanding of the role of CE, without devaluing the need for a personal experience of conversion/regeneration.[215] Thus, Evangelical thinking about CE continues to put a priority on personal conversion and faith from the earliest age possible while at the same time fully engaging the larger work of lifelong nurture, including children born into the church.

---

[209]Ibid., 140.
[210]Ibid., 139.
[211]Ibid., 149.
[212]Williams, "Christian Education," 133.
[213]Towns, *What Every*, 38.
[214]Ibid., 162-178.
[215]Estep, "What Makes Education Christian?" 40; Dettoni, "What Is Spiritual Formation?" 11-14.

Bushnell: Christian Nurture

Horace Bushnell (1802-1876) is considered by many as being "the father of both American theological liberalism and modern religious education."[216] Although his views were strongly challenged (even deemed heretical by Calvinists) in his lifetime, his writings have since become some of the most important in the development of CE in America.[217] As a Congregationalist minister in Hartford, Connecticut, Bushnell saw firsthand some of the negative aspects of revivalism and its attendant emotionalism. He particularly took issue with the notion that a child could not be a true Christian until he or she had reached the age of accountability. Robert Choun explains the prevailing notion of the time thusly—"The role of the parent was to remind the child of his or her sinful nature" until the age of accountability and the time for conversion.[218]

In 1847, the Massachusetts Sabbath School Society published Bushnell's book, *Views of Christian Nurture*, which he wrote for parents, not for Sunday school teachers who were more focused on Pestalozzi's ideas at that time.[219] The book's main proposition was "that the child is to grow up a Christian and never know himself as being otherwise."[220] While rejecting baptismal regeneration as superstition,[221] Bushnell believed that children born into Christian families were born regenerate, saying . . .

> In other words, the aim, effort, and expectation should be, not as is commonly assumed, that the child is to grow up in sin, to be converted after he comes to a mature age; but that he is open on the world as one that is spiritually renewed, not remembering the time when he went through a technical experience, but seeming rather to have loved what is good from his earliest years.[222]

---

[216] Anthony and Benson, *Exploring*, 324.
[217] Robert J. Choun, "Bushnell, Horace," in *Evangelical Dictionary of Christian Education*, ed. Michael J. Anthony (Grand Rapids: Baker Academic, 2001), 101; Anthony and Benson, *Exploring the History*, 326.
[218] Choun, "Bushnell," 101.
[219] Boylan, *Sunday School*, 147, 150-151.
[220] Bushnell, *Christian Nurture*, 7.
[221] Ibid., 25, 59-60.
[222] Ibid., 7.

The core theological concept in Bushnell's writings that allows for the state just mentioned is "the organic unity of the family,"[223] which means that, just as children can inherit depravity from their parents, so too can they inherit regeneration.[224] This state exists as long as those children are "held within the matrix of parental life."[225] Such a state is both real and potential. Instead of the child being born in depravity, the child is born in a state of regeneration and therefore ready to respond in faith when the time is right. Bushnell contends that, in the rite of infant baptism, "God engages, on his part, that it may be, and calls the Christian parent to promise, on his part, that it shall be."[226] In this way, infant baptism expressed the family's organic unity in the same way the Jewish rite of proselyte baptism included the whole family.

One final key contribution of Bushnell's reasoning is the primacy of the home in nurturing the child's faith. He describes the spiritually nurturing home in these ecclesiastical terms—"The house, having a domestic Spirit of grace dwelling in it, should be the church of childhood, the table and hearth a holy rite, and life an element of saving power."[227] Bushnell's exhortation to parents is both theological and practical. In the chapter titled "Physical Nurture, to Be a Means of Grace," he included food (quality and amount), clothing, and table manners among the range of aspects of spiritual nurture in the home.[228] To leave children to their own devices and moral development until they reach an age of reasoning is "ostrich nurture," just as the ostrich in Job 39:13-17 "deals cruelly with her young" by showing no care for their safety.[229]

A 'Catechumenical Church' in Cambodia

The Catholic Church in Cambodia has made conversion the primary role of its internal educational programs since the re-institution of religious freedom in 1993. Responding to the proselytizing scandals of Evangelicals in the refugee camps in the 1980s, the Catholic Church chose to turn from building a physical presence through church construction efforts to building a community that was respectful of the culture and of Buddhism. Destombes stated, "I insist he who wants to

---

[223]Ibid., 47-63.
[224]Ibid., 47-48.
[225]Ibid., 53.
[226]Ibid., 58.
[227]Ibid., 12.
[228]Ibid., 139-150.
[229]Ibid., 35-36.

be a Catholic must [study the Church's teachings] for three years, every week. We believe that only God can convert."[230]

François Ponchaud refers to a "catechumenical church" in Cambodia in order to emphasize the centrality of catechism. Because many who come to the Catholic Church are poor and drawn by "seeing charity in action," catechumens are carefully vetted for "inner freedom" after their initial motivations have been purified.[231] This process takes approximately three years. The first year is introductory as catechumens search their own hearts and questions. In the second year, "they are brought into contact with Jesus and his teaching."[232] Ponchaud describes the third year in detail thusly:

> When the leaders consider that faith is burgeoning, the time comes for the first stage, according to a ritual sanctioned by the Council: in the celebration of the entry into the Church, the catechumen solemnly takes "Christ as a refuge, the Word as a refuge, and the Church as a refuge." Formerly they would take Buddha, the Law and the monastic community as a refuge at the pagoda or in any Buddhist celebration. For yet another year, they deepen their faith especially through appropriate Biblical texts and liturgies.[233]

Internal Roles of Non-Formal CE—Summary

This section has considered various viewpoints on the internal roles of non-formal CE. The Evangelical views presented here all emphasize the authority and centrality of the Bible, conversion, growth, and service. All these views strive for integration between the cognitive, affective, and behavioral domains; however, Estep, Anthony, and Allison's theologically-driven CE leans towards the cognitive. Representing a shift away from traditional thinking about CE as an educational program within a local congregation, Dettoni speaks of spiritual formation as the total work of the church.

The long-standing issue of conversion versus nurture is the philosophical and theological background to the Evangelical views

---

[230] Lachlan Hastings, "Vanquished in the 70s, Catholic Church Still on the Mend," *The Phnom Penh Post*, March 25, 2005, http://www.phnompenhpost.com/national/vanquished-70s-catholic-still-mend (accessed January 7, 2017).
[231] Ponchaud, *The Cathedral in the Rice Paddy,* 282-283.
[232] Ibid., 284.
[233] Ibid.

described here. Although the fires of controversy have died down, local Christian teachers must still wrestle with the question of conversion for children born into Christian families. Horace Bushnell's writings have had a strong influence on thinking about this issue. More specific to the research context, the Catholic Church in Cambodia has made catechism (a tool typically associated with confirming the faith of those born into the church) its primary tool of conversion for a church that is still primarily made up of first-generation Christians. In so doing, the Catholic Church demonstrates that the difference between conversion and nurture may not be very clear in contexts like Cambodia.

CHAPTER 4

Literature Review and Conceptual Framework: Organizational Approaches of Non-Formal CE and Teachers of Non-Formal CE

This chapter addresses the third and fourth levels of the conceptual framework (see Figure 2.1 in Chapter 2). The third level is organizational approaches to non-formal CE, of which there are three basic models. The fourth level looks at the teachers of non-formal CE. This present chapter concludes with an overview of the fully developed conceptual framework for the research methodology to be detailed in Chapter 5.

CONCEPTUAL FRAMEWORK—LEVEL 3: ORGANIZATIONAL APPROACHES TO NON-FORMAL CE

The third level of this conceptual framework for exploring non-formal CE among AGC churches covers organizational approaches. Whereas local church non-formal CE exists within the larger context of national education systems and fulfills a spectrum of external and internal roles that are relatively common across contexts, the organizational approach of each local congregation represents its particular expression of social relationships and power structures. Each congregation's CE organizational structure reflects its values, resources, limitations, and aspirations. As Kenneth Garland stated, "The goal of any church in organizing the Christian Education ministry, regardless of its size, should be to meet as many needs as possible given the available resources."[234] Since there is normally no accreditation or formal standardization

---

[234] Kenneth R. Garland, "Organizing Christian Education in the Small Church," in *Foundations of Ministry: An Introduction to Christian Education for a New Generation*, ed. Michael J. Anthony (Grand Rapids: Baker Books, 1992), 242.

involved in setting up non-formal CE programs, each congregation's approach can be pragmatic or customized from available models.

This section considers three CE organizational models that have been prevalent in Western churches as starting points for understanding organizational approaches to non-formal CE in contexts like Cambodia. The following material draws primarily from Mark Cannister.[235] His first two models—the Functional and the Age-Group—were based on models previously described by Garland[236] and Bechtle.[237] His third model—the Group-Purpose—is a recently developed approach that works toward greater integration between education and all other aspects of church life. Figure 4.1 illustrates how these three CE organizational models relate to each other on a continuum of less-to-more integration. Following presentations of these models is a discussion of ways in which small-church dynamics affect CE organization.

Figure 4.1. Continuum of CE organizational models prevalent in Western churches

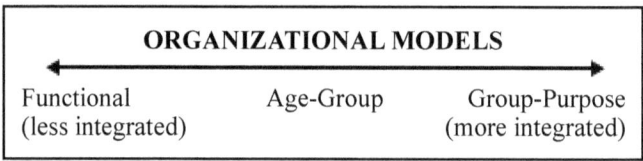

Functional Model

The Functional Model focuses on spiritual formation along programmatic lines, leaving other aspects of the church to work in parallel structures. In this model, for example, youth ministry, Sunday school, and children's church function as separate programs coordinated by a CE leadership team.[238] According to Garland, the model was common in small churches (i.e., less than two hundred members) in the West for many years and grew up around ministries that had developed within

---

[235]Mark W. Cannister, "Organizational Models of Christian Education," in *Introducing Christian Education: Foundations for the Twenty-First Century*, ed. Michael J. Anthony (Grand Rapids: Baker Academic, 2001), 150-157.

[236]Garland, "Organizing Christian Education," 242-254.

[237]Michael A. Bechtle, "Organizational Structures for Christian Education," in *Foundations of Ministry: An Introduction to Christian Education for a New Generation*, ed. Michael J. Anthony (Grand Rapids: Baker Books, 1992), 213-228.

[238]Cannister, "Organizational Models," 150-152.

local churches over time.²³⁹ Figure 4.2 illustrates how the Functional Model might look in a local church.

Garland describes four weakness regarding this model. First, the church's CE committee is often comprised of people who are not directly involved in the ministries they oversee. Second, conflicts of interest can arise as each ministry needs to recruit workers from the same limited pool of people. Third, each department needs to create its own administration, thus duplicating efforts within the same organizational structure. And fourth, conflicts can arise around the use of shared facilities.²⁴⁰

Figure 4.2. Functional model for CE organization²⁴¹

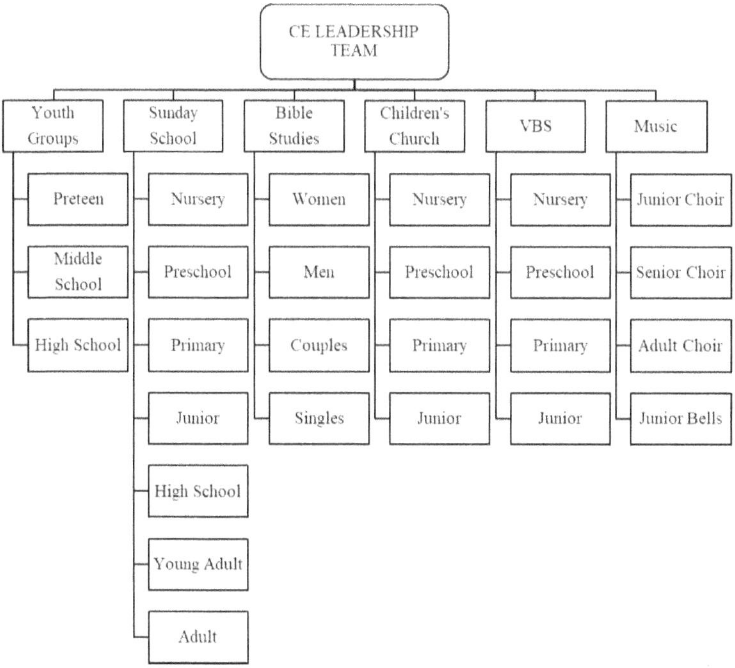

[Organizational chart with CE LEADERSHIP TEAM at top, branching into: Youth Groups (Preteen, Middle School, High School); Sunday School (Nursery, Preschool, Primary, Junior, High School, Young Adult, Adult); Bible Studies (Women, Men, Couples, Singles); Children's Church (Nursery, Preschool, Primary, Junior); VBS (Nursery, Preschool, Primary, Junior); Music (Junior Choir, Senior Choir, Adult Choir, Junior Bells)]

Age-Group Model

The Age-Group Model is today more common than the Functional Model. It typically organizes all aspects of a church's CE program by

---

²³⁹Garland, "Organizing Christian Education," 242.
²⁴⁰Ibid., 243-244.
²⁴¹Cannister, "Organizational Models," 151.

the three primary age groups—children, youth, and adults. The strength of this model is that it coordinates ministry for a given age group across program lines, leading to stronger relationships between leaders and participants. However, because it is still basically program driven, it can also tend toward fragmentation by isolating education from other aspects of church life.[242] Figure 4.3 illustrates how this model looks at a basic level of sophistication.

Figure 4.3. Age-group model for CE organization[243]

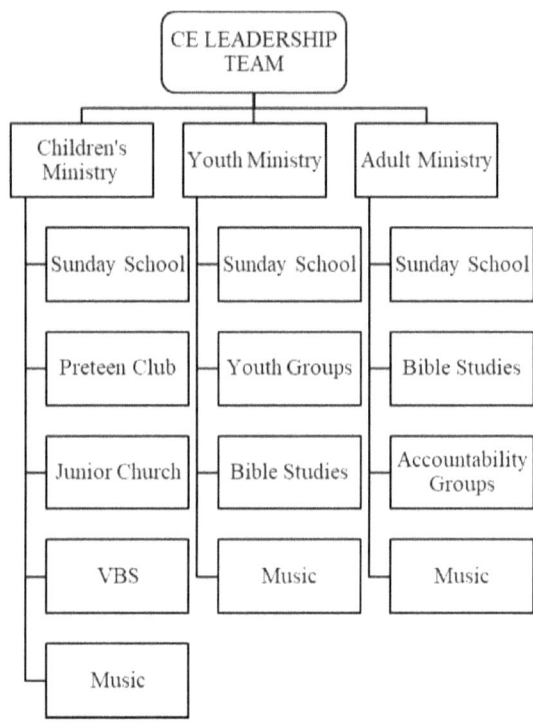

Garland endorses the Age-Group model as superior to the Functional Model because (1) it eliminates administrative duplication, coordinates recruitment across age groups, and reduces conflicts over use of facilities; and (2) it can work for a variety of church sizes. As a local church grows,

---

[242]Ibid., 152-153.
[243]Ibid., 152.

age groups can be divided and the CE Leadership Team expanded accordingly. When attendance reaches two hundred, he recommends the church consider adding a staff member who is specifically skilled in overseeing the education program.[244]

Group-Purpose Model

The Group-Purpose Model follows the age groupings of the second model and then crosscuts each age group with the five purposes of the church—worship, spiritual formation, service, evangelism, and fellowship. In this way, the entire church follows the same tradition in worship, same approach to evangelism, complementary curriculum, etc. This model is led by the Christian Ministries Leadership Team, which works to integrate all aspects of church life.[245] As Figure 4.4 shows, the strength of this model is the way in which each purpose is carried out from a unified source across programs and age groups. Among its limitations are the need for curricula that fit the desired level of integration across age groupings, strong administrative oversight to direct and maintain a complicated system, and skilled volunteers who are flexible enough to work across the age groups.

---

[244]Garland, "Organizing Christian Education," 247-248.
[245]Cannister, "Organizational Models," 153-154.

Figure 4.4. Group-purpose model for CE organization[246]

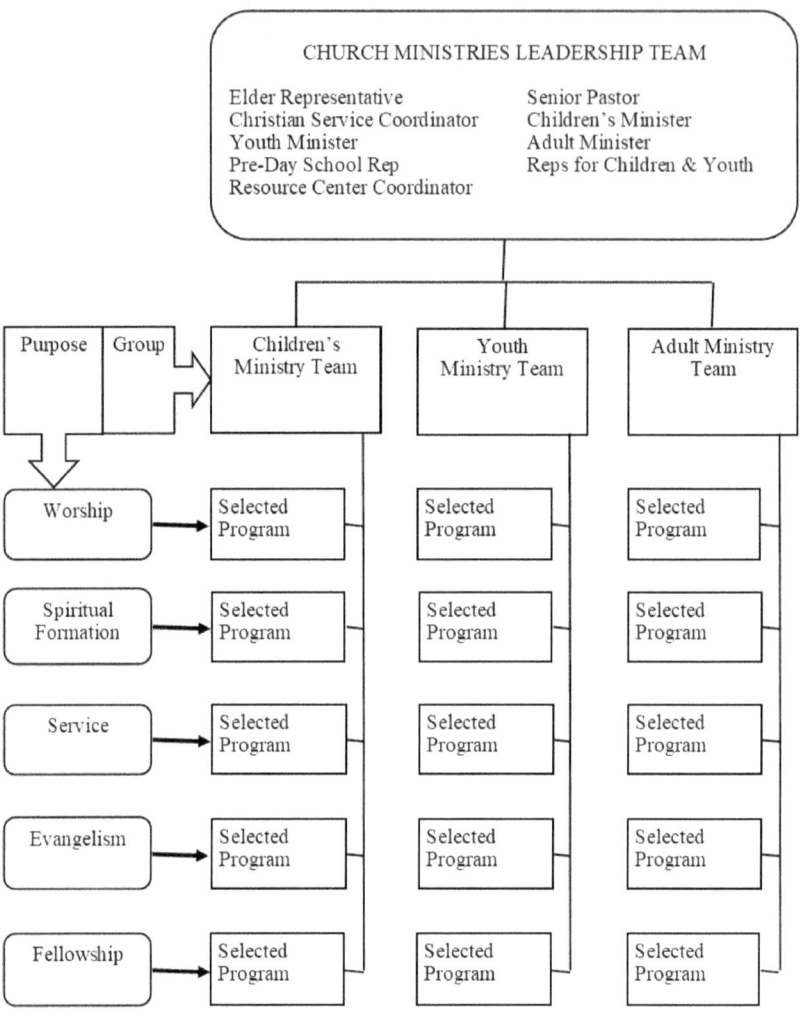

---

[246]Ibid., 154.

Organizational Considerations from Small-Church Dynamics

Mark Simpson offers some additional considerations for CE in small churches, which he defines as having less than five hundred active members.[247] He contends it's a misconception to think that "the small church is essentially a scaled-down version of the larger church,"[248] asserting instead that the special internal dynamic of small churches needs to be taken seriously because they "statistically dominate the North American church scene."[249] He characterizes small churches as having (1) a family orientation in which the minister is viewed more as family member than professional, (2) a tendency for short-term planning, (3) a high value on special events, and (4) a deeply vested leadership that is slow to change but effective at rapid communication.[250] Moreover, educational programming is apt to be the defining element because it dominates the weekly schedule and fills out the annual calendar.[251] These points are summarized in Table 4.1.

Table 4.1. Small church dynamics affecting organizational approaches[252]

1. A family orientation
2. A tendency for short-term planning
3. A high value on special events
4. A deeply vested leadership that is slow to change but effective at rapid communication
5. A weekly schedule and annual calendar dominated by educational programming

Both the Age-Group and Group-Purpose models have the potential to work well for congregations of all sizes. However, Simpson's characterization of small-church dynamics suggests that implementation of any CE organizational model must fit the local cultural context and character of each congregation in order to be effective. While the three

---

[247]Mark Edward Simpson, "Christian Education in the Small Church," in *Introducing Christian Education: Foundations for the Twenty-First Century*, ed. Michael J. Anthony (Grand Rapids: Baker Academic, 2001), 159.
[248]Ibid.
[249]Ibid.
[250]Ibid., 159-166.
[251]Ibid., 163.
[252]Ibid., 159-166.

models described above do provide useful starting points, they do not represent a standard by which organizational approaches to non-formal CE programs in contexts like Cambodia are to be measured. In my view, we must be cautious about evaluating any one of these models as better than the others or working from a sophisticated, corporate urban model to a simpler family-rural model. Rather, non-formal CE organizational approaches, both in the West and the East, need to be understood in terms of how they embody biblically informed cultural values and are shaped by local socioeconomic situations.

Organizational Approaches to Non-Formal CE—Summary

This section has considered three CE organization models (all from an American context) as starting points for exploring the organizational models that have been developed for non-formal CE among AGC churches. The Functional Model, representing the lowest level of integration, was popular for many years and developed organically with the rise of various programs in local churches. The Age-Group Model has a higher level of integration in that it is organized across age groups and activities, but it is still essentially program driven. However, as the discussion of small-church dynamics suggests, the Age-Group model can be more integrated than it appears in Figure 4.3. Lastly, the Group-Purpose Model represents a new approach to integrating all of church life around five core purposes; however, it requires a significant amount of organizational skill and resources to create and maintain an organizational structure around those core purposes.

CONCEPTUAL FRAMEWORK—LEVEL 4: TEACHERS IN NON-FORMAL CE

The fourth and final level of the conceptual framework looks at the teachers of non-formal CE (see Figure 2.1 in Chapter 2). This aspect of non-formal CE is the most unique with regard to local congregations, because each church must work with the people that are available. Walking through the levels of the conceptual framework, the educational context has a lot of influence on the quality of teachers and the teaching-learning styles that function in classrooms. Then, teachers must fulfill the external and/or internal roles of a non-formal CE program and fit within a local organizational model. As an expression of each church's culture and values, the organizational model both produces and validates teachers.

The first sub-section on Teachers of Non-Formal CE considers Sunday school teachers in 19th century America because of similarities with development of non-formal CE in contexts like those in Cambodia. The next sub-section then looks at literature on qualifications for non-formal CE teachers. Basic ones are considered first, followed by advanced qualifications, with special reference to the external and internal roles of non-formal CE. Each of the qualifications is appraised in terms of its potential importance to non-formal CE in contexts like Cambodia.

Sunday School Teachers in 19th Century America

Anne Boylan's analysis of Sunday school in America from 1790 to 1880 provides insight that can be helpful for thinking about non-formal CE in contexts like those found in Cambodia. She reports that, after the first two decades of growth in America, Sunday schools made a dramatic shift away from being philanthropic ventures with paid teachers.[253] "Throughout most of the nineteenth century, Sunday schools were the only American institutions for children that relied entirely on volunteer labor for their maintenance and perpetuation."[254]

Recruitment of teachers was an ongoing issue during that time due to geographical mobility and the custom of female teachers giving up their classes when they became mothers.[255] Thus, new recruits often were those whose lives had been influenced by their Sunday school teachers, were females, and were still in their teens and twenties. The primary recruitment tool was the "Bible classes" offered to youths as a way of combating the temptations of adolescence. The primary goal of those classes was conversion, just as it was with the children's classes. "Bible class members who did experience conversion were expected to take up teaching as a sign of their commitment and a means of developing it."[256]

One peculiar and controversial practice was the use of "unconverted" persons as teachers. More than just a means of transmitting a set of values, teaching Sunday school was also viewed by teachers as a means of their own personal spiritual development. Boylan cites a selection of diary accounts in which teachers were converted and became strong in their faith through the process of teaching. She summarizes, "Although there was disagreement on the issue, most advisors urged unconverted

---

[253]Boylan, *Sunday School*, 101.
[254]Ibid., 131.
[255]Ibid., 109.
[256]Ibid., 114.

individuals to become teachers, on the theory that teaching could lead to conversion."[257]

In conclusion, Sunday school teachers in 19th century America were young (i.e., in their teens and twenties), mostly female, and lacked formal training for teaching. Although turnover was high, teaching Sunday school was an important phase of spiritual development for many young evangelical Protestants in a nation still in its first century. The intangible benefits of teaching were powerful motivators. Said Boylan, "Teaching cemented their identification as evangelicals and provided rewards in the form of public approbation, spiritual self-improvement, expanded social experience, and broadened responsibility."[258] The same benefits may be available to young teachers in socioeconomic contexts like those in Cambodia as well.

Qualifications of Non-Formal CE Teachers

As the historical perspective above indicates, volunteer teachers have traditionally been the engine that drives non-formal CE. Need for effective lay teachers is perpetual and a primary concern for any viable non-formal CE effort. According to Michael Lawson and Robert Choun, "No church has ever had a standardized set of trained teachers. Only in our dreams will all teachers arrive at some predetermined level of expertise at the same time."[259]

This final sub-section of the literature review considers two levels of qualifications for non-formal CE teachers. With level one of the conceptual framework (Educational Context) in mind, the first sub-section lays out the basic qualifications for any level of CE program development. The second sub-section then considers advanced qualifications for volunteer teachers with reference to the external roles and perspectives on internal roles of non-formal CE presented in level two of the framework (Roles of Non-Formal CE).

---

[257]Ibid., 129.
[258]Ibid., 101.
[259]Michael S. Lawson and Robert J. Choun, Jr. *Directing Christian Education: The Changing Role of the Christian Education Specialist* (Chicago: Moody Press, 1992), 140.

Basic Qualifications of Non-formal CE Teachers

In his book, Teaching to Change Lives, Howard Hendricks describes the ideal CE teacher as 'FAT'—Faithful, Available, Teachable.[260] This succinct summary of the basic qualifications of a volunteer non-formal CE teacher is not an oversimplification. Teachers in 19th century America's Sunday school movement (described above by Boylan) were neither highly qualified nor highly educated, and the materials for training prior to 1860 "devoted more space to counseling teachers on their spiritual lives than suggesting how or what to teach."[261]

The educational context (i.e., literacy, educational levels, pedagogical experiences) and makeup of a local church determine the quality and availability of voluntary CE teachers. This dynamic is markedly different from formal educational institutions, which must meet accreditation standards and employ certified teachers. Thus, in the absence of external standards, essential qualifications for non-formal CE teachers need to be identified. Michael Bechtle's six basic qualifications for any position in a CE program (see Table 4.2) provide benchmarks for considering non-formal CE teachers in contexts like those found in Cambodia.

Table 4.2. Bechtle's basic qualifications for CE workers[262]

The worker is a Christian.
The worker is maturing in his or her Christian life.
The worker is teachable.
The worker has a love for people.
The worker should be a team player.
The worker is dependent on God.

These six qualifications for volunteer CE workers were written for the American context, which has a relatively well-educated population

---

[260] Hendricks, *Teaching*, 20.
[261] Boylan, *Sunday School*, 127.
[262] Michael A. Bechtle, "The Roles and Responsibilities of Christian Education Personnel," in Foundations of Ministry: An Introduction to Christian Education for a New Generation, ed. Michael J. Anthony (Grand Rapids: Baker Books, 1992), 238.

and a religious environment that is primarily Protestant or Catholic.[263] Even so, the qualifications are arguably relevant for any context and particularly salient for development of non-formal CE in contexts analogous to Cambodia.

Before discussing how these six basic qualifications could be understood in contexts besides America, it is important to note some qualifications not included in the list. First, the education level of a prospective teacher or worker is not given. Second, educational or professional qualifications are not required. Third, the list specifies that the worker be a 'maturing' but not a 'mature' Christian. To Bechtle, the actual level of maturity is less important than the fact of ongoing, observable growth, which is the essence of discipleship. In other words, his list of basic qualifications centers on character traits, personal faith, and a desire to work with people, seeing gifts, skills, or even potential for effectiveness as being secondary.

The six basic qualifications identified here probably sound like common sense to a Judeo-Christian context. However, they cannot be taken for granted in societies where Christianity is a minority religion, the church is largely first-generation, and many adults are only functionally literate is not a given. The following observations are made from a Buddhist context as examples:

1. People may participate in a local congregation for many months before they begin to come to personal faith. So, evidence of conversion and probably water baptism would be necessary for volunteer teachers.
2. A maturing faith would need to include basic biblical literacy and evidence of a biblically influenced worldview. Even though the Bible translation may be good, biblical concepts such as God, sin, salvation, and prayer may not correlate with Buddhist concepts. Teachers who are not mature enough in their faith to know this difference can create a lot of confusion.
3. Being teachable is critical when the church's educational approach differs from the pedagogy of the national education

---

[263]Research on American teenage spirituality in 2002 and 2003 by Christian Smith and Melinda Lindquist Denton debunked the oft-promoted assumption that America is being increasingly secular or religiously pluralistic. Christian Smith and Melinda Lundquist Denton, *Soul Searching: The Religious and Spiritual Lives of American Teenagers* (Oxford: Oxford University Press, 2005), 31.

system and is based on counter-cultural ideas about teacher-student relationships.
4. Loving people is important anywhere in the world, but it takes on strong healing connotations in places where poverty and abuse are widespread.
5. Being a 'team player' could have more to do with submission to the congregation's organizational structure than with working as a team in the Western ideal. Such submission may be difficult for individuals who have more wealth or education than those under whom they must serve.
6. Dependence on God in all areas of life (a key sign of a true disciple) is not to be taken lightly in societies where prayers and offerings are customarily made to manipulate the spirit world for one's own advantage or to alleviate suffering.

Advanced Qualifications of Non-Formal CE Teachers

The qualifications listed above are basic in the sense that they create a reasonable baseline for voluntary CE teachers. They fit the accounts of the early days of Sunday schools in England and America just as well as they fit contemporary middle-class America or a first-generation church in Asia. However, in order for a church's non-formal CE approach to be viable in the long term, they must include an educational philosophy and a teaching culture that goes beyond this 'basic' baseline while still maintaining the kind of strong lay ethos that gave the Sunday school movement its vitality over the first two hundred years.[264]

This final sub-section of the literature review considers some advanced qualifications that can contribute to the long-term viability of a local congregation's approach to CE. Two categories of advanced qualifications need to be considered. The first category relates to churches' possible external roles of non-formal CE as indicated in the second level of the conceptual framework. They must recognize that some educational programs may require special skills or training (e.g., seminars on how to use lesson materials) even for volunteer teachers. For example, if a church offers literacy classes, English classes, or after-school homework assistance, the volunteer teachers need to be more

---

[264] I mention Sunday school here and throughout this chapter because it is arguably the quintessential CE approach. Even without Sunday schools in the classic sense, local churches need viable approaches to CE in order to be spiritually healthy and growing.

than 'FAT.'[265] They also need to have a reasonable level of knowledge and skill in what they are teaching, as well as the ability to help their students learn. The requisite level of knowledge and skill does not need to be extremely high, but they need to be strong enough to ensure a class achieves its stated purpose.

The second category relates to an overall theory of Christian education. The six points presented in Table 4.3 and then discussed are taken from Jim Wilhoit's "Evangelical Theory of Biblical Instruction," in *Christian Education and the Search for Meaning*.[266] His purpose was to provide a theory of education that lay teachers could "carry into the classroom without having to consult a large number of books."[267] These qualifications are ideals that take time to develop, especially in a first-generation church context. However, they are crucial for the long-term fruitfulness of a non-formal CE program, even if not all of the teachers can attain them.

Table 4.3. Wilhoit's qualifications for CE teachers[268]

1. Biblical literacy
2. A delight in Scripture
3. Submission to the Bible
4. An appropriate method of interpretation
5. A Christian world-view
6. Use of Scripture as a tool

Biblical Literacy

Wilhoit prioritizes biblical literacy for the simple fact that "If one does not know what the Bible says, it is impossible to obey it."[269] He was writing in response to a surge in CE literature that set aside biblical literacy as "outmoded provincialism" in favor of "self-understanding, interpersonal skills, and caring for others."[270] In social contexts like those

---

[265]"Faithful, Available, Teachable." Hendricks, *Teaching to Change Lives*, 20.
[266]James C. Wilhoit, "Toward an Evangelical Theory of Biblical Instruction," in *Christian Education and the Search for Meaning*, 2nd ed. (Grand Rapids: Baker Academic, 1991), 159-170.
[267]Ibid., 159.
[268]Ibid., 159-170.
[269]Ibid., 160.
[270]Ibid., 161-162.

in Cambodia, biblical literacy on the part of teachers is highly important because the default alternative is often a worldview in conflict with the teachings of Scripture.

A Delight in Scripture

Wilhoit's focus with this point is intrinsic motivation to read the Bible. When teachers delight in the Scriptures, their students will as well. This approach to teaching is healthy for the teacher and helps students become lifelong readers of the Bible.[271] Literacy levels are an issue for CE teachers in contexts like those found in Cambodia. In some places, people simply do not read books or magazines, either for pleasure or for learning. As teachers acquire a delight in the simple reading of the text, the truths it expresses, and the experiences of the authors or characters, their motivation to read it grows. For teachers with relatively low levels of education, the practice of reading a Bible portion daily can have a dramatic impact on their reading skills over even a short period of time.[272]

Submission to the Bible

Wilhoit charges teachers with the responsibility to help students go beyond simply learning facts to reflecting on "what the Bible demands and promises and how we actually live."[273] At issue here is the authority of Scripture. Religious views regarding sacred texts vary. In some contexts, people have little personal contact with their sacred texts; whereas in others, the idea of an authoritative text may not be present at all. Therefore, when developing non-formal CE teachers in places like Cambodia, acknowledging the authority of the Bible is equal to biblical literacy in importance.

An Appropriate Method of Interpretation

The goal of CE should be more than just transmission of information or ideas to students. Instead, Wilhoit advocates for CE that teaches Christians to read and study the Bible for themselves using exegetical

---

[271]Ibid., 162.
[272]I am speaking from personal observation. Many new Christians in Cambodia excitedly testify to an increased ability to read as they develop the habit of regular Bible reading. For some, this personal change is described as a miracle.
[273]Wilhoit, "Toward an Evangelical Theory," 165.

tools appropriate for lay people.[274] This point is a rather lofty goal for non-formal CE teachers in less-developed countries like Cambodia. Even pastors who have formal training from Bible schools may struggle to have functional hermeneutical skills, much less model methods of interpretations that are appropriate for their congregation.

A Christian Worldview

Writing in response to what he understoods as an essentially secular and humanistic society, Wilhoit sees helping Christians learn "to describe and evaluate life's experiences from a biblical perspective" as an important function of CE.[275] For religious contexts like Cambodia, teachers must engage in this process continually. Cultivating a Christian worldview is as much a skill as it is a process, because it involves biblically informed critical thinking about one's own culture. To borrow Paulo Freire's idea of 'conscientization,' CE teachers need to come to such a level of biblical knowledge, delight in the text, and submission to the Bible that they begin to perceive contradictions between their culture and the Scriptures.[276] A strong Christian worldview will empower CE teachers to live out their faith publicly and to model Christian living and thinking for their students.

Use of Scripture as a Tool

Wilhoit views the Bible as a tool that "can be properly used to comfort, challenge, console, or spiritually refresh."[277] He urges teachers to help students learn how to use the Bible to minister to others. Several challenges must be considered for this ideal to become reality in contexts like Cambodia. On the one hand, cultures with an animistic worldview can easily slide into using the Bible like an amulet or a book of magical answers for all of life's problems. On the other hand, using the Bible as Wilhoit suggests can be very empowering and lead to excesses, especially for those who have never experienced responsible use of authority. CE teachers already have a high degree of authority with their students by virtue of their role, despite any lack of training. Therefore, it is critically

---

[274]Ibid., 165-167.
[275]Ibid., 168
[276]Translators note, Freire, *Pedagogy*, 35n1.
[277]Wilhoit, *Christian Education*, 169.

important that church leaders model, teach, and endorse the appropriate use of the Bible as a tool of ministry in CE programs and classes.

Teachers of Non-Formal CE—Summary

This section has considered teachers of non-formal CE from two points of view—historical and ideal. The above examination of Sunday school teachers in 19th century America is instructive because the socioeconomic dynamics at play may have similarities with the socioeconomic dynamics that shape approaches to non-formal CE in places like Cambodia. Early Sunday school teachers were teens or young adults, mostly female, and often young in their faith. By teaching Sunday school, they became cemented in their evangelical identity and reproduced that identity in their students. In this way, young, inexperienced teachers were an important element in the development of a large-scale evangelical ethos. The same effect is possible in contexts like Cambodia.

The second point of view for thinking about non-formal CE teachers is the ideal, here described in terms of basic and advanced qualifications. The basic qualifications provide a baseline, while the advanced provide a direction for growth. Neither one includes training, certification, gender, or background. Rather, they focus on personal faith and character, with the potential for growth according to each individual's gifts. Both sets of qualifications provide a useful template for studying teachers of non-formal CE in AGC churches and in contexts like those found in Cambodia.

CONCEPTUAL FRAMEWORK FOR EXPLORING NON-FORMAL CE

Non-formal CE can be evaluated from a variety of perspectives, depending on context and purpose. This literature review has considered non-formal CE in four different aspects ('levels') in order to construct a conceptual framework for conducting research into non-formal CE among AGC churches. The framework provided the main data bins for the research and informed the development of research instruments as described in Chapter 5. The findings of that research are presented in Chapters 8 through 10. Those findings were then used to construct a descriptive model that can inform research in contexts that have similar dynamics (i.e., transferability). The model is presented in Chapter 11.

Figure 2.1 in Chapter 2 presented a sideview of the four levels of this conceptual framework. Before looking at a detailed version of the framework, it would be useful to first consider the basic framework from another angle. Figure 4.5 presents the basic framework described above, the four levels shown as concentric circles to give some idea of how they interact with one another. For example, the outer circle (educational context) can influence a local church's approach to non-formal CE in several ways, such as leaving basic education gaps to fill (external roles), creating organizational expectations, and affecting teacher quality and availability.

Figure 4.5. Top view of the basic conceptual framework

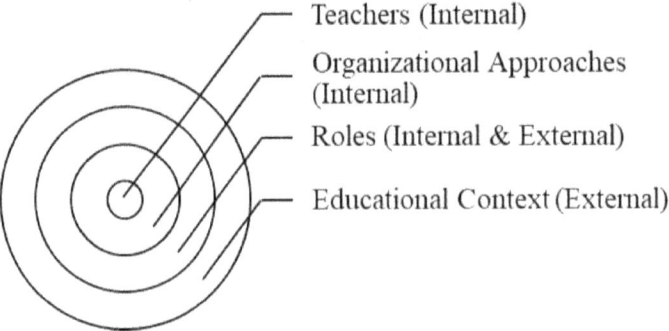

Lastly, Figure 4.6 is a detailed conceptual framework for exploring non-formal CE that includes rudimentary details for each of the four levels.

Figure 4.6. Detailed conceptual framework for exploring non-formal CE in AGC churches

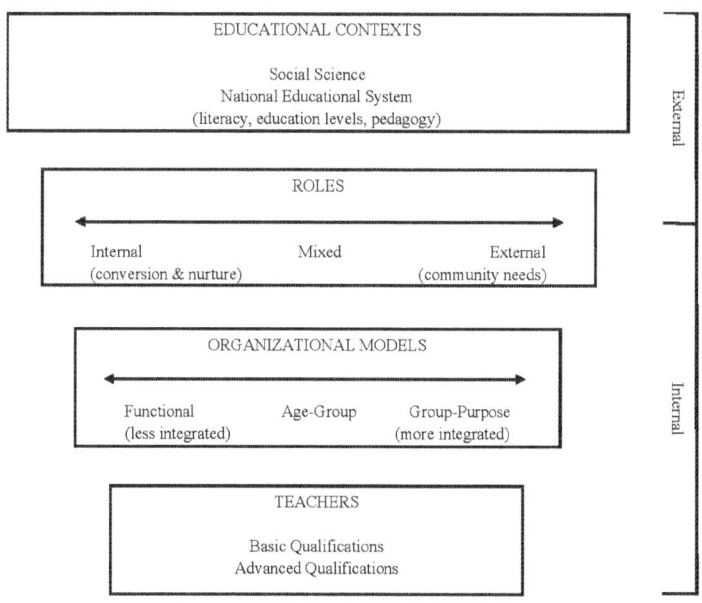

The first level is the educational contexts, which include elements that are external to a congregation's approach to non-formal CE. The social sciences provide educational philosophies that can guide pedagogy and expectations about teacher-student relationships and roles. This level also includes the formal education system in which a congregation is situated. That system affects non-formal CE in various ways, such as determining level of literacy, providing general education for teachers and students, and providing teachers and students with formal pedagogical experiences on which to base their non-formal CE experiences.

The framework's second level covers the roles of non-formal CE, which span a spectrum from internally focused efforts to externally focused efforts. Internally focused non-formal CE is concerned with conversion and nurture of congregants, while externally focused CE addresses social issues and education gaps in the society around a congregation. Mixed roles are efforts that seek to address community needs and add members to the congregation (i.e., evangelism and conversion) at the same time. Such efforts can lean toward one side of the spectrum or the other.

The third level considers the organizational model of a specific local church. Since the organizational approach is a representation of a congregation's culture and values, it can be highly customized to each situation. This level has a continuum of organizational models including the Functional (least integrated), the Age-Group, and the Group Purpose (most integrated). These three models, which are common in the West, are presented as starting points for thinking about organizational approaches to non-formal CE among AGC churches.

The fourth level looks at teachers of non-formal CE, typically volunteers with limited pedagogical training. The literature demonstrated more concern over the prospective teachers' character and spiritual life than with their education levels or backgrounds. The framework, therefore, includes two levels of qualifications or desired qualities in non-formal CE teachers. The six basic qualifications provide a baseline for non-formal CE teachers of all levels and degrees of experience, the primary emphases of these qualifications being the teacher's personal experience of conversion and desire to nurture students in their faith. The six advanced qualifications are ideals toward which non-formal CE teachers should be growing, including skills at handling Scripture and developing an integrated Christian worldview. These qualifications are deemed necessary for a local approach to non-formal CE to produce strong Christians and effective teachers over the long-term.

CHAPTER 5
Research Methodology

INTRODUCTION AND OVERVIEW

The purpose of this multiple case study was to describe, explore, and compare approaches to non-formal Christian Education (CE) among Assemblies of God of Cambodia (AGC) churches across two socioeconomic situations. The findings of the research were used to construct a descriptive model of non-formal CE among AGC churches that could be used to study non-formal CE among churches in similar socioeconomic situations.

The central question addressed by this study was—What approaches to non-formal CE have been developed by AGC churches? Six procedural sub-questions were followed to collect and analyze data from the cases:

1. How are approaches to non-formal CE organized in each of the cases? What is the rationale for each organizational approach?
2. How did the current approaches to non-formal CE in each of the cases originate and develop over time?
3. How are teachers recruited, developed, and resourced in each case? What ideas about teaching and learning influence this process?
4. What are the perceived contributions of the approaches to non-formal CE to the health and mission of each case?
5. How do approaches to non-formal CE among the cases reflect the Cambodian educational context?
6. How do approaches to non-formal CE among the cases compare across socioeconomic situations?

The exploratory nature of this research meant that the multiple case study strategy of Robert Yin utilizing 'theoretical replication' would ensure consistent data collection across cases and facilitate cross-case analysis.[278] The research's theoretical orientation is Emergent Theory, as described by Jaccard and Jacoby. In this orientation, theory emerges from descriptions, understandings, and explanations of phenomena using a variety of data types in interaction with existing theories. Emergent Theory is distinct from traditional scientific analysis in that the data are used to construct theory, not to test theory. It differs from Grounded Theory in that it is not "tied to symbolic interactionism."[279]

This chapter describes the research sample, the information needed, the research design, methods used for data collection, methods used to analyze and synthesize data, ethical considerations, and issues of trustworthiness. The sections on information needed, research design, and data collection include sufficient information for an audit of the research.

RESEARCH SAMPLE

The cases for this research were chosen using criterion sampling.[280] Staying within the delimitation of the AGC (see section "Delimitations" in Chapter 1), the primary criterion was that the church had succeeded in developing a sustained approach to non-formal CE. The cases are not a representative sample of AGC churches because most congregations do not seem to have consistent teaching or discipleship as part of their regular church life at this point in the fellowship's history.[281] Rather, these cases were chosen because they have had a measure of success in overcoming whatever conditions have hindered other churches from developing sustained approaches to non-formal CE.

A secondary criterion was the potential for developing a model that could contribute to further research.[282] Robert Stake views this quality as paramount, saying, "Balance and variety are important [in case selection]; opportunity to learn is of primary importance."[283] Following

---

[278] Yin, *Case Study Research*, 54, 160.

[279] James Jaccard and Jacob Jacoby, *Theory Construction and Model-Building Skills* (New York: The Guilford Press, 2010), 256-258.

[280] Bloomberg and Volpe, *Completing Your Qualitative Dissertation*, 248.

[281] This anecdotal statement reflects many conversations I have had with AGC leaders and missionaries who are deeply concerned about the lack of discipleship. Determining the extent of non-formal CE activities in the AGC is beyond the scope of this research.

[282] Creswell, *Educational Research*, 208.

[283] Robert E. Stake, "Case Studies," in *Handbook of Qualitative Research*, 2nd ed., ed. Norman K. Denzin and Yvonna S. Lincoln (Thousand Oaks, CA: SAGE Publications, 2000), 447.

Yin's principle of theoretical replication,[284] the research sample included two cases in the provinces and two in the capital city. The differences and similarities among the cases provided for a rich cross-case analysis. Utilizing four cases made it possible to study each one in depth, while at the same time strengthening the transferability of the resulting descriptive model.

The cases located in the provinces were labeled Prov-1 and Prov-2 and in the capital city as Cap-1 and Cap-2. All four were first-generation AGC churches (planted in the 1990s)[285] led by licensed ('full rights') or ordained pastors. Beyond these basic commonalities and the criterion of a sustained approach to non-formal CE, each of the cases had its own distinct history, development, personality, and approach to church life. Table 5.1 outlines a comparative overview of the four cases. This chapter and the next present detailed descriptions of each case.

Table 5.1. Overview of the cases

	Prov-1	**Prov-2**	**Cap-1**	**Cap-2**
Pastor				
Gender	Male	Female	Male	Male
Age	47	55	54	35
Year Became Pastor	1996 (considered founding pastor)	1997 (founder)	1994 (co-founder)	2007

---

[284] Yin, *Case Study*, 54.
[285] The fact that all four churches were planted in the 1990s is interesting, but it was not a criterion for selection.

Education	B.A. in Bible & Ministry (CBI)	A.A. in Christian Ministry (CBI) No other formal education[286]	A.A. in Christian Ministry (CBI) Professional training in education & ministry	Diploma in Bible & Ministry (CBI) B.Th., M.A. in Ministry (BCM)
Leadership	AGC district leadership (former)	Village committee member	AGC national leadership (current)	AGC national leadership (current)
Serves FT/PT	Part time	Full time	Full time	Full time
Church				
Year Founded	1993	1997	1994	1996
Church Founder	American missionaries	Current pastor	Current pastor with American missionary	Filipino missionary
Socioeconomic Makeup	Farmers, plus education sector & textiles Young families & students	Farmers Female dominated[287]	Urban middle-class Multi-generational	Urban lower/middle-class Young families & students, some elders
Size of Congregation	50-60 adults & youth 20 children	Total all groups: 91 adults & youth 113 children Main church alone: 32 adults & youth 35 children	120 adults & youth 40 children	100-120 adults & youth 30 children
Number of teachers	18	24	30	22
Outreach & Missions	2 village cell groups	Main church as "umbrella" with 6 village cell groups	Partnerships with 2 provincial church plants	Planted 7 churches; partnerships with many church plants

CBI=Cambodia Bible Institute; BCM=Bible College of Malaysia

---

[286]The pastor of Prov-2 did not have the opportunity to go to primary school. Motivated by the desire to answer the call to be a pastor, she learned to read on her own. She passed the entrance exam and graduatd from Cambodia Bible Institute's two-year program.

[287]Women fill twenty of twenty-two leadership positions (91 percent).

OVERVIEW OF THE INFORMATION NEEDED

This research required the following four categories of information[288] to answer the central question and the procedural sub-questions—contextual, demographic, perceptual, and theoretical. This section details each of these categories as it relates to this multiple case study.

Contextual Information

The contextual information required by this research fell into two general types—the background of each case and the educational situation in Cambodia. The background of each case included the church's history, development, facilities, congregational statistics, finances, guiding philosophy, organizational structure, philosophy regarding CE, and the general approach to non-formal CE. Information about the educational situation in Cambodia included the history of educational development in Cambodia, development of the national education system since the 1990s, and expectations about teacher/student roles.

Demographic Information

The demographic information required for this research included church statistics, information about the pastor, information about the teachers, and information about the classes offered in each church. The church statistics were general—attendance, monthly budget, and portion of the budget used for CE. Demographic information about the pastors included age, gender, background, family, education, and vocational experience. Information about the teachers included age, gender, family, education, vocation, core spiritual experiences (e.g., water baptism, baptism in Holy Spirit, spiritual disciplines), and the classes they teach. Lastly, demographic information about each class included attendance broken down by gender.

Perceptual Information

Perceptual information played a key role in this research by providing explanations for each church's approach to non-formal CE and a means of triangulating contextual and demographic information. Perceptual information was primarily gathered through recorded open-

---

[288]Bloomberg and Volpe, *Qualitative Dissertation*, 105-106.

ended interviews guided by two questionnaires[289] and through the Teacher Questionnaires.[290] This information provided the rationale for each church's approach to non-formal CE, how that approach developed over time, and the purposes or underlying philosophy of its approach to non-formal CE. These two types of perceptual information were complemented by class observations[291] and the researcher's field notes about church life as a participant observer.

Theoretical Information

This research design used a pre-structured approach to each case, working from the conceptual framework developed from the theoretical information discussed in Chapters 2 through 5. The theoretical information about Cambodia included research that has already been done on both Christianity and the educational situation in the nation. Information about CE in local churches included the roles of non-formal CE, organizational models of non-formal CE, and characteristics of CE teachers. This theoretical information was further informed by literature on small-church dynamics and the history of the Sunday school movements in England and the United States.

The conceptual framework developed from the literature provided the data bins to address procedural sub-questions. Table 5.2 outlines the relationships between the framework's four levels, the procedural sub-questions, and the four types of information needed for this research. The table is arranged in order of the framework levels, from the most general to the most case-specific. The order of the procedural sub-questions has been been adjusted accordingly.

---

[289]See Appendix A and B: Case Background Questionnaire and Approach to CE Questionnaire.
[290]See Appendix C.
[291]See Appendix D, Classroom Observation Protocol.

Table 5.2. Conceptual framework, procedural sub-questions, and information needed

Conceptual Framework Level	Procedural Sub-questions	Information Needed
1. Educational Contexts	5. How do approaches to non-formal CE among the cases reflect the educational context?	*Contextual*: Cambodian national education system *Demographic*: educational background of teachers and pastors *Perceptual*: views of teacher-student roles *Theoretical*: Cambodian national education system; historical interaction between CE and educational systems
2. Roles	4. What are the perceived contributions of the approaches to non-formal CE to the health and mission of each case?	*Perceptual*: vision of each case; pastors' views of CE program; teachers' views of their roles; class observations *Theoretical*: roles of CE
3. Organizational Models	1. How are approaches to non-formal CE organized in each case? What is the rationale for each organizational approach? 2. How did the current approaches to non-formal CE among the cases originate and then develop over time?	*Contextual*: organization of each case; stages of church development *Perceptual*: rationale for the organization of each case and how it developed over time *Theoretical*: organizational structures of CE

4. Teachers	3. How are teachers recruited, developed, and resourced in each case? What ideas about teaching and learning influence this process?	*Contextual*: policies for recruiting and equipping teachers; curriculum choices *Demographic*: age, gender, education, vocation, etc., of teachers *Perceptual*: ideals about teacher characteristics; experiences of teachers with recruiting and equipping; spirituality of teachers *Theoretical*: standards for CE teachers; personal spirituality of CE teachers

RESEARCH DESIGN

This multiple case study followed Robert Yin's principles for case-study research. His approach was appropriate because this current research was exploratory in nature and directed toward "a contemporary phenomenon within a real-life context" that was not under the control of the researcher.[292] The research design begins with a central question supported by six procedural sub-questions[293] that address the four levels of the conceptual framework. The data were collected using ethnographic methods designed to obtain both emic and etic perspectives. In keeping with Yin's 'replication logic,' the cases were studied in succession using the same protocol.[294] This section describes the main points of the research design, including development of research instruments, data collection methods, and methods of data analysis.

---

[292] Yin, *Case Study*, 2.
[293] Creswell, *Educational Research*, 134-135.
[294] Yin, *Case Study*, 53-54.

Development of the Research Instruments

The first phase of the research involved the development of data collection instruments. These instruments were created first in English (drawing on the literature), then translated into Khmer according to their purpose.[295] They included the following—the Invitation to Participate in the Research (Informed Consent), the Case Background Questionnaire, the Approach to CE Questionnaire, the Teacher Questionnaire, the Classroom Observation Protocol, and the Focus Group Protocol. Those instruments that required Khmer versions were revised and piloted with the help of native Khmer speakers in the faculty, office staff, and translation staff at Cambodia Bible Institute.

Data Collection Phase

The data collection phase utilized four instruments. The first two (Case Background Questionnaire and Approach to CE Questionnaire) were designed to collect contextual, perceptual, and demographic data for sub-questions 1 through 4, which focused on organizational models, roles, and teachers (see Table 5.2 above). These questionnaires gave special attention to the historical development of each church and to its philosophy about the selection and function of teachers. Originally designed to function as written questionnaires with an interview follow-up, these two instruments were used more effectively as in-depth interview protocols (see section, "Methods of Data Collection"). The Case Background questionnaire covered the origin of the church, its stages of development, its facilities, congregational statistics, its finances, personal information about the pastor, and the church's philosophy. The Approach to CE Questionnaire addressed the organizational structure of the church, its philosophy regarding CE, roles of CE in the church, selection of teachers, and training of teachers.

The third instrument was the Teacher Questionnaire. In contrast to the open-ended Case Background and Approach to CE questionnaires, the Teacher Questionnaire needed to be concise, easily understood by church members, and cover a range of topics, all without feeling laborious to respondents. The questionnaire included background/demographic questions, personal spirituality questions, teaching experience and

---

[295] I either translated the documents myself or relied on translation staff at Cambodia Bible Institute to provide primary translations from which to work.

attitude questions, and a table in which respondents were to rate five teacher/student roles.[296]

This Teacher Questionnaire required the most theoretical grounding, revising, and piloting of all the data collection instruments. In addition to demographic information, it needed to capture contextual and perceptual information that would flesh out the experiences of teachers and their roles in the church. Ann Boylan's analysis of the Sunday school movement in America from 1790-1880 pointed to the importance of information about the teachers' personal spirituality, influences on their spiritual growth, the personal involvement of teachers in the lives of their students, and the spiritual benefits teachers can receive from teaching in the church.[297] In keeping with the classical Pentecostal orientation of the AGC, the questionnaire also asked whether teachers had been baptized in the Holy Spirit with the evidence of speaking in tongues and whether they continued to speak in tongues as part of their ongoing experience.

The section in the questionnaire titled "Roles of Teachers" asked respondents to rate five models of teacher roles as weak, good, or very good for teaching in the church. The purpose of that question was to capture respondents' perceptions about teacher roles in the context of the national educational system in Cambodia (conceptual framework level one). Table 5.3 lists those five roles and how they were presented in the questionnaire. The first three approaches (taken from historical educational psychology) have been influential in the popular understanding of CE. The last two represent Western thinking about CE. Each approach was carefully worded for the questionnaire, keeping in mind the educational levels and non-professional nature of the respondents. Additionally, the role of the teacher in John Dewey's developmental approach has traditionally been labeled 'Coordinator.' This term is used for management in the Khmer language (nek krobkrong); so I lifted the label 'Equipper' from the definition as an alternative.

---

[296]Creswell, *Educational Research*, 385-387.
[297]Boylan, *Sunday School*, 1988).

Table 5.3. Five teacher models[298]

Originator/ Proponent	Approach	Teacher's Role	Description in the Questionnaire
Jean Jacques Rousseau	Romantic	Gardener	As a gardener takes care of plants, teachers nurture students to reach their potential as they naturally grow.
Mortimer Adler et al.	Transmissive	Technician	As a teapot pours liquid into a cup, teachers provide students with important knowledge and abilities.
John Dewey	Developmental	Equipper [Coordinator]	Teachers equip students with the knowledge and understanding they need for successful lives.
Jim Wilhoit et al.	Transformative	Guide	Teachers lead students to experience truths that will transform their lives.

---

[298] The first four models are adapted from Wilhoit, *Christian Education*, 74-102, 114; the fifth model (Fello w Travelers) is from Westerhoff referenced in Catherine Stonehouse and Scottie May, *Listening to Children on the Spiritual Journey: Guidance for Those Who Teach and Nurture* (Grand Rapids: Baker Academic, 2010), 22.

| John Westerhoff | Pilgrimage | Fellow Traveler | Teachers and students are on the same journey in which they are learning from each other. |

The Teacher Questionnaire went through seven drafts in English and three in Khmer as I narrowed down the questions and refined the wording. Revision of the wording required a lot of consultation with Cambodian colleagues. The number of open-ended questions was limited so that respondents could fill out the four-page questionnaire in fifteen to twenty minutes. Four Cambodian church leaders/pastors and two church members volunteered to pilot the questionnaire.

The fourth data collection instrument was the Classroom Observation Protocol (see Appendix D). The purpose of this instrument was to collect qualitative data about teaching approaches and teacher/student interaction to triangulate with the Teacher Questionnaire and the Approach to CE Questionnaire. Development of the protocol began with a study of classroom evaluation forms used by elementary schools. However, I determined that those tools were of limited value to my research because they were keyed to professional teaching standards rather than to collecting data about non-professional, nonformal teaching.

The final version of the Classroom Observation Protocol consisted of three pages. The first (General Observations) was based on the four variables of CE described by Richards and Bredfelt—learner, teacher, curriculum, and location.[299] The second page was a table with twenty items divided into three categories. Items for the category "Lesson Content and Delivery" were developed from evaluation tools I created for teaching homiletics. Theoretical bases for the items in the categories "Engagement Between Teacher(s) and Students" and "Spiritual Atmosphere" were books written by Elmer Towns[300] and Howard Hendricks[301] for CE teachers and the historical analysis of Sunday school in America by Boylan.[302] The third page included eight possible questions for a semi-structured, recorded interview with the teachers

---

[299] Richards and Bredfeldt, *Creative Bible Teaching*, 311-313.
[300] Towns, *What Every*.
[301] Hendricks, *Teaching*.
[302] Boylan, *Sunday School*.

following their class. The questions were translated into Khmer and refined with native Khmer speakers.

Member Checking

According to Peter Knight, focus groups can be an effective way to "explore provisional findings either by summarizing them to a selection of participants or by bringing the findings to other groups of stakeholders in the inquiry."[303] Focus groups give researchers a chance to test their interpretations and clarify unresolved questions about the data. One pitfall with focus groups, however, is that they "should be used to inform thinking, not determine it," because there is an immediacy to the ideas expressed that may not reveal how deeply those ideas are held or how pervasive is their influence.[304]

The member-checking phase involved meeting with focus groups from each case for about one hour. Focus group participants included the pastor, teachers, and non-teaching leaders. I requested that both men and women be included. The Focus Group Protocol was designed around the four levels of the conceptual framework (see Appendix E, "Focus Group Protocol"). The first part of the protocol involved presenting summary findings of the research regarding the organizational model, the teachers, and roles of the case's approach to CE. The second part focused on the first and broadest level of the conceptual framework—educational context.

Cross-Case Analysis

The research's cross-case analysis phase was completed after the member checking phase, which involved reviewing and summarizing data on a case-by-case basis for presentation to the participants. Adding in perceptions and other information collected from the focus groups, the analysis phase involved a comprehensive review of all data. Matrices and displays of data were constructed to facilitate analysis within cases, across cases, and across the two socioeconomic situations. Lastly, the findings that emerged from the analyses were used to construct the descriptive model presented in Chapter 11.

---

[303] Knight, *Small-scale Research*, 70.
[304] Ibid., 117.

DATA COLLECTION

Data collection for all four cases took place between March and July 2018, and focus groups for member checking were conducted in September 2018. Each site was visited an average of twelve times, with an average of 43.6 total contact hours[305] per case. The sites were studied in this order—Prov-1, Cap-1, Cap-2, and Prov-2.[306]

The multiple case study research utilized these data collection methods—participant observation, in-depth interviews, document reviews, questionnaires, and classroom observations. The following subsections detail the theoretical basis for each data collection method, the manner in which it was implemented, and adjustments that were made in implementation.

Participant Observation

Throughout the entire data collection process, my stand was that of a participant observer. According to Brian Hoey, participant observation "represents the dual role of the ethnographer" that enables them to include both emic and etic perspectives in their data.[307] The potential richness of the data gathered through participant observation, however, must be weighed against the pitfalls of observer bias through intentional or unintentional manipulation of events.[308]

As an Assemblies of God missionary serving the AGC,[309] I was warmly welcomed into church life as a member of the broader fellowship. I worshipped with the congregation (sitting in the back where I could observe the entire room), gave in the offering, and even performed a few ministerial functions, including leading in prayer, giving impromptu devotionals, and preaching. In the spirit of reciprocity, I gave rides to church members and hauled materials to and from the capital city. On a few occasions, I encouraged teachers in their work and, when requested, offered suggestions. Keeping the pitfalls in mind, I did not intervene when teachers were unprepared, lacked basic Bible knowledge, or struggled to manage unruly students.

---

[305] The term 'contact hours' refers to time spent on site, including conducting interviews, following up on questionnaires, participating in church life, etc.

[306] The order of study was a matter of convenience, not intention.

[307] Brian A. Hoey, "A Simple Introduction to the Practice of Ethnography and Guide to Ethnographic Fieldnotes," *Marshall University Digital Scholar* (June 2014), 2-3, http://works.bepress.com/brian_hoey/12 (accessed December 2, 2017).

[308] Yin, *Case Study*, 102; Bloomberg and Volpe, *Qualitative Dissertation*, 252.

[309] See Chapter 1 section "The Researcher's Background with the AGC."

In-Depth Interviews

The Case Background Questionnaire and the Approach to CE Questionnaire were originally designed to be filled out by the pastor or a knowledgeable leader in preparation for a recorded interview. When I arrived to meet with the pastor of the first case, I found that he had only written answers to about 20 percent of the questions.[310] I proceeded to interview him and the assistant pastor, making notes on the questionnaire myself. The process worked so well that I used these two questionnaires as semi-structured interview protocols for the remainder of the research. Robert Yin characterizes this data-gathering approach as in-depth interviews in which the respondent is like an informant that provides information, perceptions, and corroboration of information or impressions.[311]

Document Reviews

According to Yin, "The most important use of documents [in case study research] is to corroborate and augment evidence from other sources."[312] However, he warns that the perspective and the purpose of the documents for that community must be understood.[313] In Peter Knight's words, documents "are not 'objective' witnesses."[314] With these caveats in mind, I found the review of documents to be a rich source of contextual and perceptual information that could be triangulated with information from interviews, questionnaires, and observations.

This sub-section details the documents that were reviewed for each case in chronological order. Apart from those documents that are footnoted as translations in the following paragraphs, all documents were in Khmer with no English versions. Table 5.4 lists those that were reviewed for each case.

---

[310]The other three pastors did not write any answers in advance.
[311]Yin, *Case Study*, 107.
[312]Ibid., 103.
[313]Ibid., 105.
[314]Knight, *Small Scale Research*, 118.

Table 5.4. Documents reviewed by case

Prov-1	Prov-2	Cap-1	Cap-2
• Constitution • 2018 plan for activities and expenses	• Children's curriculum: *The Greatest Journey; Beloved Child* • Vision and mission statement • Leadership organizational chart • Vision and mission statement of the preschool • Vision and mission of the youth • Three-year activity plan • Synopsis of the church's history • "River of Life" pictorial history of the church	• Constitution • Children's lessons: *Superbook: Church Edition*	• Constitution • Sunday bulletins • *Intentional Moves* lesson books • *Intentional Moves* manual (source material, Philippines)

The first case (Prov-1) provided two important documents for this research. The first was the church's constitution, which had been adopted and filed with the Ministry of Cults and Religion in 2016. The second document was a 37-page plan for the church's activities and expenses for 2018. It included a week-by-week outline of the lesson topics for the children's classes. I reviewed these two sources for the main ideals of the church, its organizational structure, and qualifications and responsibilities for leadership and ministry positions. I also reviewed them thoroughly for references to teaching and discipleship.

The second case (Cap-1) had two documents for review. The first was the church's constitution, which had been adopted and filed with the Ministry of Cults and Religion in 2009; it was reviewed in the same manner as Prov-1. The second document was the Khmer version of the Superbook: Church Edition[315] curriculum that the church was using in its children's Sunday school classes. I reviewed this material giving special attention to lesson elements and ease of use for teachers.

The third case (Cap-2) had three documents for review. The first was the church's constitution, which had been adopted and filed with the Ministry of Cults and Religion in 2008; it was reviewed in the same manner as Prov-1. The second type of document was the Sunday bulletins that were produced during this study period; these bulletins listed positions and names of ministry leaders, weekly attendance numbers, and announcements about church life. The third type of document was Intentional Moves,[316] the three-part lesson series the church was using for its Life Groups; it was reviewed for general content, structure, and approach. (The Intentional Moves lesson booklets had been revised and translated into Khmer from materials produced by the Philippines General Council of the Assemblies of God. I was able to download and review the English version of the Intentional Moves manual[317] as source material, giving special attention to its philosophy of discipleship and strategies for implementation.)

The fourth case (Prov-2) was unique in terms of documents for review. The church did not have a constitution but did have two documents that were applicable to this research. The first was the lesson material for its children's classes, which I reviewed for lesson elements and ease of use for teachers. The church was using two curricula— *The Greatest Journey*[318] (produced by Samaritan's Purse) and *Beloved*

---

[315]Christian Broadcasting Network, *Seavpov vises: merean kromchumnum* [Superbook: church edition], Khmer version (Phnom Penh, Cambodia: Christian Broadcasting Network, 2014).

[316]Sur del Rosario, Glenn Howard Lucas, and Lawrence Romero, *Khachumrunh dowy chetana* [Intentional Moves], 3 parts, revised Khmer version (Phnom Penh, Cambodia: Cambodia School of Missions, n.d).

[317]The Philippines General Council of the Assemblies of God, *Intentional Moves Training Manual* (ICI Ministries: The Philippines, 2015), http://www.iciphilippines.org/wp-content/uploads/2015/01/IM-manual-Empowered-Local-Churches.pdf (accessed June 6, 2018).

[318]Samaritan's Purse, *Domnar chivit da l'ah bomphot* [The Greatest Journey], Khmer version (Phnom Penh, Cambodia: Samaritan's Purse, 2017).

Child[319] (created locally by a Filipina missionary working with several Cambodian children's teachers).

The second Prov-2 'document,' which detailed the church's vision and mission, its three-year activity plan, and its history, were handwritten or hand-drawn items for public display. The church's vision and mission was displayed on a large sheet of chart paper on the front wall of the main hall next to a diagram of the leadership structure (complete with the names and photos). The vision and mission of the church-run community preschool was hand painted on the front outside wall of the church building.

Three other documents, also handwritten on large sheets of chart paper but not being displayed, included (1) vision, mission, and activities of the youth, (2) list of activities of the church for the next three years, and (3) a three-sheet synopsis of the church's history from 1997 to 2018. Lastly, complementing that synopsis was a pictorial history titled 'River of Life' that had been drawn on a three-meter by one-meter sheet of fabric and displayed on the left wall of the main hall. I took digital photos of all these documents and made full reference translations; I also took video footage of the pastor and another leader explaining both the River of Life and the leadership structure diagram.

Teacher Questionnaires

The sampling approach used for the Teacher Questionnaire was site sampling, which attempts to collect data from an entire group of specifically identified people.[320] The sample called for in this research was everyone who fulfills the role of a teacher in each case. The final sample included all teachers at all four sites (total of ninety-four). Only one teacher declined to participate.

I originally created a protocol for administering the Teacher Questionnaire to a group of teachers at the same time. The fourth page had four questions that I planned to ask each teacher in a short, recorded interview. This process was quite successful with the first case (Prov-1). However, with the second case (Cap-1), due largely to the busyness of urban life, it was impossible to gather the teachers together for questionnaires and interviews. So I worked from a master list of teachers and gathered the questionnaires whenever I had the opportunity. I found their written answers to the open-ended questions on the last page to be

---

[319]Rowena S. Estrebilla, Phun Thurain, and Voeun Rotha, *Khmeng somnop [Beloved Child]* (Takeo Province, Cambodia: Partners Against Poverty (Western Australia), 2016).

[320]Knight, *Small Scale Research*, 122.

both detailed and insightful. Some answers went well beyond what I had recorded in the interviews at Prov-1. Therefore, I followed this approach for the remaining two cases.

Classroom Observations

Implementing the Classroom Observation Protocol was one of the most challenging aspects of data collection due to the range of approaches, skill levels, and age groups represented in the cases. Considering time and opportunity constraints, the goal was to observe a variety of classes from each case, with the primary purpose being to triangulate observations with data from the questionnaires, class information sheets, and focus groups. Table 5.5 lists the classes that were observed in each case; the age range of each class is in parenthesis where applicable.

Table 5.5. Classroom observations by case and age group

	Prov-1[44]	Prov-2	Cap-1	Cap-2
Children*	1. Main church 2. Main church	1. Main church 2. Village site 3. Village site 4. Village site	1. Younger (3-7) 2. Older (7-12)	1. Younger (3-7) 2. Older (7-12) 3. Older (7-12)
Youth	3. Youth class 4. Youth class	5. Bible class 6. Bible class	3. Youth class	4. Life Group (18-25)
Adult		7. Village site 8. Village site	4. Women 5. Men 6. Discipleship	5. Life Group (25-35) 6. Life Group (35+)

*Children's classes include all ages together unless otherwise designated.

---

[32] Adult classes were not held during the case study period.

Two adjustments had to be made in the design and implementation of the Classroom Observation Protocol. The first was made to the second page after the first day's use. The scale and arrangement of items proved to be too cumbersome, so I revised the descriptors and regrouped some of the items (see Appendix D for the final version.)

The second adjustment was made to the third page, which listed eight possible questions for a semi-structured, recorded interview with the teachers following their classes. This procedure was successful with the first case because we were able to find relatively quiet places to talk, and the teachers were comfortable with the approach. However, in the second case, the teachers were uncomfortable with the formal recorded interview, plus finding find a place to talk without distractions and noise was difficult. As a result, I adjusted my approach to an informal conversation (observation sheet in hand) to follow up on aspects of the class and hear the teachers' thoughts about the curricula. This change worked well and yielded the insights needed to round out the observation. Therefore, I applied this approach to the remainder of the research.

Focus Groups

The purpose of the focus groups was to present summary findings of the research to a selected group of knowledgeable participants for their corroboration, responses, and clarifications. I requested that each group include the pastor, two pillar leaders who were not necessarily teachers, and two to three teachers who were not pillar leaders. I also requested male and female representation in the group.

The Focus Group Protocol had three sections (see Appendix E). The first section was greetings and introductions, including a video roll call of the participants for the record. The second section dealt with the three lower levels of the conceptual model—organizational model, teachers, classes, and roles. During this time, I presented the data I had collected from their church regarding teacher demographics, teacher spirituality, and attitudes toward teaching. I also discussed my findings on the roles of CE in their church.

The third section addressed the first and broadest level of the conceptual framework—educational context. For this part, the participants were invited to discuss the five teacher roles described in the Teacher Questionnaire in terms of strengths, weaknesses, and rankings for teaching in the church. I presented them with the results of the questionnaires filled out by their teachers and gave them a chance to respond. Then I asked them to describe which models were the most common for teachers in the government education system (primary and secondary). Lastly, I asked them to discuss how their approach to CE reflects or differs from the national education system.

ETHICAL CONSIDERATIONS

The gold standard of ethics in ethnographic research is summarized in the Belmont Principles adopted by the United States government in 1978. Those principles require researchers to act with justice, beneficence, and respect toward their research subjects. The principle of respect is embodied in policies of informed consent.[322] In this research, the risk to individual participants was minimal because the research was not directed toward personal stories and experiences. However, as those ultimately responsible for each congregation and for allowing this research to proceed, pastors had a right to understand the nature and purpose of the study, how the researcher would mitigate potential risks to them and their congregations, and their right to withdraw at any time.[323] In the case of this research, a letter of invitation to participate in the research to address the concerns of informed consent was presented to the pastors. The research then proceeded with their permission.

Three ethical issues were of concern in this research. First, as David Fetterman observes regarding ethnographic research, anonymity was virtually impossible due to this study's public nature.[324] With that in mind, I explained to the pastors that I would respect the internal affairs of the church and only openly share information that would be considered public knowledge (e.g., what children's curriculum was being used). I kept individual information secure and informed pastors that I would only share general or aggregate information with them. Second, because of my role as a missionary serving the AGC and the benefit I received from their participation, I felt an ethical obligation to participate in church life in the spirit of reciprocity. Third, I had to be aware of power dynamics[325] because of my status as a missionary and the director of the Bible school. Regarding teachers, I had to avoid making them feel that their performance was being evaluated or that they were being coerced

---

[322]LeCompte and Schensul, *Ethnographic Research,* 287-289.
[323]Ibid., 290.
[324]David M. Fetterman, *Ethnography: Step-by-Step,* 3rd ed., Applied Social Research Methods Series, vol. 17, ed. Leonard Bickman and Debra J. Rog (Los Angeles: SAGE Publications, 2010), 147.
[325]The issues involved in power dynamics include 'positionality' (social position) and 'situationality,' that is, "specific privileges and disadvantages inherent in an individual's social role or status." LeCompte and Schensul, *Designing and Conducting,* 30.

into participating. Regarding pastors, I had to show deference to their position and gratitude for the privilege of studying their churches, both in private conversations and in public interactions.

ISSUES OF TRUSTWORTHINESS

Researchers use a variety of terms to discuss trustworthiness or validity in qualitative studies. Bloomberg and Volpe describe three standards by which qualitative research can be judged for trustworthiness—credibility, dependability, and transferability.[326] This section discusses the ways in which this multiple case study research upheld these standards.

First, *credibility* is the quality of accurately reflecting the social world of the research participants.[327] This research addressed credibility by triangulating between a variety of sources of data, bracketing the researcher's reflections, checking impressions with participants throughout the process, and member checking with focus groups. Beyond the case study participants, I also checked my impressions with Cambodian colleagues and foreign missionaries who know the context well.

Second, *dependability* "refers to whether one can track the processes and procedures used to collect and interpret data."[328] This research was designed, organized, and conducted to facilitate analyzing data and to make auditing possible. Since case study research cannot be duplicated in the strictest sense, I have presented my methodology in such a way that another researcher should be able to review my data and see explicitly how I arrive at my findings.

Third, *transferability* "refers to the fit or match between the research context and other contexts as judged by the reader."[329] This research, therefore, does not claim to be a representative sample or to be generalizable to a larger population. Rather, it presents findings from a specific socioeconomic context and Christian tradition that should resonate with similar socioeconomic contexts and Christian traditions. The transferability of findings is strengthened by detailed contextual information and by clear data collection procedures. Using theoretical replication,[330] this research utilized a single protocol with four cases

---

[326] Bloomberg and Volpe, *Qualitative Dissertation*, 112-114.
[327] Ibid., 112-113.
[328] Ibid., 113.
[329] Ibid.
[330] Yin, *Case Study*, 54.

representing two socioeconomic contexts in Cambodia—provincial and capital city. The consistency in types of data was the basis for cross-case analysis, drawing findings, and constructing a model that could aid in the study of comparable socioeconomic situations.

CHAPTER SUMMARY

This chapter presented the methodology of this multiple case study into approaches to non-formal CE among AGC churches. The research sample involved four cases in two socioeconomic situations—provincial and the capital city. Four types of information were needed to answer the six procedural sub-questions—contextual information, demographic information, perceptual information, and theoretical information. The chapter also presented the research design in terms of phases of the research, the conceptual framework, procedural sub-questions, data sources, and methods of data collection.

Informed consent was obtained using a letter of invitation to participate in the research. During the collection of data, the privacy of individuals and churches was respected, a spirit of reciprocity was maintained, and the researcher endeavored to be sensitive to power dynamics. Regarding the trustworthiness of the research, explicit steps were taken to ensure that the findings accurately reflect the social world of the cases (credibility) and that the research can be audited (dependability). These steps strengthen the transferability of the findings to similar socioeconomic situations.

The chapters that follow present the findings of this research and how those findings can inform thinking about non-formal CE in socioeconomic situations like those represented in the cases. Chapters 6 and 7 present each of the cases on its own terms, including origins, development over time, core ideals, organizational structures, and general approaches to non-formal CE. Chapters 8 through 10 present a detailed cross-case analysis of the data and a series of findings from the analyses. Then, Chapter 11 walks through a descriptive model of approaches to non-formal CE among AGC churches constructed from the findings listed at the end of Chapter 10. Lastly, Chapter 12 summarizes the findings of the research, offers ideas for implementation of the findings, and suggests directions for additional research.

CHAPTER 6
Presentation of the Cases: The Provincial Cases

INTRODUCTION AND OVERVIEW FOR CHAPTERS 6 AND 7

The purpose of this multiple case study was to describe, explore, and compare approaches to non-formal CE among AGC churches across socioeconomic situations. The data from this research were used to construct a descriptive model for thinking about non-formal CE among churches in similar socioeconomic contexts, which will be presented in Chapter 11. The study involved four cases—two AGC churches located in the provinces (labeled Prov-1 and Prov-2) and two located in the capital city (labeled Cap-1 and Cap-2).

Chapters 6 through 10 present the research's findings following the levels of the conceptual framework constructed in Chapter 4. Table 6.1 lists the levels of that framework along with the procedural sub-questions and sources of the information. Chapters 6 and 7 address the first three sub-questions on a case-by-case basis. Chapters 8 through 10 present a cross-case analysis and the findings for each part of the conceptual framework. Then Chapter 11 will present a descriptive model of AGC non-formal CE approaches based on the findings set forth at the end of Chapter 10.

Table 6.1. Conceptual framework levels, procedural sub-questions, and sources of information

Conceptual Framework Levels	Procedural Sub-questions	Sources of Information
Organizational Models	1. How are approaches to non-formal CE organized in each case? What is the rationale for each organizational approach? 2 How did the current approaches to nonformal CE among the cases originate and then develop over time?	Case Background Questionnaire Approach to CE Questionnaire Interviews with pastors and leaders Church documents
Roles	3. What are the perceived contributions of the approaches to non-formal CE to the health and mission of each case?	Approach to CE Questionnaire Interviews with pastors and leaders Church documents Class observations
Teachers	4. How are teachers recruited, developed, and resourced in each case? What ideas about teaching and learning influence this process?	Approach to CE Questionnaire Interviews with pastors and leaders Teacher Questionnaire Class observations
Educational Context	5. How do approaches to non-formal CE among the cases reflect the educational context?	Focus Groups Teacher Questionnaire Class observations
	6. How do approaches to non-formal CE among the cases compare across socioeconomic situations?	

Each of the four cases in this study worked out their own distinct approach to non-formal CE. This chapter and the next present each of the cases on its own terms, with minimal cross-case analysis, in the following manner:

1. I introduce each case in a way that highlights its personality and the core ideals that inform its approach to non-formal CE.
2. I walk through each case's origins, development, and current status. These narratives shed light on how that case has evolved, particularly regarding non-formal CE.
3. I present a profile of each case's pastor. These profiles are important because AGC pastors are the primary influence as to the spirituality, values, and personalities of their churches. While all four cases had group leadership structures, the pastors were ultimately the ones in charge. During the interviews, I found them to be knowledgeable in all areas of ministry and directly involved with many, if not most, aspects of church life.
4. I take a macro-look at each case through its vision/mission statement in relation to CE and its organizational model. I consider the development and key functions of each organizational model separately. (I will return to these organizational models in Chapter 8 for cross-case analysis, with specific attention to the role of CE in each model.)
5. I provide information on the non-formal CE classes offered in each case, including level of participation and teacher perceptions about the functions of their classes.

PROV-1: GROWING TOGETHER THROUGH RESPONSIBILITY

Prov-1 was located two hundred meters off the national highway about 43 km from the capital city, Phnom Penh. The church yard was one of the most pleasant I have seen in Cambodia, having playground equipment for children and a small pavilion. Like many Cambodian churches, a simple, open room was the focal point for much of church life, including worship, children's classes, youth meetings, planning meetings, and fellowship meals. It was referred to by several names—

meeting room (*bonthop brachum*),[331] big room (*bonthop thom*), worship place (*kanlaing tvaybongkhom*).

Prov-1's Origins, Development, and Current Status

The church was started in 1993 by two female American missionaries who were healthcare professionals. The current pastor assumed leadership in 1996 immediately after graduating with the first class of students at Cambodia Bible Institute (CBI). He was considered the original pastor, and Prov-1 was part of the first generation of AGC churches.

The church went through a series of developmental stages before coming into its current form and structure. From 1996 to 2003, various Filipino missionaries worked with it. From 2000 to 2005, its ministry focused on a program called Community Health Evangelism.[332] Then in 2006, it made a permanent shift toward educational programs, including English, computers, educational support, and a preschool called Seeds of Life.[333] Lastly, the years 2006 to 2013 were significant in the development of Prov-1. Working with a female Malaysian missionary, the church expanded its facilities, matured in its thinking about church ministries, and began to write its core documents. It has not been in formal partnership with a missionary since 2013.

Prov-1 was the smallest of the four cases in terms of numbers, the congregation consisting of fifty to sixty adults and youth plus about twenty children. Its reported monthly budget was in in the $301-$500 range. The pastor and assistant pastor were the only paid ministers, each receiving part-time pay for working afternoons Monday through Saturday plus, of course, Sundays. About 10 percent of the church's budget went toward CE.

---

[331]The transliterations of Khmer words are my own. The Khmer language does not have a standardized transliteration at this time.

[332]Also known as the CHE Program, the "E" being later changed to mean "Education."

[333]During the timeframe of this study, facilities were being constructed for Seeds of Life, with a plan to grow it into a K-12 Christian school. Prov-1 does not consider Seeds of Life a regular ministry of the church; therefore, it was excluded from this study.

Prov-1 Pastor's Profile

The pastor of Prov-1 was male, forty-seven years old, and had been married for twenty-one years. He was born into a farming family in a neighboring province along with four siblings. He and his wife had three children ranging in age from seven to eighteen. Having completed high school and passed the comprehensive exams, he was in the first class of students at CBI, receiving his certificate in 1995. He upgraded his theological education at CBI to a three-year diploma in 2005 and to a B.A. in Bible and Ministry in 2015.

Prov-1's Vision in Relation to Non-Formal CE

The pastor stated the vision of the church thusly—"To see the people of [name of the area] receive salvation." He affirmed that this had been the church's vision since the beginning. I recorded in my field notes that this statement was repeatedly referred to in the church's services, planning discussions, documents, prayer times, and testimonies.

When asked how Prov-1's approach to CE fit with its vision, the pastor explained that they wanted "to see people become personally responsible in their faith, live it out, and help others so that others see Jesus through their lives." The word "responsible" (*thothuol khos throv*)[334] in that statement was a key one for understanding the church. One Sunday after service, I asked him, "What makes your church work the way it does?" He explained that they always worked in groups; none worked alone. They wanted to make sure that no one had a load that was too heavy and that everyone had opportunities to take responsibility. In summary, taking responsibility was seen as essential to growing in one's faith, and CE was an important way for that to happen.

Description, Development, and Key Functions of Prov-1's Organizational Model

Prov-1 functioned without a formal organizational model for many years. Over time, however, they came to realize that roles were too unclear and disorganized. So such a model was developed and finalized in 2016 (the official version including photographs of each person) and was registered with the government, along the church's constitution.

---

[334] The word in Khmer literally means "to accept wrong/right."

Figure 6.1 is a representation of Prov-1's organizational model. I added *(in italics)* the number and gender breakdown of those who were responsible for each ministry.

Figure 6.1. Prov-1 organizational model

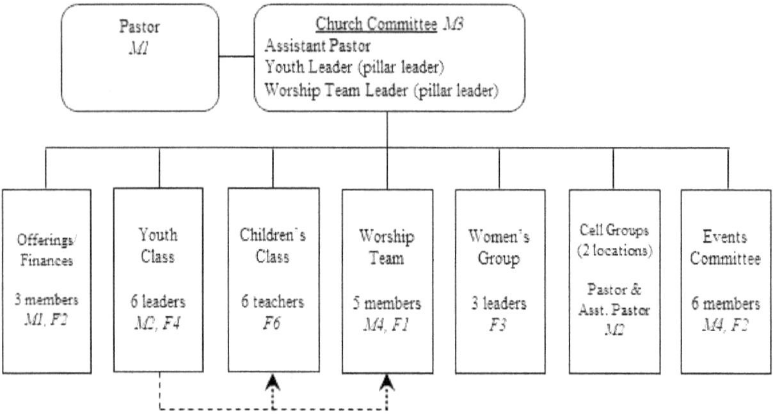

```
              Pastor                Church Committee M3
               M1                   Assistant Pastor
                                    Youth Leader (pillar leader)
                                    Worship Team Leader (pillar leader)

  ┌──────────┬──────────┬──────────┬──────────┬──────────┬──────────┬──────────┐
Offerings/  Youth     Children's  Worship    Women's    Cell Groups   Events
Finances    Class     Class       Team       Group      (2 locations) Committee

3 members   6 leaders 6 teachers  5 members  3 leaders  Pastor &      6 members
M1, F2      M2, F4    F6          M4, F1     F3         Asst. Pastor  M4, F2
                                                        M2
```

A few characteristics of Prov-1's organizational model need to be considered. First, the pastor was intentionally positioned *beside* the church committee to show that he worked closely and shared responsibility for the church with it.

Second, the top tier of leadership included two people identified as "pillar leaders" (*nekduknoam bongkol*). The church committee was prescribed by the constitution, but the pillar leaders were identified as being such based on their character.

Third, the arrows I added leading from the youth class to the children's class and the worship team indicate that these two areas of ministry were *de facto* functions of the youth class. Although not under the leadership of the youth, the people who served in them were all from the youth class. Teaching children and leading worship were two important ways that young people began to assume responsibility in Prov-1. This dynamic meant that a significant amount of ministry within the church was carried out by single people in their teens and twenties.

Lastly, Figure 6.1 shows thirty-five roles with responsibilities in the church. Even though some people filled two (even three) roles, the numbers indicate that about half of this congregation of fifty to sixty adults and youth had ministry responsibilities. In terms of gender, the top leadership of Prov-1 was all male, but women slightly outnumbered men eighteen to seventeen in all roles combined. Prov-1 had the strongest male representation and most even gender representation among the four cases. The numbers also show that youth were a significant ministry force, accounting for seventeen out of thirty-five (48.6 percent) of all ministry roles.

Prov-1's Class Information

The church had classes for children, youth, worship, and women and desired to develop a class for men as well. Activities were concentrated as much as possible on Sundays because of the busyness of the members. Prov-1 also had four village cell groups, which it considered outreaches that could become church plants. These cell groups were not counted as members of the congregation.

Perceptions of Roles of Specific Classes at Prov-1

The Class Information Sheet listed nine common purposes for CE classes that cover a spectrum of internally—and externally—focused functions.[335] Internally focused functions are directed toward those who are already a part of the church, while externally focused functions are directed toward people not part of the church. Evangelism is an internal function when directed toward people in the church (e.g., confirmation of salvation) and a mixed function when it is directed toward those outside with the purpose of bringing them into the church. Table 6.2 lists the functions that Prov-1 teachers marked as being true for their class. Three of the teachers added that their classes also taught health and civic morals.[336]

---

[335] See the last page of the Approach to CE Questionnaire, Appendix B.
[336] I am using the term "civic morals" to describe lessons related to living in society, such as how to do household chores, show respect to the elder, and negotiate traffic.

Table 6.2. Functions of classes at Prov-1

	Church					Village Cell Groups						TOTALS
	Child	Youth	Worship	Women		1a Youth	1b Child.	2	3	4		
Bible knowledge	X	X	X	X	4	X	X	X	X	X	5	9
Discipleship	X	X	X	X	4	X	X	X	X		4	8
Fellowship		X	X	X	3	X	X		X		3	6
Helping community	X				1	X	X	X			3	4
Evangelizing community	X				1			X	X	X	3	4
Preparing for ministry		X	X	X	3							3
Other: health, civic morals	X				1			X	X		2	3
Relationships w/community		X			1							1
Confirming salvation												0

Here are a few observations that can be made from Table 6.2. First, looking at the classes in aggregate, increasing Bible knowledge was considered the main function of Prov-1 classes, followed closely by discipleship and then fellowship. Second, the regular classes, when viewed separately from the village cell groups, emphasized the internally focused functions of discipleship, increasing Bible knowledge, fellowship, and preparing people for ministry. Only the children's class was concerned with the community because it included children from families not part of the church. Third, in terms of teaching, Prov-1 engaged the community most directly through its village cell groups.

PROV-2: SERVING THE COMMUNITY HOLISTICALLY

Prov-2 was located 5 km off a national highway about 53 km from Phnom Penh in an area where the Assemblies of God had a lot of history. The government school on this little road was established in the early 1990's in partnership with the Assemblies of God, a unique status that has been maintained to this day.

The church itself had two features that stand out immediately. First, its main building functioned as both a church and a community preschool. The walls, inside and out, were painted with popular cartoon characters, happy children at play, and large alphabet and number charts. In addition to these colorful images, the main hall had ruler-straight, hand-painted Scripture verses like Psalm 18:2; Malachi 3:10; 1 John 2:1; and John 14:6 to remind everyone that God's call motivated what they did in that space.

Second, the original church building on the property has been used as a cucumber co-op since 2017. Every morning, about 1,000 kg of produce were brought in by the community and hauled out in vans by a company called *Lo-as Thmei* (New Sprout), a program of World Vision Cambodia. Prov-2 took no fees from the people because this co-op was part of its holistic service in their community. I have introduced Prov-2 with these images because they epitomize the church's understanding of what it means to "answer God's call" and to "live as an example, as light, in actions, words, and love, by taking Jesus as the principle."[337]

However, Prov-2 had different priorities in the beginning. A three-meter-long sheet titled River of Life in the main hall recorded the church's history from 1997 to 2012 in hand-drawn pictures. The first part depicted it as a group of people meeting under a house surrounded by lack of development, lack of sanitation, gambling, and domestic violence. Then, beginning in 2000, the pictures changed and multiplied significantly with images of happy children going to school and playing in the church yard, creation of the preschool, agricultural development, and sanitation improvements, including construction of hygienic toilets for 240 families—the church being instrumental in bringing this about. That shift to holistic, community-focused ministry defined Prov-2 and provides us with a critical lens for understanding its approach to non-formal CE.

Prov-2's Origins, Development, and Current Status

Prov-2 was founded by the current pastor in 1997, joining the three other AGC churches already in the area since 1994. The pastor herself had become a believer in one of those churches. However, sensing God's call to establish a church in her own village, she established Prov-2 with the blessing and encouragement of the other churches.

Prov-2 had the most documented history of the four cases in this study. As already described briefly above, the two key documents were

---

[337] These words are taken from the Vision Statement and Mission Statement of Prov-2, which is posted on large, white chart paper encased in plastic at the front of the main hall. (My translation.)

the River of Life pictorial history and a summary of the church's history handwritten on three large sheets of chart paper for public display titled History of [name] Church, 1997-2018. This latter documentation divided the church's history into the following three stages:

- *Stage One (1997-2000).* The church met under the pastor's current house. Many people who had joined them at first left because the focus was entirely on spiritual needs. They became disillusioned when the material benefits they imagined they would receive did not materialize.
- *Stage Two (2000-2008).* The historical account began, "In the year 2000, the church began to build a building to make it easier to meet for worship and prayer." Funds for that building came through a Filipino missionary, while much of the labor came from the community and the church. Because the land was public land, Prov-2 started a community preschool in 2002 with fifty-three students. Also, the church committee worked with international agencies and the community to bring improvement in various areas, such as sanitation, agriculture, and domestic violence.
- *Stage Three (2008 to the present).* Prov-2 entered into a partnership with World Vision Cambodia (WVC), which has endured to the present and has facilitated many of their social programs. WVC gave about one half of the money needed ($4,700) to construct the main hall (the building with the colorful paintings) in 2015. Other funds came from a Korean donor, with the men in the church and community providing the labor. Also, this stage was characterized by growth in a variety of areas, including community programs and village cell groups.

The pastor described the overall structure of Prov-2 as a 'big church' (*kromchumnum thom*) with six village 'cell groups' (*krom kaoseka*) under its 'umbrella' (*chat*). One village cell group was about 12 km to the east, one was 0.5 km to the south, and four were to the west at distances of 7 to 10 km. Table 6.3 shows the number of people involved in the various groups that made up Prov-2. The community preschool is added in at the bottom because it was considered a ministry of the church (unlike Prov-1 and Cap-2).

Table 6.3. Total of all groups at Prov-2

	Adults	Youth	Children	TOTALS
Main church	20	12	35	67
Village cell groups				
South	12		4	16
East	32		25	57
West 1	5		25	30
West 2	10		10	20
West 3			7	7
West 4	5		10	15
TOTALS	**84**	**12**	**116**	**212**
Preschool			45	
OVERALL TOTALS	**84**	**12**	**161**	**257**

Being under the 'umbrella' of Prov-2 meant that the village cell groups were considered part of the church and covered by its legal standing with the government. However, some of these groups were also 'semi-autonomous,' meaning they had their own leaders and handled their own finances.

Prov-2's monthly budget fell into the $301 to $500 range. Offerings and expenses in the village cell groups were separate. The pastor received a part-time salary but served the church full-time; she was the only paid minister. The preschool teachers received a modest monthly offering from the church. Including the offerings for the teachers, the church spent about 60 percent of its monthly budget on CE.

Prov-2 Pastor's Profile

The pastor of Prov-2 was female, fifty-five years old, married for thirty-eight years, and the mother of five children. Born into a farming family in the village where she lived, she and her husband were farmers. When she became a Christian, she had no formal education. Thus, when sensing God's call to start a church in her village, she realized that to be a pastor she needed to learn to read and write.[338] Also, she determined that

---

[338] The Khmer language is Sanskrit-based with thirty-three consonants and twenty-three vowels.

all her children would get a college education. At the time of this study, three of them had graduated from university, one had started but did not graduate, and the fifth was in his third year. The pastor herself graduated with a two-year degree from CBI in 2006.

Prov-2's Vision in Relation to Non-Formal CE

Prov-2 had its vision and mission statements handwritten on white chart paper encased in plastic and displayed in the front of the church's main hall. The following is my translation of those statements:

Vision: [We] want to see all people receive salvation (from children to adults), equipped to become leaders that humble themselves, submit, are united, have relationships with those around them, and live as light by reverencing God, and are able to make disciples to the glory of God, especially taking Jesus as the example and answering the call of God.

The mission of the church:
1. Live as an example, as light, in actions, words, and love, by taking Christ as the principle
2. Answer the call of God
3. Commit to being servant-leaders

Both statements began with expressing a desire to see people receive salvation, with the remainder focusing on the nature, attitudes, and actions of the church. My observations confirmed that the people at Prov-2 intentionally and persistently endeavored to live out these ideals in a way that they believed was transforming their community. When I asked the pastor and one of the leaders to describe the church's personality, they said that their ministries were for helping the community, regardless of religion. They described those ministries as 'unselfish,' meaning without coercing people to become Christians.

When asked about the relationship of CE to this vision, they explained that the main goal of CE was for people to believe and be saved. They especially liked to use the term *sko-al preah* ('know God'). Their approach to CE centered on knowing the Bible because knowing it led to knowing God and to salvation. They described teaching as one of five functions of their church —teaching, service/ministry, development/agriculture, liaising with agencies that can help the community, and visitation/evangelism.

Description, Development, and Key Functions of Prov-2's Organizational Model

Prov-2's organizational model had been in place for about eight years, but its essence was there from the beginning of the church. Figure 6.2 is a reproduction of the chart on display in the front of Prov-2's main hall, safely encased in plastic. The chart was hand-drawn on large, white chart paper and bordered with red construction paper. Each box contained the positions, names of individuals, and their photographs. I added the brackets identifying the church committee, gender information, and arrows connecting the youth leaders to the worship leaders and the leaders of children's teachers.

Figure 6.2. Organizational model of Prov-2

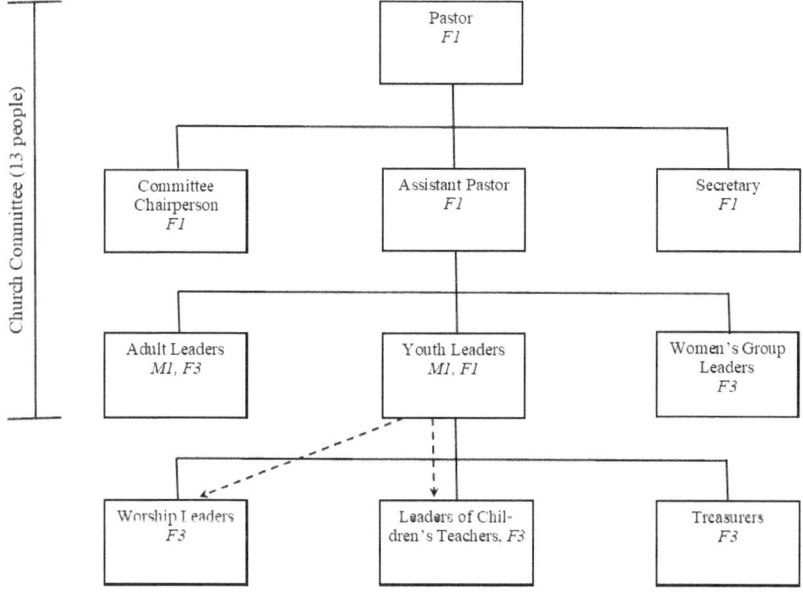

This organizational model was hierarchical, each tier indicating levels of authority and responsibility. The pastor led the church (top tier) in close coordination with the three individuals in the second tier. The church committee was made up of the pastor plus the twelve people in the second and third tiers. The committee chairperson had the power to call the committee together, and the secretary kept the official records for the committee and the church. The treasurers (bottom right, fourth tier) handled the money for all ministries in the church. Lastly, the arrows indicate that the youth leaders oversaw the worship and children's ministries.

This figure shows there were twenty-two individual roles filled by twenty women and two men, making it by far the most female-dominated of the four cases. No one at Prov-2 held more than one position in the organizational structure. While a few people were from the cell groups, most were from the main church, which was made up of about twenty adults and twelve youth (see Table 6.3 above). This high level of responsibility among members at the main church said a lot about the church's ethos and suggested a possible explanation for the breadth of Prov-2's reach.

Prov-2's Class Information

The church's CE classes for children and youth plus the community preschool were held at the main facility. The six village small groups had six classes for children and three for adults. The preschool was considered a ministry of the church (not parachurch), although the children were not counted as church members. All classes met weekly except the preschool. The children's classes at the main church and the south village cell group used *The Greatest Journey*[339] curriculum, while the other children's classes at the village cell groups used *Beloved Child*.[340] The community preschool used the government curriculum. The youth class used materials the teacher had studied as a CBI student. Lastly, the adult groups in the village either studied lessons prepared by the leader or books the teacher thought would encourage their faith.

Perceptions of Roles of Specific Classes at Prov-2

Table 6.5 displays the functions of each class at the main church and in the village cell groups as understood by its teacher. The following points stand out when examining this table. First, the functions of the preschool marked here go well beyond that of an externally focused program to serve the community. Although running a regular preschool program, the teachers had strong spiritual motivations, which they shared openly with the children and their families. Second, while the village

---

[339] Samaritan's Purse, *Domnar chivit da l'ah bomphot* [The Greatest Journey], Khmer version (Phnom Penh, Cambodia: Samaritan's Purse, 2017).

[340] Estrebilla, Thurain, and Rotha, *Khmeng somnop*.

Presentation of the Case: Provincial Cases 121

cell groups were concerned with community engagement, the teaching in these groups still focused on traditional internal CE functions, such as discipleship, Bible knowledge, and evangelism.

Third, the teachers of the youth Bible class in both the main church and village cell groups all marked "preparing for ministry." This class explicitly existed to develop young people for ministry (especially the teaching of children). I did not, however, see them carrying out this function in my observations of the three children's classes and two adult classes in the village groups. So, it begs the question as to what *all* the teachers filling out my Class Information Sheets understood by this phrase.[341] One possible explanation draws on the phrase "answer the call of God" in Point 2 of Prov-2's vision statement above. I heard this phrase often in their preaching and teaching. I hold the tentative conclusion that it is equivalent to "serve God" (i.e., "understand and obey God's will for your life"). This observation highlights their explicit desire for all church members to be prepared to serve God and obey his will for their lives.

Table 6.4. Functions of classes at Prov-2

	Main Church				Village Cell Groups							Totals
	Child.	Youth Bible Class	Preschool		South	East	West 1	West 2	West 3	West 4		
Discipleship	X	X	X	3		X	X	X	X	X	5	8
Bible knowledge		X	X	2	X	X	X	X	X	X	6	8
Evangelizing community	X	X		2	X	X	X	X	X	X	6	8
Preparing for ministry		X		1	X	X	X	X	X	X	6	7
Confirming salvation		X	X	2	X				X	X	3	5
Fellowship		X	X	2	X		X			X	3	5
Providing mutual care		X	X	2				X	X	X	3	5
Relationships w/community		X	X	2			X	X		X	3	5
Helping community			X	1				X	X	X	3	4
Other:			Prepare to enter 1ˢᵗ grade									

---

[341] I used the term *pointekech* in the form. This term is relatively formal, covering both recognized ministry and lay ministry in the church. The term *ka-bomrar* is the word for 'serving' in the broadest sense and the word used in the phrase 'serving God.'

CHAPTER 7
Presentation of the Cases: The Capital City Cases

CAP-1: BUILDING A CULTURE OF GRACE

Cap-1 was located on a quiet street in the heart of Phnom Penh near an imposing foreign embassy compound and the 'dike road' (an elevated ring road at what used to be the edge of the city). On my first research-oriented visit, I watched a university student give her testimony in front of the whole church as the last step in her preparation for water baptism. This seemingly confident, well-spoken young lady began to get choked up as she shared her story. When she asked the pastor for help, he stepped up beside her, gently placed his hand on her shoulder, and quietly prayed for a couple of minutes. Everyone waited. When she regained her composure, she talked about the transformation Jesus had wrought in her life. The crowd's response was that of a proud family watching a daughter come of age.

This simple vignette was the culmination of months of preparation nurtured by Cap-1's culture of grace. During its baptism class, new believers would come to understand their experience of transformation in scriptural terms and would craft their testimony in order to share it with the church, family, and friends. This informal form of teaching (i.e., sharing one's testimony) was the first goal of CE at Cap-1. As the pastor explained it, the church's approach to CE relied on the truths of Scripture to persuade people in their hearts, not on church rules or by coercion from leaders to motivate people. He called this ethos a "culture of grace." It was the defining characteristic of Cap-1 and the lens for understanding its approach to CE.

Cap-1's Origins, Development, and Current Status

Cap-1 was the second Assembly of God church to be established in Cambodia. Meeting in the home of a missionary, it was started by the current pastor and a female American Assemblies of God missionary in 1992 or 1993. After some time, the church rented space in an international school and then rented a house, with assistance from a different missionary. In 1998, the current property was purchased, and the main hall plus lower floor of the back building was built. The total cost was $100,000, with 10 percent being raised by the church and 90 percent provided by Assemblies of God World Missions (US). In 2002, a second floor was added to the back building and another small, two-story building in the back corner of the property was built.

The pastor divided Cap-1's historical development into two phases. He called the first phase "dependence on missionaries" (beginning in 1992 or 1993) and the second phase "walking on [our] own" (taking place between 1996 and 1997). A number of people left the church as missionary leadership yielded to Cambodian leadership, marking a defining moment for Cap-1. The pastor said, "Those who stayed were very strong. And we began to walk on our own." They have held to that path ever since.

Cap-1 had about 120 adults and youth plus 40 children. Although there was no formal membership, the pastor had a semi-formal way of classifying the people in the church. Of those 120 adults and youth, about 50 had ministry responsibilities, another 50 did not have responsibilities but were always present, and the remaining 20 were part of the church but attended inconsistently.

Financially, Cap-1's budget exceeded $1,000 per month. About 30-40 percent of that budget was spent on CE, including half-salaries for two people who worked in a youth educational outreach program that uses some of Cap-1's office space. The pastor served full-time and received full-time compensation; and the two assistant pastors also received compensation. Unlike the other three cases in this study, Cap-1 had sufficient facilities for CE, some of which were used primarily for that purpose.

Cap-1 Pastor's Profile

The pastor was male, fifty-four years old, had been married twenty-nine years, and he and his wife had two grown children. He was born and raised with eight brothers and sisters in a village not far from where Prov-2 was located. His father was a schoolteacher who later became one of the founding AGC pastors in that area. Cap-1 pastor's wife, a teacher by profession, was serving as the principal of a K-12 Christian school. The pastor graduated from high school and became a government high school teacher after completing two years of pedagogical training. He left his teaching position because he felt God calling him to the ministry. He was in the first class of students at CBI but graduated from the two-year program with the second class in 1998. Besides his training at CBI, he completed a two-year leadership development program with Asian Access and a two-year program with Langham Preaching. At the time of this study, he was a member of AGC's national executive committee.

Cap-1's Vision in Relation to Non-Formal CE

Cap-1 took time to carefully formulate its vision in the early years and has never veered from it—"to declare the Good News of Jesus." The first page of the constitution stated the church's vision as follows: "[Name] Church is committed to taking responsibility to bring the Good News of salvation and transformation to people living in sin, that they may come into the kingdom of God and become a people of praise, giving glory to God in all things."

The outworking of this vision involved three components—declaring the Good News, a 'culture of grace,' and the importance of elders. When I asked how its approach to CE related to the vision, the importance of elders came to the forefront. The pastor said that teaching was directed first to the elders and leaders then to the church through them. The elders and leaders bore primary responsibility to continuously bring the church back to the proclamation of the Good News and to ensuring that all ministries remained true to the vision. The 'culture of grace' was the underlying principle by which the leadership persuades (not educates)[342] the church to live out this vision.

Description, Development, and Key Functions of Cap-1's Organizational Model

Cap-1 did not have a published organizational model. Thus, Figure 7.1 is my construction created from the pastor's sketch, which I presented to him for correction and feedback. He confirmed that this model had been in place since the beginning. I added (*in italics*) information about the number of positions and gender representation in each box.

The church committee was made up of nine people—the pastor, the two assistant pastors, and six elders. These elders had been church founders; some no longer had leadership responsibility, while others were among the pillar leaders of Cap-1. Each of the seven ministries

---

[342] The pastor was very clear in this distinction. The word he used for educate' (*ab'rom*) is a term that can carry forceful connotations.

identified in the figure was led by an individual recognized as a pillar leader. At the time of my research, discussion was underway about changing the elder committee to include more pillar leaders and leaders from the younger generations.

Figure 7.1. Cap-1 organizational model

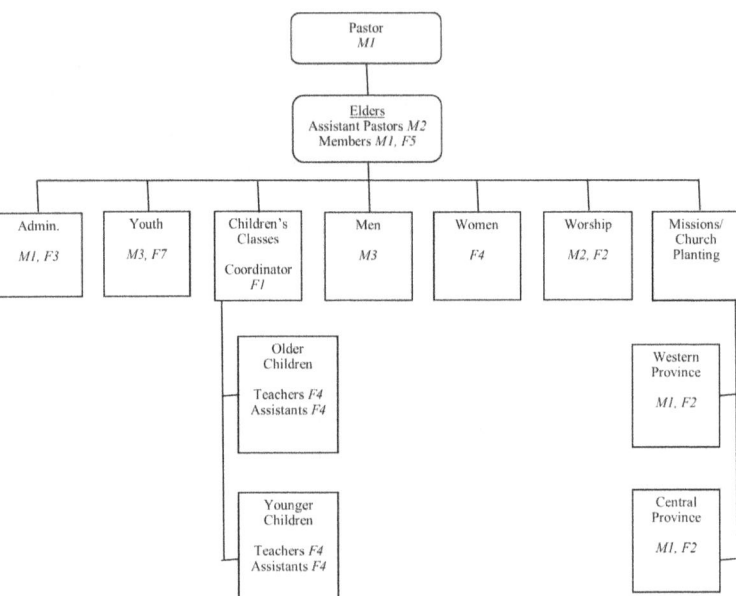

Figure 7.1 provides data about the roles and gender representation in Cap-1's organizational model. All three of the formally recognized pastors were male, but the church committee (i.e., pastors plus elders) was almost evenly split between men and women. The children's teachers were all female (sixteen). Removing them from the count of ministry roles still left a ratio of about two females to one male. So, while the top leadership was male, women filled most of the ministry roles overall. The total number of roles came to fifty-seven, which represented nearly one-half of the congregation's 120 adults and youth.

Cap-1's CE Classes Information

Cap-1 had two types of classes—regular and occasional. Regular classes were taught weekly at the church for specific groups on an ongoing basis. The children's class, held during the Sunday service, used *Superbook* curriculum that had been translated into Khmer.[343] Each week of the month was taught by a different teacher accompanied by an assistant teacher. The youth, women's, and men's classes met before the Sunday service. The youth teacher used various books from which to teach. The men's and women's classes had a peer-teaching approach, with a different class member teaching each week. The women shared from literature they read or from their own personal devotions. The men discussed whatever text was in the annual Bible-reading plan for that day. The teaching in these two classes was more devotional than systematic.

The discipleship class was special among the regular classes in content, approach, and function. As discussed in the sub-section "Cap-1's Vision in Relation to Non-Formal CE," that class was the one in which the leaders and teachers were taught. Although anyone could join the class, it was specifically designed for people with responsibility. The pastor taught the class personally, providing opportunity weekly for leaders to meet with him, to communicate with one another, and to make plans. At the time of the study, this class was run in partnership with the Christian Life Program of CBI. With the course materials being provided by CBI, the participants could earn certificates from CBI for completing ten books in the program.

Cap-1 also had occasional classes. One was a three-month-long marriage-preparation class between the pastor and the couple. The pastor also led a water baptism class twice a year over a period of about three months that was timed with the church's two largest outreaches of the year—Christmas and Parents Day (June). This particular class covered basic beliefs, and helped the participants prepare their testimony and identify their gifts for serving in the church. Additionally, the pastor had an informal preaching class with three young men in the church who were part of the preaching schedule. Cap-1 also hosted a parachurch youth educational outreach program run by an international organization, which offered courses in English and computers.

---

[343]Christian Broadcasting Network, *Seavpov vises: merean kromchumnum* [Superbook: church edition], Khmer version (Phnom Penh, Cambodia: Christian Broadcasting Network, 2014).

Perceptions of Roles of Specific Classes at Cap-1

Table 7.1 presents the perceptions of the teachers as to the functions of their classes at Cap-1. Only the regular classes have been included. Their responses led to the following three general observations. First, the strongest categories were Bible knowledge, fellowship, and mutual care; these perceptions rang true with my class observations, including the idea of mutual care in children's classes.[344] Second, setting aside the men's class, the functions were almost entirely internal in focus; this finding fits the discussions above about the church's philosophy of ministry. Although Cap-1 had an outward-focused vision (i.e., proclaiming the Good News), the teaching was decidedly inward-focused in order to equip people to carry out that vision. Third, some of the functions marked for the men's group are hard to explain because I did not receive any information about community-oriented activities by this class.

Table 7.1. Functions of regular classes at Cap-1

	Younger Children	Older Children	Youth	Women	Men	Discipleship	TOTALS
Bible knowledge	X	X	X	X	X	X	6
Providing mutual care	X	X	X	X	X	X	6
Fellowship	X	X	X	X	X		5
Discipleship			X		X	X	3
Preparing for ministry					X	X	2
Confirming salvation			X				1
Relationships w/community					X		1
Helping community					X		1
Evangelizing community					X		1

CAP-2: MOBILIZING THE CHURCH THROUGH LIFE GROUPS

Cap-2 was a youthful church located in a double shop house that opened onto one of the capital city's main thoroughfares just a short walk from the Royal University of Phnom Penh. Its cell groups or home groups were originally organized family-style or by neighborhood (i.e., block). Over time, the church's young family base matured, and life in the capital city became more hectic and crowded. Thus, the people became

---

[344] For example, teachers had children pray for each other.

'uncomfortable culturally' with having groups in their homes. So, Cap-2 adapted by shifting from disseminated small groups that provided fellowship and care to Life Groups that discipled and mobilized. It also shifted to homogenous groups led by peers or near peers. Part of that strategy included concentrating activities on Sunday mornings in every available space at the church (including under the stairs) in order to maximize the time that people had available.

I have introduced Cap-2 in this way to bring out themes that were important for understanding its approach to non-formal CE. First, that approach was somewhat shaped by efforts to maximize a restricted physical space (i.e., a double shop house with no yard) and to thrive in a crowded city. Second, Cap-2 was constantly evaluating what it was doing and thus adapting. At the time of this study, even though Life Groups were in their first generation, the leaders were already thinking about how to make adjustments when groups multiplied. Third, single people and families in their mid-20s and 30s were the driving force of Cap-2's ministries and church life (a point that will be very apparent when looking at demographics in Chapter 9). Fourth, these three dynamics converged to find their expression in the Life Groups. These Life Groups were not simply a CE model or mobilization strategy but the outworking of Cap-2's self-understanding and the philosophical driver of its approach to non-formal CE.

Cap-2's Origins, Development, and Current Status

The church was founded in 1996 by a female missionary from the Philippines. At first, it met in the missionary's house, then it moved into a student center, and finally into its current facilities in 1998. Cap-2 was a unique first-generation AGC church. The founding missionary was guided by indigenous-church principles and planned from the outset to establish a contextualized church with a Cambodian pastor. Her plans were proceeding step by step until factional fighting between political parties became military action in July 1997, forcing her to leave the country for several months. During that time, the young man she had been mentoring to become the pastor kept the church going. From then on, he was considered its first pastor.

The truly unique aspect of Cap-2's story is that it was the only AGC church to have gone through a pastoral change not precipitated by the death of the founding pastor. Cap-2 has had three pastors, and their terms of service corresponded to the church's developmental stages. The first pastor (1997-2002) was credited with getting the church established and contextualizing its church culture. The second pastor (2002-2007), chosen to serve while the now-current pastor was getting his theological education, was credited with creating the church's constitution, setting up cell groups/home groups, and expanding the church's ministries to include youth and sports. The third and current pastor was installed as senior pastor when he returned from earning his B.Th. in Malaysia in 2007. His ministry has seen continued church planting, the addition of community service or social ministries, and the establishment of an English congregation in 2009.

At the time of this study, Cap-2 had about 120 adults and youth plus thirty children. It also had an English congregation of fifty to seventy people led by the founding missionary. (The relationship between these two congregations will be further explored in the sub-section on Cap-2's organizational model.) The church's budget was more than $1,000 per month, approximately 5 percent of which was spent on CE. The pastor was the only minister that received compensation.

Cap-2 moved into its present facilities, which was a single shop house on a corner, in 1998, with a second shop next door purchased in 2004. Then In 2005, the two buildings were joined, and the roof was renovated into an enclosed main hall. The building purchases and renovation costs totaled about $100,000, the funds coming from Hong Kong, the United States, Australia, and church members. Cap-2 owned the building, but there were seven different owners of the land underneath them, including apartments, small businesses, and two government offices (a police station and a *sangkat* [district] office).

Cap-2 Pastor's Profile

The pastor of Cap-2 at age thirty-five was the youngest of the pastors in this study and the only one born and raised in Phnom Penh. His father was a motorcycle taxi driver, his mother was a domestic cook, and he was the second of their four children. The pastor had been married for ten years, and he and his wife had three children ages two months to eight years. They served as partners in ministry. She ran the church's daycare and led its women's ministry; she also served on AGC's national women's ministry committee. He was the youngest member of the AGC's National Executive Committee.

After graduating from high school, the pastor attended CBI, earning a three-year diploma in 2005, then a B.Th. from the Bible College of Malaysia (BCM) in 2007, and four years later an M.A. in Ministry from BCM. He reported that his time in Malaysia had a significant impact on his philosophy of church administration, which will be apparent in the sub-section on Cap-2's organizational model.

The pastor served his church full-time and received full-time compensation. Additionally, he had two other significant ministry endeavors. He was the academic dean of Cambodia School of Missions since its founding in 2009; and he had been on Christian radio since 2013, hosting both a program on the life of Christ (15-minute segments) and a call-in counseling program (one to two hours live).

Cap-2's Vision in Relation to Non-Formal CE

The mission statement of Cap-2 appeared on the pastor's business card in both Khmer and English, which read, "Committed to be the Light of God in bringing the gospel and life transformation to people who live in darkness." The pastor explained that this statement was really about Cap-2's vision for church planting nationwide. At the time of this research, the church had planted seven new works and had partnered (*dai ku*) with countless other church plants.

Regarding CE, the pastor explained that everything the church did was weighed against its mission statement. The theme chosen for 2018 overtly connected CE to that statement as follows: "Every believer must be a student of the Word." That theme was not intended to get everyone to join Bible classes, but rather to encourage everyone to be a student of the Word in all four main functions of the church—worship, discipleship, fellowship, and mission/ministry. The term 'discipleship' did not refer to CE classes; for in the pastor's view, CE was not just formal classes but "life sharing experience with each other."[345] Additionally, teachers were facilitators who were to encourage discussion. According to him, the most important question was, "How does the Bible really relate to real life?" He wanted teachers as facilitators to work with the experiences and questions of their students to bring biblical principles out in a way that would help them to be serious students of the Word.

---

[345]Unless otherwise noted, quotations of the Cap-2 pastor are his own words in English.

Description, Development, and Key Functions of Cap-2's Organizational Model

Cap-2 formalized its organizational model and filed it with the Cambodian government's Ministry of Cults and Religion as part of its required license renewal in 2017, although the essence of the model had been in place since adoption of the church's constitution in 2008. The constitution called for a four-part leadership structure—pastor, pastoral team, church board, and ministry coordinators. The pastor formulated much of his philosophy of church governance when pursuing his B.Th. in Malaysia, where he had opportunity to study the organizational structure of the church he attended. For instance, following that church's example, Cap-2's weekly bulletin listed all the church positions and ministry coordinators to constantly remind people of their roles. The bulletin list included fifteen positions covering twenty-six individual roles, which were filled by about twenty persons.

Figure 7.2 is a faithful reproduction of Cap-2's organizational model, including its shape and the order of the boxes. I added information as to the number and gender of individuals *(in italics)*, age ranges for Life Groups, dashed arrows to show relationships, and the designation 'community service' for certain ministries. The pastor explained that the shape of the model was necessary to fit everything on a single sheet of paper. (The shape does not indicate a philosophy of governance.)

Key leaders of Cap-2 were the pastor, the pastoral team, and the ministry coordinators. These coordinators, whom the pastor and the pastoral team had selected or invited to serve, were responsible for the regular functions of the church. Members of the church board were not counted among the key leaders because they were elected and met only three to four times a year to make major decisions for the church.

Figure 7.2. Cap-2's organizational model

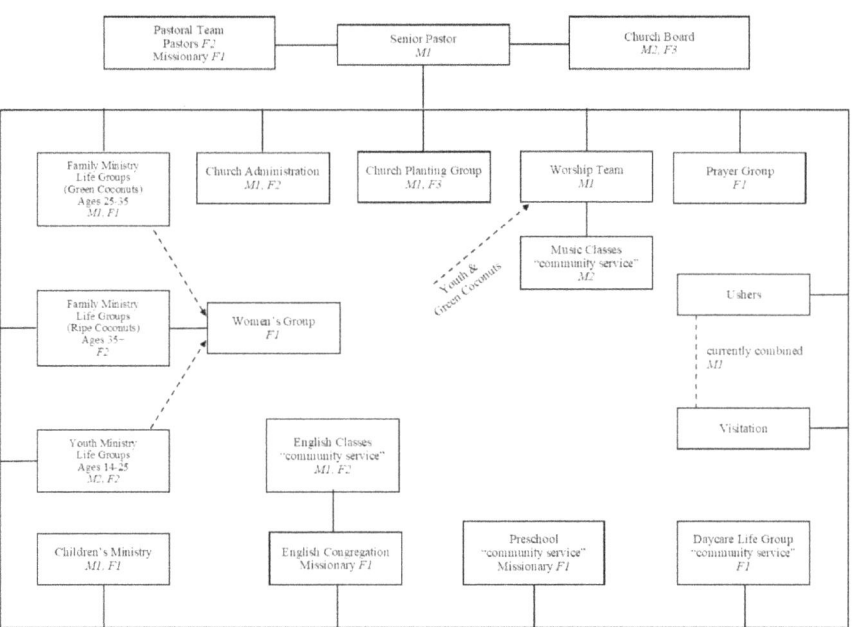

In addition to its unique shape, Cap-2's organizational model had a few important characteristics that differentiated it from the other cases in this study in these four ways:

1. Unlike the other three cases, which relied on committees and a high level of integration, this church's ministries were led by people with delegated responsibility. For example, the pastor did not lead a Life Group; instead, he led in the adoption of the program, guided its development, and invested in the leaders.
2. Forming the philosophical core of the model were the Life Groups. If or when the vision of the leadership is eventually realized, the four Life Group boxes will come to represent many groups and a major portion of church life.
3. Cap-2 had a semi-autonomous English congregation included in its organization, which was led by the founding missionary. That congregation ran the English classes and the preschool (no connection line in their model). Although considered part of Cap-2's overall reach, its participants/adherents were not

counted as church members, and Cap-2 was not responsible for their ministries.
4. The English classes, music classes, preschool, and daycare are all labeled 'community service.' They were offered as services to the community and thus are not considered core ministries of Cap-2. (As with Prov-1, because these ministries received fees for childcare or formal education, they did not fall within the delimitations of this study.)

Cap-2's organizational model included a total of forty roles, compared to a congregation size of about 120 adults and youth. The number of lead individuals was less than the number of roles because some filled more than one role. For example, members of the church board were also ministry coordinators. Additionally, a few of the positions in this model were undertaken by members of the English congregation (e.g., English teachers, music teachers, and the founding missionary). Further, it must be noted that women filled positions in a ratio to men of almost two to one across the model. At the top level, the senior pastor was male, but the pastoral team was all female. Women outnumbered men across the various ministries twenty to eleven.

Cap-2's CE Classes Information

The primary forms of non-formal CE at Cap-2 were Sunday school for children and the Life Groups divided by ages for youth and adults (called 'Green Coconuts' and 'Ripe Coconuts'), plus a special Life Group consisting of the daycare staff. The assistants in the children's classes did not teach. The Life Groups for older youth and Green Coconuts had coordinators in addition to teachers because they already had multiple groups. As will be seen in Chapter 9, this was an important demographic for Cap-2. Altogether, sixty-one youth and adults were in Life Groups, approximately one half of the congregation. The children's classes had twenty boys and seven girls, which was unique among the cases. I can say from my class observations that it created an interesting (e.g., lively) classroom dynamic.

All Cap-2 classes utilized teaching material chosen by the leadership. The Sunday school class for the older children used AGC's doctrinal booklet.[346] Teachers for the younger children taught stories from a children's Bible. The Life Groups used Intentional Moves, a four-book discipleship and mobilization program based on material produced by the Philippines General Council of the Assemblies of God.[347] Cap-2 had translated the first three books, with some revisions for the context in Cambodia but were planning to use the AGC doctrinal booklet in place of the fourth book.

While the classes described here were "the key elements for the church to function," Cap-2's organizational model (Figure 7.2) includes additional educational efforts labeled 'community service.' The English and music classes were offered in cooperation with the English congregation as a service to the community on an ad hoc basis, and the students in these classes could connect to either congregation. The preschool was run by the English congregation as a formal education service that was physically and legally separate from the church. They had plans to develop it into a Christian school.

Perceptions of Roles of Specific Classes at Cap-2

Table 7.2 presents the functions of the classes at Cap-2 as understood by the teachers or ministry coordinators. The children's classes focused on discipleship, Bible knowledge, and preparing for ministry (possibly thinking of children and assistant teachers). They built relationships and evangelized the community through the neighborhood children who attended. The daycare staff Life Group, which was purely internal, focused on discipleship. The other four Life Groups prioritized Bible knowledge, fellowship, and mutual care, which were core values discussed in the church's philosophy above. An additional purpose of these Life Groups was to prepare people for ministry, especially as future Life Group leaders. The youth (18-25) and the 'Green Coconuts' were the core demographic of the church and a main point of entry for new people. And the 'Ripe Coconuts' were a group of older ladies who were providing mutual care for one another, serving God with their gifts (including domestic and foreign missions trips), and helping

---

[346]*Statement of Faith of the Assemblies of God of Cambodia*, Khmer language, revised (Phnom Penh, Cambodia: Assemblies of God of Cambodia, 2011).

[347]The Philippines General Council of the Assemblies of God, *Intentional Moves Training Manual* (ICI Ministries: The Philippines, 2015), http://www.iciphilippines.org/wp-content/uploads/2015/01/IM-manual-Empowered-Local-Churches.pdf (accessed June 6, 2018).

with community outreaches. In summary, the classes at Cap-2 were largely focused on church members but were doing so in order to fulfill their vision "to be the Light of God in bringing the gospel and life transformation to people who live in darkness."

Table 7.2. Functions of classes at Cap-2

	All Children	Daycare Staff	Youth 14-18	Youth 18-25	Green Coconuts	Ripe Coconuts	TOTALS
Bible knowledge	X		X	X	X	X	5
Discipleship	X	X	X		X		4
Fellowship			X	X	X	X	4
Preparing for ministry	X		X		X	X	4
Provide mutual care				X	X	X	3
Relationships w/community	X		X	X			3
Confirm salvation				X	X		2
Evangelizing community	X					X	2
Helping community						X	1

SUMMARY OF CHAPTERS 6 AND 7

These two chapters presented the four cases in this study in terms of their origins and development, core ideals, organizational structures, and general approaches to non-formal CE. They were similar in that they are all first-generation AGC churches engaged in sustained efforts at non-formal CE from their earliest stages of development. They formulated their approaches to CE independent of each other, learning from their own experiences and drawing on different sources for ideas and materials. Prov-1 was a mid-sized church (by Cambodian standards), but the other three were among the largest AGC churches (150-200 people).

Prov-1 was a well-established church in a small community. It was led by a man in his 40s who had a B.A. degree from CBI. The value placed on education was seen in the educational levels of its members (see demographics in Chapter 9), in its preschool with over 200 children, and in its ambitious vision to build a Christian school in the community. Not surprisingly, CE was central to Prov-1's church life. Its approach to CE was driven by the conviction that believers grow in their faith through taking responsibility in the church's ministries and outreaches.

Prov-2 was the largest of the cases in terms of members/adherents. It was led by a pastor in her 50s who had no formal education apart from a two-year degree from CBI. Although the main church of about twenty adults and twelve youth was relatively small, its 'reach' was astonishing as the people worked to serve their community and surrounding villages holistically. Prov-2's organizational model and highly integrated approach to ministry were unique among the cases (and possibly among AGC churches). The women who led this church infused all its ministries and social engagements with a clear sense of calling and purpose. Teaching was Prov-2's dominant activity.

Cap-1 was a middle-class church in the heart of the capital city. It was led by a pastor in his 50s who had a two-year degree from CBI plus about six years of professional training in education and pastoral leadership. He was a skilled teacher and used that gift strategically to build the church's 'culture of grace,' which motivated people to serve God according to their gifts. Its organizational structure and approach to CE gave special place to the role of elders, who were caretakers of the vision of this inter-generational church.

Cap-2 was a church of young adults and young families. It was led by a pastor in his 30s who had graduated from CBI and then went on to earn a seminary degree. Cap-2 had an active children's ministry (much like the other cases); however, Life Groups drove its approach to non-formal CE and provided the primary platform for mobilizing people for service. Although teaching was fundamental to every aspect of church life, Cap-2 thought about discipleship in broader terms as people connected the Word to real life with the help of teacher-facilitators.

CHAPTER 8
Cross-Case Analysis and Findings: Organizational Models and Roles

INTRODUCTION AND OVERVIEW FOR CHAPTERS 8 THROUGH 10

In Chapters 8 through 10, the data from the four cases cover the four primary aspects of non-formal CE among AGC churches–organizational models, roles of non-formal CE, non-formal CE teachers, and educational context. Each of the chapters' four main sections presents an analysis of the data across cases, interacts with relevant literature, and identifies the findings from the analyses that are used to construct the descriptive model of non-formal CE among AGC churches, which is presented in Chapter 11. Chapter 10 concludes with a summary and list of the twelve findings (Table 10.7).

However, before discussing data analysis, I want to explain why the main sections of Chapters 8 through 10 are ordered differently from the levels of the conceptual framework. The literature review in Chapters 2 through 4 was used to construct a conceptual framework with four levels that were ordered from external (educational context) to mixed-external/internal (roles of non-formal CE) to internal to the cases (organizational models and teachers). Another way of characterizing these four levels would be from most general to most case-specific. The purpose of the conceptual framework was to create data bins, refine the research design, and inform the development of the data collection methods and instruments.

The organization of Chapters 8 through 10 reflects a different kind of relationship among the four aspects of non-formal CE. I begin with the organizational models of the cases because they formally express the overriding values of each church. Thus, the roles and teachers fit within that structure and embody those values. In practical terms, the organizational model and the duly appointed leadership determine the roles of non-formal CE (internal and external), the organization of classes, who will teach those classes, and the values that will be embodied in the teachers and their relationships with students.

The educational context ubiquitously surrounds the church. It provides formal education and creates educational norms that each church interacts with in its approach to non-formal CE. However, the primary point of interaction is at the level of the teachers. Therefore, I found it natural to address the data on educational context following the sections on teachers.

Table 8.1 (copied from Table 6.1 in Chapter 6) lists the levels of the conceptual framework with the procedural sub-questions and sources of the information. Chapters 6 and 7 addressed the first three procedural sub-questions on a case-by-case basis. Now Chapters 8 through 10 address all four levels of the conceptual framework and examine the data for all the procedural sub-questions, except for the second sub-question.

Table 8.1. Conceptual framework levels, procedural sub-questions, and sources of information

Conceptual Framework Levels	Procedural Sub-Questions	Sources of Information
Organizational Models	1. How are approaches to non-formal CE organized in each case? What is the rationale for each organizational approach? 2 How did the current approaches to non-formal CE among the cases originate and then develop over time?	Case Background Questionnaire Approach to CE Questionnaire Interviews with pastors and leaders Church documents
Roles	3. What are the perceived contributions of the approaches to non-formal CE to the health and mission of each case?	Approach to CE Questionnaire Interviews with pastors and leaders Church documents Class observations

Teachers	4. How are teachers recruited, developed, and resourced in each case? What ideas about teaching and learning influence this process?	Approach to CE Questionnaire Interviews with pastors and leaders Teacher Questionnaire Class observations
Educational Context	5. How do approaches to non-formal CE among the cases reflect the educational context?	Focus Groups Teacher Questionnaire Class observations
	6. How do approaches to non-formal CE among the cases compare across socioeconomic situations?	

ORGANIZATIONAL MODELS AND NON-FORMAL CE

Chapters 6 and 7 presented the organizational models on a case-by-case basis in terms of their development and functionality. This present section now analyzes those models in comparison to each other and to the literature. The analysis first focuses on the relation of non-formal CE to each case's organizational structure. Then the focus moves to the overall role of teaching in the organizational models. The section concludes with the introduction of Finding 1.

Analysis of the Four Cases

One purpose of this study was to compare approaches to non-formal CE across socioeconomic situations. The differences between provincial and capital city churches will be sharply delineated in some of the analysis below, but this is not true of the organizational models. Prov-1 and Cap-1 had models that strongly resembled each other (see Figures 6.1 and 7.2 in Chapters 6 and 7, respectively). The pastor led, along with a church committee, and the ministries of the church were divided into a clean, linear list.

Cap-2's organizational model, although configured in a unique way, had many elements in common with Prov-1 and Cap-1 (see Figure 7.2 in Chapter 7). If Cap-2's model is converted from a rectangular into a linear configuration, then all three of these models might look much the same. When it comes to leadership style, the leadership of Prov-1 and Cap-1 integrated the model from the top through direct involvement. In contrast, Cap-2 disseminated leadership by delegating authority and responsibility to the pastoral team and to ministry coordinators.

Differing from these three cases, Prov-2's three-tiered hierarchical model brought all the various ministries and functions into relationship with each other in a strongly integrated way (see Figure 6.2 in Chapter 6). Of the twenty-two positions in its model, thirteen worked together as the church committee (the pastor plus the top and middle tiers). Of the nine remaining positions (bottom tier), three of them served the entire model as treasurers. During my time with Prov-2, I observed this integration in action, with everyone seemingly working in concert.

The function of the youth ministries in relation to children's classes and the worship teams was a characteristic that set the provincial churches apart from the capital city churches. In Prov-1, all the children's teachers and worship leaders were students and leaders in the youth ministry. They carried out these functions under the supervision of top-level leaders. At Prov-2, the youth ministry was directly responsible for leading worship and teaching the children's classes. In contrast, at Cap-1 and Cap-2, the worship and children's ministries were separate from the youth ministries, although the youth were a source of teachers and worship team members. These dynamics will be explored in more detail in the sub-section Teacher demographics.

Mark Cannister describes three CE organizational models that are prevalent in Western churches. He orders the models from less integrated to more integrated. That order being the functional model, the age-group model, and the group-purpose model.[348] His discussion of the three focuses on integrating CE with the whole church versus CE becoming a stand-alone ministry within the church. The first two models (functional and age-group) try to keep CE programs integrated through CE leadership teams. The group-purpose model, on the other hand, tries to integrate CE into the whole church by crosscutting the age groups with the five purposes of the church, using the term 'spiritual formation' instead of CE.

Trying to compare the cases in this study with Cannister's three CE organizational models is challenging because none of the cases had CE as a separate ministry. They all had some affinity with the functional

---

[348]Cannister, "Organizational Models," 150-157.

and age-group models because their organizational structures were built around specific groups of people and ministries that developed over time. Only Cap-2's approach had some commonalities with Cannister's group-purpose model. Teaching was not overtly pervasive in Cap-2 the way it was in the other cases. Rather, Cap-2 wanted everyone to become a student of the Word in the four main functions of the church—worship, discipleship, fellowship, and mission/ministry. These four functions compared to the five purposes in the group-purpose model—worship, spiritual formation, service, evangelism, and fellowship.[349]

The four cases did not readily fit the three Western CE organizational approaches described above, but rather strongly resonated with small-church dynamics. Mark Simpson says that small churches (less than five hundred members) have the following five common dynamics that affect their approach to CE and, by extension, their organizational structure—(1) a family orientation, (2) a tendency for short-term planning, (3) a high value placed on special events, (4) a deeply vested leadership that is slow to change but effective at rapid communication, and (5) a weekly schedule and annual calendar dominated by educational programming.[350]

Regarding Simpson's first point (family orientation), all the cases in this study had a 'family feel' in their interactions, worship services, and activities. As to his second point (tendency for short-term planning), all the cases made annual plans. Prov-1, Cap-1, and Cap-2 created planning calendars with all church ministries (Prov-1's annual planning book being more than thirty pages). Prov-2 worked from an annual agenda. None of the cases had multi-year formal plans; however, they all had long-term projects in the works on indefinite schedules.

Concerning the third item in Simpson's small-church dynamics (high value on special events), all the cases built their calendars around seminars, church outings, outreaches, and national holidays, which they used for such events. Prov-1 even had an events committee drawn into its organizational model (see Figure 6.1 in Chapter 6). Cambodia's official public holidays totaled thirty-seven days per year, four of which are three days long. Traditionally, people work six or seven days a week; thus, these many holidays create a seasonal rhythm to life. The cases in this study followed that cultural pattern in the way they planned frequent special events.

---

[349]Ibid., 154.
[350]Simpson, *Christian Education*, 159-166.

Simpson's fourth item (deeply vested leadership) is probably the most important for understanding how the four cases function. As mentioned in the last chapter, three of the cases were led by the founding pastors, and the founding missionary of Cap-2 was still part of its pastoral team. I observed that the pastors and church committees functioned as the churches' caretakers by keeping ministries aligned with their vision and by appointing ministry leaders and teachers. Indeed, the provincial churches depended on vested leadership for long-term viability because the youth often left the community for education and work. This dynamic will be explored further in the discussion on Teacher Demographics below. As to rapid communication, I was astonished at how quickly and smoothly the leaders made program changes in response to developing circumstances. More than once, I arrived at a site to observe a class or event, only to find that an unplanned 'opportunity' had superseded it. At the same time, I saw how people readily adjusted; no one seemed upset at having their plans changed on short notice.

Simpson's fifth point (dominance of CE in church activities) was largely true of the cases in this study. Non-formal CE took up a significant amount of their weekly activities and planning. All four of the churches had a single Sunday worship service per week, which was the focal point of church life. Non-formal CE formed a large portion of what took place on Sunday morning. Indeed, the sub-section Teacher Demographics below will show that all the cases had a significant proportion of their people involved in teaching.

Overall Role of Teaching in the Organizational Models

Again, I want to note that, even though none of the cases had a CE department or CE committee, non-formal CE pervaded their organizational models and church activities in highly integrated ways. Table 8.2 categorizes the parts of each model in terms of the priority of teaching. These characterizations, which were made by the pastors and leaders, are supported by my observations. Note that the table lists boxes/roles in each case's model, not individuals.

Prov-1 and Prov-2 had similar categorizations and balance with regard to the role of teaching in their organizational model, teaching being a high priority in both. Out of the nine boxes in Prov-1's model, teaching was a primary responsibility for five and one aspect of another two. That church's constitution explicitly emphasized the teaching priority. It listed seventeen positions with their qualifications and responsibilities, with ten of those calling for the individual to be able to teach.

Out of the ten boxes in Prov-2's organizational model, four had teaching as a primary function, and three more engaged in teaching as one aspect of their roles. The remaining three boxes were administrative, although the persons in those roles taught as well. While not included in the church's organizational model, I have nonetheless added the six village cell groups to the list since they were regular ministries of Prov-2.

Table 8.2. Overall role of teaching in the organizational models

	Teaching as a Primary Function	Teaching as One Aspect	Teaching Not a Function
Prov-1	Pastor Assistant Pastor Youth Class Children's Class Cell Groups (2)	Worship Team Women's Group	Offerings/Finances Event Committees
Prov-2	Pastor Assistant Pastor Youth leaders Leaders of Children's Teachers [Village Cell Groups (6)][4]	Adult leaders Women's group leaders Worship leaders	Church Committee Chairperson Secretary Treasurers
Cap-1	Pastor Assistant Pastors Youth Children's Classes Men Women Missions/Church Planting	Worship	Administration

---

[351] The village cell groups are not in the organization model, although they are direct ministries of Prov-2. See the sub-section "Origins, Development, and Current Status of Prov-2" in Chapter 6 for a description of the relationship between the main church and the village cell groups.

Cap-2[5]	Children' Ministry	Pastor (preaching) Life Groups • Youth (ages 14-25) • Green Coconuts (ages 25-35) • Ripe Coconuts (ages 35+) • Daycare staff	Visitation Ushers Prayer Group Administration Board

Cap-1's organizational model was the most strongly weighted toward CE. The pastor described teaching as the primary function of seven out of the nine roles. As with Prov-1 and Prov-2, its worship ministry included an element of teaching, while administrative roles did not teach.

Cap-2's organizational model gave teaching a different emphasis compared to the other three. According to the pastor, only the children's ministry engaged in teaching as its primary function. Although the pastor did not teach a class or lead a Life Group, preaching was considered a form of teaching in this study. Thus, the pastor fit the category of teaching as one aspect. Because direct teaching was only one element of discipleship and mobilization at Cap-2, Life Groups naturally fit into the category of teaching as one aspect.[353] Lastly, Cap-2 had the largest group of boxes in the non-teaching category. As with the other cases, administrative roles did not teach. Only Cap-2 considered the other three non-teaching activities (i.e., prayer, ushering/hospitality, and visitation) as being ministries in their own right.

Section Conclusion and Finding

The four cases in this study were among the oldest, largest, and most developed Assemblies of God churches in Cambodia. None of the four had a CE department in its organizational structure. Consequently, the Western CE organizational models described in the literature did not

---

[352]The English congregation has been excluded because they are not members of Cap-2. The 'community service' ministries have been excluded because they are not considered part of regular church life. See the sub-section "Cap-2 Class Information" in Chapter 7 for more information.

[353]See the sub-section "Cap-2's Vision in Relation to Non-Formal CE" in Chapter 7 for more discussion about this point.

resonate. Rather, Simpson's list of small-church dynamics seems to fit well the data and inner workings of these cases. This analysis of the organizational models is the basis for the first finding, which reads:

Finding 1: The congregations in this study functioned like small churches in which non-formal CE pervaded their organizational models and dominated church activities.

One important observation needs to be made with respect to this finding. The four churches were small compared to those in other contexts, and their organizational models were not very complex. Given time, as these churches grow and become more sophisticated, they may develop CE departments like the Western models, especially the capital city churches. Even so, Prov-2 (the largest of the four) suggests that it could develop organizational approaches that have little resemblance to the Western models. Regardless of how these four cases evolve in the future, Finding 1 will still likely hold true for other AGC churches that are following them in development.

ROLES OF NON-FORMAL CE

Chapters 6 and 7 presented the classes taught at each of the case churches with details relating to attendance, curriculum, functions, etc. In the first sub-section below, I examine the roles of non-formal CE by looking at the types of classes conducted across the cases. Then I analyze the perceptions of roles of classes in terms of their internal-external focus and their functions. Following that analysis, I relate these findings to the literature on internal and external functions of CE. I conclude this section with the presentation of Findings 2, 3, and 4.

Class Information Across Cases

Table 8.3 provides a comparative list of the classes taught in the four cases. Those classes are divided into the following four categories:

- Regular. These were considered part of normal church life, with most of them meeting on a weekly basis and most of the students considered as being church members.
- Additional. Prov-2's community preschool is listed as 'additional' instead of 'parachurch' because it was considered a ministry of the church to the community; Cap-1's pre-marital and water baptism classes are likewise listed as 'additional' because they were supplemental to its regular programs.

- *Ad hoc*. These classes were offered to meet specific needs for as long as they were needed and teachers were available.
- Parachurch. Three of the churches had formal education programs which I have labeled 'parachurch' because they were administratively separate from the church.

This study is primarily concerned with the regular classes and their functions in church life. Therefore, the table creates a fuller picture of the cases by including educational activities that are not part of this study.

Table 8.3. Classes taught in the cases

	Prov-1	Prov-2	Cap-1	Cap-2
Regular	Children (all ages)	Children (all ages)	Older children	Older children
			Younger children	Younger children
	Youth	Youth Bible class	Youth	Youth Life Groups
	Women		Women	Adult Life Groups
			Men	
			Sat. discipleship class	
	Worship			
	Village cell groups (4)	Village cell groups (6)		
				Daycare staff Life Group
Additional		Community preschool	Pre-marital Water baptism	
Ad hoc	Water baptism	Water baptism	Preaching mentoring	Water baptism
				Youth Alive
				English classes
				Music classes

| Parachurch | Preschool/ Christian school | | Youth educational outreach | Preschool/ Christian school |

Certain types of classes were offered by all the cases, with some variations. First, all the cases had children's classes. The provincial cases put all the children together, while the capital city cases divided them into two age groups. Second, all four had classes for youth. Prov-1, Cap-1, and Cap-2 had youth classes for the purpose of general discipleship. In contrast, Prov-2's youth Bible class was to prepare the students to be teachers because teaching children was one of the responsibilities of the youth in that church. This approach was similar to the practice of using Bible classes to create cadres of teachers from among the youth during the Sunday school movement in the United States in the 1800s.[354] Third, all the cases had water baptism classes. Cap-1's pastor was systematic and cyclical with this class, each cycle lasting about three months. The other three cases either met with candidates a few times prior to the service or met with them individually for informal teaching. The goals of Cap-1's baptism class were to confirm the people's faith and prepare them to serve according to their gifts. The main purpose of the other three water baptism classes was to make sure that people understood what they were doing and had truly come to faith in Christ. None of the cases had a class for new believers. When asked why, they all said that people were considered members once they had received water baptism.

Table 8.3 also highlights some differences across socioeconomic contexts. The provincial cases had networks of village cell groups, an approach common in rural Cambodia. These cell groups were organically connected to the main church through the leaders. Prov-2's 'umbrella' approach (described in detail in Chapter 6) was similar to several other AGC church networks in that area. The pastor of Prov-2 was pragmatic about these relationships, recognizing that some of the village cell groups may choose to become separate congregations while others may not develop to that level or may choose to remain under the main church indefinitely. Prov-1's village cell groups were treated more like outreaches, thus not counted among church members. The key point of connection between main churches and cell groups in both cases was CE.

---

[354]Boylan, *Sunday School,* 134. The use of the same term 'Bible classes' is incidental but interesting.

Table 8.3 shows the capital city churches had non-formal CE covering the entire range of ages and generations in the church. Cap-1 addressed men and women through traditionally structured groups, with devotionally oriented peer teaching/sharing. Cap-2 addressed the generations through age-ranged Life Groups. Ideally, the Life Groups brought people together (both men and women) from across backgrounds. However, the people tended to prefer groups with their friends, especially the older women. If the Life Groups grow as expected, this dynamic will evolve in the coming years. The provincial churches did not have much CE directed toward adults because of a generation gap, which will be discussed below under Teacher Demographics.

Perceptions of Roles of Classes

Procedural sub-question #3 asks, "What are the perceived contributions of the approaches to non-formal CE to the health and mission of each case?" The key phrase in this question is 'perceived contributions.' This sub-section is not as concerned with what the classes actually did but rather how leaders and teachers perceived the focus and function of their classes. The information for Table 8.4 was collected during the focus groups, and the information for Table 8.5 was tabulated from the Class Information Sheets.[355]

Table 8.4 presents those classes that were considered a regular part of church life on a continuum from internally-focused to externally-focused. Internally-focused classes are for people already a part of the church, including those who are not believers. These types of classes nurture believers in their faith and bring people in the church to a point of personal faith. At the other extreme of the continuum, externally-focused classes seek to benefit the community regardless of affiliation with the church. Mixed-focus classes both benefit the community and seek to bring people into the church (e.g., evangelism). Classes are left-justified, centered, or right-justified to show relative positioning on the continuum.

---

[355] See the last page of the Approach to CE Questionnaire, Appendix B.

Table 8.4. Internal-external focus of classes

	Internal	Mixed	External
Prov-1	Children Youth Women	Village cell groups (4)	(none)
Prov-2	Children's class (main church) Youth Bible class	Village cell groups (6)	Community preschool
Cap-1	Discipleship Men Women Children	Youth	Mission, western province Mission, central province
Cap-2	Life Groups • Youth (ages 14-25) • Green Coconuts (ages 25-35) • Ripe Coconuts (ages 35+)	Children Life Group—daycare staff Youth Alive English classes Music classes	(none)

The internally-focused classes in the table are standard for a healthy church, with one interesting exception. Cap-2 placed its children's classes in the mixed part of the continuum because several children came who were not part of the church. Cap-1's youth class and Cap-2's daycare staff Life Group are both on the left side of the mixed part of the continuum because they were internally-focused classes that brought people in from outside the church. Cap-1's two missions to the provinces involved monthly teaching support to two church plants. Although they could be considered mixed because they had a church focus as opposed to a community focus, nonetheless Cap-1 saw them as a ministry to people outside the church.

Prov-2's community preschool was the quintessential externally-focused ministry, even though it was held in the church's main hall. The preschool existed to benefit the community, regardless of religion or social status. As a member of the village council, Prov-2's pastor registered births. So as children approached school age, she would have the preschool teachers meet with the parents to persuade them of the importance of education for small children. The preschool helped children develop the skills needed to succeed in the first year of the government system. When they were ready, the preschool worked directly with the local elementary school to facilitate the children's entry into first grade. The main part of the preschool's mission statement (painted on the front of the church building) made this partnership explicit to "partner with all levels of government, in order to collect information and statistics of children in the community, and to communicate additionally to parents about the importance of educating small children." (translation mine)

Teacher Perceptions about the Functions of Their Classes

Chapters 6 and 7 examined the ways in which teachers perceived the roles of each of their classes on a case-by-case basis. Table 8.5 presents teacher perceptions of the functions of their classes in summary fashion for cross-case analysis. The numbers represent the frequency with which each function was chosen by the teachers. For example, if five out of six teachers marked 'Bible knowledge,' then the frequency number is 0.83 (five divided by six). The purpose of this analysis was to discover critical emphases and to provide a means of cross-case comparison (and not to speak in absolute terms about the activities in the classes).

The first six functions listed in the table are internally-focused (discipleship through preparing for ministry). 'Bible knowledge' received the highest number across all cases (0.93), with almost all teachers marking this function for their class or group. As one leader at Cap-1 explained in the focus group, "The Word of God is the main thing. People will know God through His Word, and living will follow." This conviction matches the core idea of Richards and Bredfeldt's transformative approach to CE. The goal of their approach is life transformation through engagement with the Bible in all three of Bloom's domains of learning—cognitive (head), affective (heart), and behavioral (hands).[356] The holistic view of CE is discussed in the section "Reflecting on the Educational Context" below.

---

[356] Richards and Bredfeldt, *Creative Bible Teaching*, 135-138.

Table 8.5. Cross-case analysis of class functions

	Prov-1	Prov-2	Cap-1	Cap-2	Prov's	Cap's	ALL
Internally-focused							
Bible knowledge	1.00	0.89	1.00	0.83	0.95	0.92	0.93
Discipleship	0.89	0.89	0.5	0.67	0.89	0.59	0.74
Fellowship	0.56	0.56	0.83	0.67	0.56	0.75	0.66
Preparing for ministry	0.33	0.78	0.33	0.67	0.56	0.50	0.53
Provide mutual care	0.00	0.56	1.00	0.50	0.28	0.75	0.52
Confirm salvation	0.00	0.67	0.17	0.33	0.34	0.25	0.29
Externally-focused							
Evangelizing community	0.44	0.89	0.17	0.33	0.67	0.25	0.46
Relationships with community	0.11	0.56	0.17	0.50	0.34	0.34	0.34
Helping community	0.44	0.44	0.17	0.17	0.44	0.17	0.31

The function 'Discipleship' received the second highest number across the cases (0.74). The provincial cases teachers marked it more often than did the capital city cases teachers—0.89 and 0.59, respectively. The provincial cases were consistent on this point from the way their leaders spoke in public to the responses of the teachers. In contrast, the capital city teachers' responses did not match the priority regarding discipleship that was expressed by the capital city leaders and church documents. This result may indicate some lack of clarity as to the meaning of discipleship in the minds of some teachers.

AGC churches did not have a clear term for discipleship. I used *kabongkart sus* in the questionnaire, which literally means 'creating students [disciples].' Many AGC churches used this term to refer to nurturing believers to maturity, but it could also carry the idea of evangelism. The term did not raise any red flags during the piloting phase of instrument development, the field observations, or the interviews. Moreover, the leadership of Cap-1 and Cap-2 used the term to denote discipleship, not evangelism[357] when they talked about their philosophy of CE. For example, the pastor of Cap-2 went to great lengths to emphasize that discipleship (in a broader sense than direct teaching) was the primary purpose of his church's Life Groups.[358] Even so, only three out of five Life Group leaders at Cap-2 marked 'discipleship.

---

[357]They typically use other terms for evangelism such as *kabrakas domnung la-ah*, which literally means "declaring the Good News."
[358]See the sub-sections "Cap-1's Vision in Relation to Non-Formal CE" and "Cap-2's Vision in Relation to Non-Formal CE" in Chapter 7.

'Confirming salvation' was chosen by the fewest number of teachers, with a frequency rating of 0.29. The term I used in the Class Information Sheet was *ka-bancheak ta monuh khnong kromchumnum ban tway kluon*—literally, "confirming that people in the church have given themselves [idiom for receiving salvation]." This function was intended to address the conversion of people within the church. Churches, including these cases, talk about *ka-tway kluon* (receiving salvation) a lot. However, three of the cases did not associate this function with CE (ratings of 0.00, 0.17, and 0.33), Prov-2 being the exception with a rating of 0.67.

One question in the Teacher Questionnaire asked, "Do you give your students opportunities to receive salvation [*tway kluon*] in class? If so, how often?" Table 8.6 records their responses by case. Looking at all responses in aggregate, about two-thirds of the teachers said that they gave their students those opportunities in class. Some of the teachers who responded 'no' explained that their students were all believers, which was certainly true for some classes. However, two explanations were instructive of teacher attitudes about this question—(1) "because they are all children with parents who are believers" and (2) "because children do not yet understand."

Table 8.6. Teachers giving students opportunities to receive salvation in class

	Prov-1	Prov-2	Cap-1	Cap-2	TOTALS
Yes	7	16	13	15	51
No	7	5	8	6	26
If yes, how often?					
Weekly		2		1	3
1-2 times per month	1	6	7		14
Once in a while	6	6	6	14	32

Most teachers who said that they gave students opportunities to receive salvation in class said that they did so 'once in a while.' Their reasons are instructive. A few mentioned doing so on special occasions/

programs or during specific lessons. Several wrote about watching to see when their students were ready. One capital city teacher explained that he invited students to receive salvation after they had been coming for about three months and thus had a chance to hear about Jesus. Sensitivity to the students' spiritual condition is exactly what Elmer Towns recommended when he addressed the matter of how well teachers know their students.[359] For my own part, I did not observe in twenty-four different class observations a single instance of teachers inviting their students to *tway kluon* (receive salvation).

Returning to Table 8.5, 'Fellowship' and 'Provide mutual care' received higher frequency ratings with the capital city churches than with the provincial city churches. While all the cases had frequent times of fellowship and providing mutual care, the capital city churches explicitly included those elements in their approach to CE. I noted this in my observations as teachers led children to pray for one another and as older women shared with younger women the secrets they had learned about dealing with husbands who were not believers. Two possible explanations for this difference on the part of the provincial cases were (1) the prominent place of children's ministry in their church activities and (2) the practice of having the youth and young adults teach a large portion of their non-formal CE.

The function 'Preparing for ministry' received mixed responses across provincial and capital city churches. Prov-1 and Cap-1 had low ratings in this category (0.33 for both), while Prov-2's and Cap-2's ratings were significantly higher (0.78 and 0.67, respectively). The explanation for this result likely lies in the information on the specific classes.[360] Prov-2 and Cap-2 used teaching as a means of mobilizing their people through village cell groups and Life Groups, respectively. In contrast, Prov-1 marked its youth, worship, and women's classes as preparing people for ministry, but not its children's class and its five village cell groups; and Cap-1 had a specific class designed to prepare people for ministry.

The bottom three functions in Table 8.5 are community-focused. Again, the mobilizing emphases of Prov-2 and Cap-2 were pronounced as they had the highest numbers for 'Relationships w/community' (0.56 and 0.50, respectively), while Prov-1 and Cap-1 had little non-formal CE directed toward community relationships (0.11 and 0.17, respectively).

---

[359]Towns, *What Every*, 38.
[360]See Tables 6.2, 6.4, 7.1, and 7.2 in Chapters Six and Seven.

However, when it comes to 'Helping community' and 'Evangelizing community' through CE, the provincial cases had higher numbers than the capital city cases. The reason for this difference probably was in their direct community engagement through village cell groups, inclusion of lessons on civic morality in children's classes, and Prov-2's community preschool.

Table 8.7 provides a summary of the data on class functions in the perspective of the teachers. The overall numbers show that the functions of non-formal CE in all four cases were largely internally-focused (0.67). However, the overall rating of 0.37 for externally-focused functions indicates that they also placed a measure of importance on people who are outside the church. This result fits those displayed in Table 8.4 regarding internally—and externally—focused classes. Lastly, the provincial cases reported a stronger external focus than the capital city cases in their approach to CE.[361]

Table 8.7. Summary of data on class functions

	Prov-1 & -2	Cap-1 & -2	OVERALL
Internally-focused functions: Discipleship, Bible knowledge, Confirming salvation, Fellowship, Mutual care, Preparing for ministry	0.59	0.63	0.61
Externally-focused functions: Relationships w/community, Helping community, Evangelizing community	0.48	0.25	0.37

Roles of Non-Formal CE Compared to the Literature

Turning now briefly to the literature on internal and external roles of non-formal CE, the internal roles represented in this study line up with the Evangelical views expressed in the literature. The Bible is the foundation, primary content, and authority of CE in these churches. It also determines the main desired outcomes, the first of which is a

---

[361] As explained above, these results do not include parachurch programs and *ad hoc* classes.

personal saving faith in Jesus Christ.[362] All four cases stated as much in their vision and mission statements.

A question remains that eluded this study—How do AGC churches view the process of conversion? As stated above, I did not witness any calls to a crisis conversion experience either in classes or in church services. AGC churches do not seem to be touched by the historical-conversion-vs.-nurture-controversy of the West. Instead, I would suggest that the approach of these cases be labeled 'conversion through nurture.' The idea espoused here is part of Cap-1's 'culture of grace.' Although shorter and less systematic, this approach has an affinity with the catechumenal approach to conversion of the Catholic church in Cambodia.[363] The tentative point here is that these AGC churches have made non-formal CE such a pervasive element of church life that it is a key means by which people come to personal saving faith in Jesus Christ without Western-style crisis conversions. This ethos reflects Cheryl Bridges Johns' description of Pentecostal churches as "teaching communit[ies]" in which all expressions of church life bring everyday experience into dialogue with God's revelation (Scriptures) under the energizing and guiding work of the Holy Spirit.[364]

The external roles of CE in these cases reflect the attitudes captured in the research of Tejedo and of Miller and Yamamori. Tejedo argued that Pentecostals are drawn to engage their communities holistically because they see God's holistic involvement in creation in the Bible.[365] Miller and Yamamori use the term 'Progressive Pentecostals' to describe Pentecostals who feel inspired by the Holy Spirit to "holistically address the spiritual, physical, and social needs of people in their community."[366] They note that educational programs are one of the hallmarks of Pentecostal efforts at social transformation.[367]

All four of the cases engaged their communities through education. Regarding non-formal education for the community, the provincial cases had monthly lessons for children that included showing respect to elders, washing clothes, "going poo" in the right places, and navigating traffic safely. Regarding formal education, three of the cases had such programs, while the other hosted a supplemental educational program

---

[362] Williams, "Christian Education," 132-133.
[363] Ponchaud, *The Cathedral*, 282-283.
[364] Johns, *Pentecostal Formation*, 86, 121, 124.
[365] Tejedo, *The Church*, 2.
[366] Miller and Yamamori, 2.
[367] Ibid., 75-79.

as a youth outreach. These four cases did not have resources to match the churches described in the Miller and Yamamori study that were filling educational gaps, but they were engaging their communities in meaningful ways through CE.

Section Conclusion and Findings

This section has examined perceptions about the roles and functions of non-formal CE across the cases. The analysis leads to three findings that are useful for understanding how these four AGC churches approached non-formal CE. As noted in Finding 1 (see the previous section), non-formal CE was pervasive in the organizational models and accounted for a significant portion of the weekly activities. The analyses in this present section show that most of the non-formal CE activity was directed toward people who were already part of the church. The primary goal of these churches' CE approaches collectively was the personal faith of individuals through nurture, as opposed to crisis conversion experiences. Finding 2 summarizes this analysis:

Finding 2: The non-formal CE of the cases in this study had a strong internal focus that emphasized Bible knowledge, discipleship, and personal faith through nurture.

Further, the analyses here indicate that the churches in this study engaged their surrounding communities through both formal and non-formal CE. Although outside of the scope of this research, formal CE was an expression of each church's understanding of its mission to bring transformation to the community and to serve it in holistic ways. All the cases engaged their communities through non-formal CE in varying degrees. The capital city cases' primary engagement was through non-formal CE that took place within the framework of regular church life and through mission/outreaches. The provincial cases had a stronger level of social engagement, that being through weekly village cell groups, monthly children's lessons on civic morals and hygiene, and formal education programs. Prov-2 had the highest level of engagement of all the cases by working in direct partnership with the government for community development. This summary leads to Findings 3 and 4:

Finding 3: The cases in this study used education (non-formal and formal) as one of their primary means of social engagement.

Finding 4: The provincial cases in this study had a stronger level of social engagement through non-formal CE than did the capital city cases, particularly through village cell groups.

CHAPTER 9
Cross-Case Analysis and Findings: Non-Formal CE Teachers

INTRODUCTION

This chapter presents a cross-case analysis of information about non-formal CE teachers in the four cases in this study. The first section describes how teachers were selected and equipped in each of the cases. The second section analyzes the teachers' evaluations of the five teacher models presented in the Teacher Questionnaire (see Appendix C). This section brings the 'voices' from the focus groups into this analysis, for studying their evaluation of these models helps us discover the attitudes and roles that they consider ideal for non-formal CE teachers.

The third section considers teacher demographics, which include age, marital status, education level, and background of the teachers with respect to their churches. Cross-case analysis of demographics is especially helpful for understanding the core dynamics of provincial versus capital city cases. The fourth section looks at the spiritual life of the teachers; it probes the key influences on their spiritual development and their current devotional lives.

The data about non-formal CE teachers in the four cases work through a wide range of themes beyond the limits of a single chapter. Therefore, Chapter 10 continues this discussion by considering the teachers' personal perspectives and experiences. Chapter 10 also includes a presentation of Finding 5 through Finding 11.

SELECTION AND EQUIPPING OF THE TEACHERS

All four cases were deliberate in the process of selecting CE teachers, with the top leadership responsible for making appointments. They sought genuineness of a potential teacher's faith, faithfulness to the church, willingness to submit to leadership, and evidence of their gift of and love for teaching. Teaching experience was not required and education level not specified. Interestingly, Bible knowledge was not mentioned as a qualification; whereas in Wilhoit's list for CE teachers, biblical literacy is the prime qualification.[368] In short, the values that the churches' leadership looked for line up almost exactly with Michael Bechtle's basic qualifications for CE workers,[369] those values being:

- The worker is a Christian.
- The worker is maturing in his/her Christian life.
- The worker is teachable.
- The worker has a love for people.
- The worker should be a team player.
- The worker is dependent on God.

The following sub-section looks at the process of teacher selection in each of the cases.

Processes for Selecting the Teachers

Prov-1

The first requirement for becoming teachers at this church was that prospective teachers were 'taking responsibility,' meaning they were already faithfully serving in some way. They could either request to teach or be invited by the pastor and church committee. Of all the cases, Prov-1 had the most systematic and formal approach to selecting teachers. Table 9.1 lists the qualifications and responsibilities for children's teachers as it appeared in the church's constitution. These items were also spelled out in a three-page, two-year service agreement signed by the pastor, all other members of that ministry, and the individual, in that order. Prov-1 was the only case with a formal service agreement and its qualifications/responsibilities were the most comprehensive of all the cases. They are presented here because they represent the ideals that I heard from all the pastors in this study.

---

[368] Wilhoit, *Christian Education*, 160.
[369] Michael A. Bechtle, "The Roles and Responsibilities of Christian Education Personnel," in *Foundations of Ministry: An Introduction to Christian Education for a New Generation*, ed. Michael J. Anthony (Grand Rapids: Baker Books, 1992), 238.

Table 9.1. Qualifications and responsibilities of children's teachers at Prov-1

Qualifications	Responsibilities
• For those married, must have one wife or husband • Must be able to keep church matters private • Must be able to serve the church and others • Must have a heart to take care of and protect people • Must have a good reputation • Takes responsibility for their family and shows love to Christ • Teachable and able to take correction • Able to cooperate and encourage one another in service • Spiritually mature • Have the qualities in 1 Timothy 3:1-7 and Galatians 5:22-23 [full text included] • Gives the tithe and above the tithe in voluntary offerings, promised offerings, benevolence offerings, and other offerings • Is gifted to teach children • Is at least 15 years old • Submits to church leadership • Is an example to others • Attends worship services faithfully	• Can prepare lessons and teach clearly • Prepare the annual plan • Visit and encourage children • Preach to children • Give counsel to children • Correct children • Participate in various training sessions • Evaluate and make activity reports every month for the pastor and committee • Must make a disciple [to take their place] before leaving this ministry or finishing the term

Prov-2

This church did not have written qualifications and responsibilities for CE teachers. When I asked the pastor to elaborate, she said they follow the same process and standards for choosing teachers as for selecting people for all positions in the organizational model. They look for the Fruit of the Spirit (Galatians 5:22-23), character along the lines of what Paul required of overseers and deacons (1 Timothy 3), evidence of gifting to teach, and willingness to serve others, which included submission to church leadership. One key characteristic they watched for was the desire to be trained. Willingness to go to training workshops and seminars indicated that the person was interested in teaching. Prov-

2's top leadership did not appoint teachers too quickly, having learned from past mistakes. They preferred to take a few months, if necessary, to allow for adequate prayer, fasting, and observance. Then the final decision was made in a private meeting in which they discussed the individual's character using as a check list the nine-point Fruit of the Spirit (Galatians 5:22-23).

Cap-1

This church followed the same principles and steps in selecting teachers as it did in selecting leaders for any position in its organizational model. The most important qualifications looked for were a transformed life, gifting for a specific area of ministry, fruitfulness in ministry, and faithfulness to the church. The higher the level of responsibility, the longer the process required for appointment; while the lower the level of responsibility, the more the leadership wanted to 'encourage' people to serve. Oftentimes, people would be recognized for their ministry by their group or their peers before they received responsibility. Cap-1's leadership would watch for this dynamic to help them identify people for ministry positions. Ultimately, the church committee reserved the prerogative to appoint all teachers by publicly laying hands on and praying over them. The committee members would do so with all seriousness, citing Paul's admonition to "not be hasty in the laying on of hands" (1 Timothy 5:22, ESV). Every January, a special service was held to anoint and pray over those who work in all areas of ministry for the coming year, including teachers.

Cap-2

Like the other cases, Cap-2's approach to selecting CE teachers was driven by the qualities they valued—spiritual maturity, gifting, and potential, especially that which was seen in relationships with others. Did the people listen to individuals and follow their lead? Did people seek counsel from them? In other words, the leadership was looking for those with mature faith and influence. Like the other three cases, Cap-2's pastoral team directly appointed teachers. However, they differed from the other cases in that they valued influence because their non-formal CE centered on Life Groups, plus their understanding of discipleship was broader than direct teaching.

Table 9.2 records the answers of the teachers in all four cases to the questions, "How did you begin teaching in the church?" and "Who encouraged you to begin teaching?" Not surprisingly, pastors and church leaders were cited the most frequently. Secondary influences included missionaries, friends, and others in the church. An additional influence that showed up in three of the cases was 'personal desire to teach,' which indicated the stirring of a gift in the people's lives. Lastly, Prov-1 had five people who talked about wanting to become teachers because of their experiences as students, especially in children's classes. This observation relates to Ann Boylan's analysis of America's early Sunday school movement. For many years, the main source of new teachers was students whose lives had been deeply influenced by their Sunday school teachers.[370]

Table 9.2. Influences on becoming teachers

Prov-1		Prov-2		Cap-1		Cap-2	
Church leaders	7	The pastor	14	The pastor	14	The pastor	12
Being a student	5	Church leaders	7	The pastor's wife	10	Child. ministry leader	5
Children's class (4)		Relationship with God	3	Missionary	3	Missionary	3
The pastor	4	Peers, family	3	Church leaders	3	Church leaders	2
Missionary	4	Teachers	2	Friends/ people at church	2	Friends	2
Personal desire	3	Personal desire	2			Personal desire	2

Means of Equipping the Teachers

This research also asked how the cases equipped their CE teachers. Two points need to be made up front. First, all the cases were interested in training the teachers, especially children's teachers. Second, all the cases engaged in in-service training. (Except for Life Group leader training at Cap-2, none of the cases engaged in pre-service training.) Third, all

---

[370]Boylan, *Sunday School*, 101.

the cases utilized informal training methods for children's teachers by having new teachers work with experienced ones. Table 9.3 records the teachers' responses regarding the training they had received.

Table 9.3. training received by teachers

Prov-1		Prov-2		Cap-1		Cap-2	
Seminars	8	Informal training	11	In-house training	9	Cell group training	5
Guests (often foreign)	8	Seminars	8	Sat. discipleship class	7	In-house child. ministry	4
Other teachers	4	Bible school (CBI)	8	Missionaries	3	Seminars	4
Church leaders	3			Seminars	3	Bible school (CBI, CSM[4])	2
Bible school (CBI)	2						
		No training	3			No training	1

The provincial cases were more *ad hoc* in their approach to training. Prov-1 was proactive about having their children's teachers attend seminars and inviting guests to come work with them occasionally. Prov-2 invited guests to conduct training sessions, sent teachers to training programs conducted by groups that produced curriculum, and equipped teachers through CBI's Christian Life Program.[372]

Table 9.3 shows that teachers in the provincial cases were primarily equipped via seminars and informal training. While all four cases cited seminars, that source topped the list for Prov-1 and came in second for Prov-2. The most frequently cited form of training for Prov-2 teachers was informal training, which included watching the pastor, being mentored by the youth leader, and learning from other leaders and teachers. Prov-1 echoed this experience with the answers 'other teachers' and 'church leaders.'

---

[371]Cambodia Bible Institute, Cambodia School of Missions.
[372]The Christian Life Program is part of Global University's School of Evangelism and Discipleship. CBI offers it as a lay ministry development program in partnership with local churches.

Responses from teachers in the capital city churches show that they leaned toward in-house training for their equipping. Cap-1 had new children's teachers work as assistants with experienced teachers,[373] conducted in-house training through teachers' meetings, invited guests to do occasional training, and sent teachers to training programs offered by organizations. Cap-2 conducted two seminars per year for its Life Group leaders that focused on core values and strategy development. In the past, Cap-2's children's pastor conducted in-house training with four areas of emphasis—vision and calling, teaching skills, preparing and using lessons, and annual planning. More recently, the church had been sending its teachers to training seminars offered by outside organizations.

In conclusion, here are two of my observations regarding teacher training in these four study cases. First, all were proactive with teacher training because teaching was foundational to their values and church life. Only four individuals across the four cases reported having received no training at all. Second, my class observations did not always support the information I had received regarding training from the leaders and from the Teacher Questionnaire. The quality of teaching was mixed in all four of the cases. Some teachers delivered their lessons skillfully and engaged their students effectively, with a few teachers being exceptionally creative and engaging. At the same time, there were teachers with years of experience and training who were unable to control their students and/ or were unclear about what they were trying to teach.

When observing classes, I was particularly interested in lesson content and delivery, teacher-student engagement, classroom management, and spiritual atmosphere (see Appendix D, "Classroom Observation Protocol"). Based on my observations, I noted two areas of difference between effective and not-so-effective teachers. First, the effective teachers seemed to have an innate gift for connecting with their students, style of teaching notwithstanding. Second, it was curriculum that made the difference for most teachers. Those who created their own lessons or taught stories from a children's Bible tended to lack a clear main idea. In contrast, those who had attended seminars sponsored by the organizations that produced the curriculum seemed to be more clear, confident, and effective.[374] Both simple training and structured, context-

---

[373]Assistant teachers are teachers-in-training. The approach is more formal than that utilized by the provincial churches.

[374]In addition to the lesson with a story and a main idea, the curricula I examined also provided teaching guidance, a memory verse, reinforcing activities, and songs that went with the lesson.

appropriate[375] curricula made a notable difference in effectiveness. Although this observation may seem outdated in Western contexts, nonetheless, it is relevant to first-generation churches and teachers in contexts like those found in Cambodia.

EVALUATION OF 'IDEAL TEACHER MODELS'

The previous section described ideal characteristics of teachers from the point of view of the church leadership. This section now shifts to the teachers and considers their views of ideal models for teaching. The Teacher Questionnaire had asked them to rate five teacher models as 'Weak,' 'Good,' or 'Very Good' for teaching in the church. The five models used in the questionnaire were discussed in detail in Chapter 5 (see Table 5.3).

Table 9.4 presents the teachers' rankings of those five models from the questionnaire. The rankings were tabulated by counting how many respondents marked them as weak, good, or very good. Once the rankings were established, I assigned numerical values to each in order to give equal weight to all the cases regardless of the number of respondents. Ties were assigned identical numerical values between the two rankings (indicated by dashes). Table 9.5 then used the numbers behind the rankings in Table 9.4 to present rankings by socioeconomic contexts and an overall ranking for all the cases combined.

Table 9.4. Rankings of teacher models by case

	Prov-1	Prov-2	Cap-1	Cap-2
Strongest	Equipper	Equipper	Guide	Guide
	Tea Pot - Guide	Tea Pot - Guide	Fellow Traveler	Fellow Traveler
			Equipper	Gardener
	Fellow Traveler	Gardener	Gardener	Equipper
Weakest	Gardener	Fellow Traveler	Tea Pot	Tea Pot

---

[375]By 'context-appropriate' I mean suitable to the teachers, not contextualized to Cambodian culture.

Table 9.5. Rankings of teacher models by socioeconomic contexts

	Prov-1 & Prov-2	Cap-1 & Cap-2	All Cases
Strongest	Equipper	Guide	Guide
	Tea Pot – Guide	Fellow Traveler	Equipper
		Gardener - Equipper	Fellow Traveler
	Fellow Traveler - Gardener		Tea Pot
Weakest		Tea Pot	Gardener

The purpose of this exercise in the Teacher Questionnaire and the follow up discussion in the focus groups was to probe ideals about non-formal CE teacher roles. The perspectives expressed did not necessarily reflect the historical meanings of these models. Rather, as respondents 'read' the models through their own experiences, they revealed their ideals about teaching in the church. At the same time, they expressed ideals that contrasted sharply with their own experiences in the national school system. These perspectives will be important for the discussion in the section "Reflecting on the Educational Context" toward the end of Chapter 10.

My analysis of these results was driven by these two questions—(1) Which model did they think was the strongest for teaching in the church, and why? and (2) Which model did they think was the weakest for teaching in the church, and why? As Table 9.4 reveals, the four cases were well-matched by socioeconomic contexts. So the following discussion brings the provincial voices together and the capital city voices together.

Provincial Cases Rankings

The provincial churches thought the Equipper model was good because it emphasized the competence of the teacher and success of the students. One Prov-1 teacher said, "The teacher has resources to share. If the students apply them, they will be successful." A female Prov-2 teacher commented, "The teacher needs to have good experience and know the truth;" and one male Prov-2 leader explained, "The teacher gives the students what they need for success. Students depend on the teacher. The teacher is responsible to help the students be able to succeed."

The provincial cases viewed the Fellow Traveler model as being unsuitable for non-formal CE. The Prov-1 focus group objected to it because it represented an impossibly high and impractical standard for teachers. One leader said, "It is hard to do this. It is hard for the teacher to live up to such a standard. Hard because people cannot share life like this." A Prov-1 teacher remarked, "[Teachers cannot live life with their students.] Students have to live their own lives. Teachers can teach and show the way, but the teacher cannot go with them." The Prov-2 focus group also thought it was unrealistic, concluding that "Teachers do not have this kind of relationship with students. It is very hard for a teacher to have this kind of role in the lives of their students." One female leader, commenting with proverbial succinctness, said, "Both are ignorant. If [one] falls, [they] fall down the same."

In addition to the Fellow Traveler and in contrast to their questionnaire responses, Prov-2's focus group decried the Tea Pot model with a chorus of passionate voices. One female leader explaining on behalf of everyone, "The model is just putting in, nothing else. No other help. No nurture. The model shows the teacher just filling a role. That's all. Done."

Capital City Cases Rankings

Both capital city focus groups were unanimous and adamant in their condemnation of the Tea Pot model as being the weakest for non-formal CE. The Cap-1 group had much to say about it. A retired high school teacher described it as "teaching by force" (*bongrean dowy bongkom*). The pastor rejected it as "not concerned with the depth of understanding of the students." A teacher critiqued its poor example, "The teacher is not receiving; pouring out, but not taking in; not a good example to the students." And a career educator said, "This image is an oversimplification. There is more to it than this." Meanwhile, the Cap-2 focus group rejected it because the teacher was characterized as being unconcerned about the lives of the students. The pastor explained, "Our [church] culture does not really like people who just give information and skills without caring about the fruit."

The capital city cases rated the Guide model as the best for non-formal CE. Cap-2 liked the image of a guide who knows the way. Cap-1 liked the model because it put the teacher in a position of leadership and responsibility, for the teacher must have more experience than the students and share that experience. One children's teacher was drawn to the emphasis on transformation, saying, "Transformation of life is important. We can teach them what a transformed life is like, how to live it, how to put the old life aside."

Disagreeing with the provincial cases, the capital city cases thought that the Fellow Traveler was a good model for teaching in the church.

Unlike the image of the Guide as a leader, the Fellow Traveler spoke to them of a close relationship between teachers and students. This result matches the capital city churches' emphasis on fellowship and mutual care in the functions of their classes (see Table 8.5). Cap-2's pastor said that the Fellow Traveler shares in the challenges that students face and goes with them. One Cap-1 children's teacher, speaking at length about what this model meant to her, said that she was moved by the love between teachers and students and the way they prayed for each other for "problems big and small."[376]

Summary

The teachers in the four cases preferred the models of the Equipper and the Guide for teaching in the church because those models depict teachers as competent, responsible, and concerned for the growth and success of their students. They also liked the close teacher-student relationship depicted in the Fellow Traveler. They strongly rejected the Tea Pot model because of its focus on knowledge transmission without attention to the development of students. Lastly, they rejected some aspects of the Fellow Traveler, such as the notion of radical equality between teachers and students[377] and what they felt were unrealistic expectations about teacher participation in the lives of their students.

TEACHER DEMOGRAPHICS

This Teacher Demographics section consists of these five sub-sections—numbers and gender, age, marital status, education level, and background in the churches where they teach. The tables present information about all teachers and then information about the children's teachers as a subset.[378] I am treating children's teachers thusly because teaching children can be one of the most resource-intense areas of ministry in a church and often the first ministry opportunity for young people. This dynamic was true for three of the four cases. Alternatively,

---

[376]I had the privilege of observing her class and seeing this teacher model in practice.

[377]This view is a corollary of teacher competency. It applies to situations where they are expected to know more than the students but does not apply to peer-teaching situations. So the Fellow Traveler was both loved and loathed.

[378]Some children's teachers also teach youth or adults.

because Cap-2's non-formal CE centered on Life Groups, I have included its Life Group leaders as a second subset, where applicable.

The statistics in this section includes data from all the teachers in all the cases, except for one children's teacher who declined to participate. The tables present the data case-by-case, by provincial cases and capital city cases, and then tabulate or average across all the cases, as applicable. Total numbers have been added across the cases without weighting. Mean and median numbers have been averaged across cases with equal weight by case, regardless of the number of teachers.

Numbers and Gender of the Teachers

Table 9.6 lists the number of teachers in each of the four cases and their gender. Looking at the All Teachers row, the first crucial observation is the ratio of females to males. Cap-2 had the narrowest, with a female-to-male ratio of 1.8 to 1. Prov-2 had the greatest difference, with female teachers outnumbering male teachers 5 to 1. Averaged across all the cases, female teachers outnumbered male teachers 3 to 1.

Table 9.6. Numbers of teachers by case with gender representation

	Prov-1	%	Prov-2	%	Cap-1	%	Cap-2	%
All Teachers	18		24		30		22	
Male	6	33.3	4	16.7	7	23.3	8	36.4
Female	12	66.7	20	83.3	23	76.7	14	63.6
Children's Teachers	8		20		15		7	
Male	0		2	10	0		2	28.6
Female	8	100	18	90	15	100	5	71.4
Life Group Leaders							14	
Male							6	42.9
Female							8	51.7
Ratio of Teachers to Church Size (adults & youth)	1:3.3		1:4		1:4		1:5.5	

The ratios change dramatically when we look at children's teachers. Prov-1 and Cap-1 had no male children's teachers; and in Prov-2, only two out of twenty were male. Cap-2 had the largest portion of male children's teachers—two out of seven. Additionally, children's teachers made up the largest group of teachers in three of the cases. In Prov-1 and

Cap-1, about half of their teachers taught children, and in Prov-2, some 83 percent of its teachers (twenty out of twenty-four) taught children. Cap-2 had the smallest proportion of children's teachers, that being 31.8 percent (seven out of twenty-two); however, its Life Group leaders made up a subset twice the size of the children's teachers (63.6 percent).

Reasons for the large number of children's teachers differed across the cases. Children's teachers in all the cases worked in groups or pairs. For instance, Prov-1's, Cap-1's, and Cap-2's teachers were scheduled on a rotating basis following the weeks of the month. Prov-1 teachers worked in pairs or threes, switching between the role of teacher and assistant teacher. Cap-1 children's classes all had a teacher and an assistant who was in training to become a teacher. Cap-2 had non-teaching assistants to help with class management; they were not considered teachers-in-training and thus excluded from this study. Lastly, Prov-2 deployed its teachers across its village cell groups. Although assigned to work together, this arrangement was fluid, based on the teachers' locations and skill level. Both provincial churches employed a strategy of informal training by assigning newer teachers to work with more experienced ones.

The bottom row of Table 9.6 shows the ratio of teachers to congregation size.[379] Those ratios ranged from 1 person out of 3.3 involved in teaching to 1 out of 5.5. The average of all cases was 1 out of 4.2. Although the ratio was a slightly tighter for the provincial cases than for the capital city cases, the point is nonetheless obvious—a large portion of the adults and youth in these cases (23.8 percent) were involved in teaching. This significant proportion supports Finding 1, which is that non-formal CE pervaded the organizational models of the cases and dominates church life.

Age Ranges of the Teachers

Table 9.7 displays age-range statistics about all teachers in the four cases. The mean and median ages show a sharp distinction between the provincial and the capital city cases. The difference in the mean age of provincial teachers and capital city teachers was 11.5 years (25.6 and 37.1 years, respectively). Comparing the median ages reveals an even sharper distinction, with a difference of 15.2 years (20.3 and 35.5,

---

[379]The church size used in this ratio includes only adults and youth because they are potential teachers.

respectively). The reason for this was the place of children's classes in the organizational arrangements of the provincial churches, where they were either under the youth ministry (Prov-2) or a *de facto* function of the youth ministry (Prov-1).[380] Prov-2 was at the extreme end of this spectrum, with a median age of 17. Almost two-thirds (62.5 percent) of their teachers were between the ages of fifteen and eighteen.

Table 9.7. Teachers' age ranges

Ages	Prov-1	Prov-2	Cap-1	Cap-2	Prov's	Cap's	All
15-22	7	16	3	3	23	6	29
23-29	6	1	6	3	7	9	16
30-39	3	4	8	12	7	20	27
40-49	2		3	2	2	5	7
50-59		3	3		3	3	6
60+			7	2		9	9
Mean	26.6	24.6	39.3	34.8	25.6	37.1	31.3
Median	23.5	17	37	34	20.3	35.5	27.9
Actual range	16-47	15-55	17-67	21-68	15-55	17-68	15-68

Examination of the generational spread of teachers in the cases also highlights dramatic differences between provincial and capital city churches. A large majority of teachers in the provincial cases were in the 15-22 and 23-29 age ranges. Prov-1's oldest teacher was age 47, while Prov-2 had a gap in the 40-49 age range, followed by three teachers in their 50s (the pastor and two pillar leaders). Cap-1 had the most even spread of teachers age-wise across generations; and Cap-2 had a key generation, with more than half in the 30-39 age range. Notably, Cap-2's pastor was 35 years old, and nine of the twelve individuals in this age range had been a part of the church at least fifteen years.

The differences in the generations of teachers between the provincial churches and the capital city churches were related to (1) their approach to church ministries and (2) educational and economic opportunities.

As to (1), children's ministry was a function of youth ministry in the two provincial churches, as already discussed above. By linking

---

[380]For further discussion on this dynamic in the provincial cases, see the section "Organizational Models and Non-Formal CE" above and Figures 6.1 and 6.2 in Chapter 6.

youth and children's ministry, provincial churches normalized teaching children as an entry-level ministry for young people who were growing in their faith. On the negative side, young people were in a transitional stage in life.

As to (2), educational and economic opportunities had an impact on who was available to teach and how long they were likely to do so. The data in Table 9.7 clearly demonstrate this dynamic in the provincial cases. The lower-age range teachers at Prov-1 were high school students who lived in the area and university students who returned home each weekend. Most of the lower-age range teachers at Prov-2 were still in high school, hence the median age of 17. From my conversations with these young teachers at Prov-2, I found that most of them had plans to go to the university in the capital city, after which they would seek employment away from their home village. Prov-1 faced a similar situation, but its distance from the capital city and potential for employment in the area (although limited) mitigated against this dynamic.

The capital city cases were less affected by these dynamics because there were more educational and employment opportunities in the city. This social stability seemed to have resulted in more teachers across generations and proportionately fewer in the 15-22 age range. Additionally, these two cases' children's ministries were not linked to the youth ministries. With regard to young teachers, Cap-1 had two in their teens and two who were still in school. Cap-2's youngest teacher was twenty-one years old, and only one teacher (age twenty-two) was still in school.

Table 9.8 displays statistics for children's teachers and Life Group Leaders. The age differences between children's teachers in provincial and capital city churches were pronounced, just as they were for all teachers in Table 9.7. Children's teachers formed a large portion of teachers in three of the cases, Cap-2 being the exception because Life Group leaders formed the largest group of teachers and because children's teachers' assistants were not teachers-in-training.

Life Group leaders comprised a unique group in this study. Cap-2's key generation appeared again in the Life Group leaders, with nine of the fourteen in the 30-39 age range. That placed the mean and median age for Life Group leaders at 37.9 and 35, respectively, which was far higher than the mean and median for children's teachers and all teachers (see Table 9.7).

Table 9.8. Ages of children's teachers and life group leaders

Ages	Prov-1	Prov-2	Cap-1	Cap-2	Prov's	Cap's	All	Cap-2 LG's[14]
15-22	4	16	3	3	20	6	26	1
23-29	3	1	5	2	4	7	11	1
30-39	1	3	4	2	4	6	10	9
40-49			2			2	2	1
50-59								
60+			1			1	1	2
Mean	22.9	19.8	32.1	26.4	21.4	29.3	25.3	37.9
Median	22.5	16.5	28	24	19.5	26	22.8	35
Actual range	16-30	15-38	17-61	21-36	15-38	17-61	55-61	22-68

Table 9.8 highlights the relative youth of children's teachers in the provincial cases. Three of the seven at Prov-1 were teenagers and still in high school. Prov-2 had fifteen such teachers between ages fifteen and eighteen, hence the median age of 16.5. Again, this result was the product of connecting children's ministry to youth ministry and the need to move out of the area for higher education.

The dynamic described here regarding provincial children's teachers is similar to the practices documented by Ann Boylan for Sunday school teachers in 19th century America—i.e., recruitment of teachers being an ongoing concern and the majority being females in their teens and 20s, for whom teaching Sunday school provided a unique and important place in society.[382] Their tenure as teachers was often interrupted by geographical mobility and/or giving up their classes when they became mothers.[383] The provincial cases in this study faced similar issues as the emphasis on education was encouraging more young people to finish high school and go on to the university, which led to employment away from their home villages.

---

[381] Life Groups.
[382] Boylan, *Sunday School*, 114.
[383] Ibid., 109.

Marital Status of the Teachers

Table 9.9 displays information about the marital status of the teachers in this study. The provincial cases had a large proportion of unmarried teachers, and an even larger proportion amongst children's teachers. Again, these data matched the prominence of children's ministry in the provincial churches and the positioning of children's classes with youth ministry. Neither of the provincial cases had teachers who were divorced or widowed.

In contrast, the two capital city cases had more married than unmarried amongst all teachers, although the numbers shifted toward singles for children's teachers. They also had teachers who were divorced and widowed. Cap-2's divorced teachers reflected the makeup of this church's membership; while Cap-1's six widowed teachers reflected the value it placed on elders and the strength of its women's class, which was led by peer teachers. Of Cap-1's six widowed teachers, two were children's teachers—one being in her forties and the other being a retiree who had been part of the church for twenty-five years.

Table 9.9. Marital statuses of teachers

	All Teachers				Children's Teachers				LG's
	Prov-1	Prov-2	Cap-1	Cap-2	Prov-1	Prov-2	Cap-1	Cap-2	Cap-2
Single	13	18	10	6	7	18	8	4	2
Engaged			1						
Married	5	6	12	12	1	2	5	3	9
Divorced			1	3					2
Widowed			6	1			2		1

Education Levels of the Teachers

Gathering information about the teachers' educational levels was important for two reasons. First, it was one more way to analyze their approaches to non-formal CE case-by-case and across cases; and second, their education level was a potential point for substantial interaction with the literature on non-formal CE, which was largely Western in orientation.

The sub-section "Processes for Selecting Teachers" above cited the literature about qualifications and desired characteristics of non-formal

CE teachers. That discussion did not address age, social situation, or education level, because non-formal CE teachers were volunteers and assumed to be (or ought to be) church members in good standing. Perhaps one reason for this gap in the discussion is the universal access to education in the West and historic ideals about who should teach in the church. Elmer Towns was one of a few voices that spoke regarding potential teachers who may have been passed over as being 'unqualified.' His words speak to teachers in contexts like Cambodia—"Without a lot of education, church officer experience, or public recognition, you can influence a life for Christ."[384]

Table 9.10 presents data on how far the teachers in the four cases had progressed in their formal education. The numbers in rows 'Elementary,' 'Grades 7-9,' and 'Grades 10-12' include both adults who did not progress past primary or secondary education and young people who were still in high school. The row 'University-level study' displays the numbers and percentages of those who had some level of tertiary education. (The highest level achieved by any teacher was a master's degree.) Prov-1, Cap-1, and Cap-2 all had teachers in this category. The row 'HS completed' records the numbers and percentages of teachers who completed their secondary education, including those who went on to tertiary education and those who did not.

Table 9.10. Education levels of teachers

	Prov-1	%	Prov-2	%	Cap-1	%	Cap-2	%		
All Teachers										
Elementary			1		2		1			
Grades 7-9	1		7		4		3			
Grades 10-12	4		12		7		3			
HS completed	14	77.8	4	16.7	21	70	18	81.8		
University-level study	13	72.2	4	16.7	17	56.7	15	68.2		
									Cap-2	%
Children's Teachers									LG's	

---

[384] Towns, *What Every*, 17.

Elementary			1						
Grades 7-9			5		2		1		1
Grades 10-12	4		12		6		2		2	
HS completed	5	62.5	3	15	10	66.7	6	85.7	13	92.9
University-level study	4	50	2	10	7	46.7	4	57.1	11	78.6

The number of teachers who completed high school provides a benchmark with the national education system. Although it still had a way to go to catch up with other nations in the region, Cambodia made a lot of progress in rebuilding its educational infrastructure since the 1990s. For example, Tandon and Fukao reported gains in net secondary enrollment from 16.6 percent in 2000 to 35.1 percent in 2012.[385] Unfortunately, secondary completion was still quite low, the National Institute of Statistics (NIS) reporting in 2016 the rate of completion for upper secondary education as being just 6 percent.[386]

Based on the NIS report and my own perceptions of the educational situation from living in Cambodia for many years, I assumed that the education level of non-formal CE teachers would be relatively low, especially in the provincial cases. However, Table 9.10 shows my assumption was incorrect. While most of the previous tables have highlighted sharp differences between the provincial and the capital city cases, this table presents a different picture. Prov-1, Cap-1, and Cap-2 all had high school completions of at least 70 percent for all teachers. In the capital city cases, the percentage was held down by middle-aged and older teachers who did not have the opportunity to finish their secondary education. Although Prov-1 did not have older teachers, it did have three teachers who were still in high school; so, its percentage of secondary completions will go up if those young people continue to teach after finishing high school.

Prov-2 was unique among the cases with regard to its teachers' education levels. Only four had completed high school (16.7 percent),

---

[385]Tandon and Fukao, *Educating the Next Generation*, 1, http://dx.doi.10.1596/978-1-4648-0417-5 (accessed June 9, 2015).
[386]National Institute of Statistics, *Cambodia Socio-Economic Survey 2016* (Phnom Penh, Cambodia: Ministry of Planning, October 2017), 48, https://www.nis.gov.kh/index.php/en (accessed November 26, 2018).

only three plus the special case of the pastor[387] had tertiary-level education, and fifteen were currently in the 9th, 10th, and 11th grades. Most, if not all, of those fifteen had plans to go on with their education; and due to the area's limited educational and economic opportunities, they would likely leave the community as they progressed in their education.

Looking at the children's teachers, the percentage of high school completions moved downward for Prov-1, Prov-2, and Cap-1. The lower numbers at Prov-1 and Prov-2 followed the policy of using youth for children's teachers, whereas Cap-1's numbers were lower because the older teachers had lower education levels. The percentage of high school completion in Cap-2 rose from 21 percent to 36 percent, mirroring the age range of its children's teachers and the effect of the key generation's leadership in this ministry. In contrast, over 90 percent of Cap-2's Life Group leaders had completed high school, and 78.6 percent had university-level training. The reason for this result was that most Life Group leaders were from Cap-2's key generation (ages 30-39).

This information and discussion about non-formal teacher education levels led to one conclusion that applies to all four cases—all these churches had a culture that values and encourages formal education. The pastors set the tone through their own educational achievements. Then, without neglecting the gifts of the older generations who had limited educational opportunities, these churches encouraged their youth and young adults to go as far as they could in formal education as being part of following God's will for their lives and developing their God-given gifts. The result was a strong level of secondary–and tertiary-level education across the cases. Prov-2 was not an exception in this regard, because most of its young people would likely reach similar levels of education in time.

Church-Related Backgrounds of the Teachers

Tables 9.11 and 9.12 present information about the backgrounds of teachers in relation to their churches. The information covers the following four aspects of that relationship—how long they had been in their church, how long they had been a believer, whether they had been baptized in water, and how many years they had been teaching. Table 9.11 provides the background information for all teachers, whereas Table

---

[387] The pastor of Prov-2 is a special situation in Table 9.10. She completed an associate degree at Cambodia Bible Institute without primary or secondary education. See the sub-section "Prov-2 Pastor's Profile" in Chapter 6 for more information.

9.12 provides it for the children's teachers at all churches plus Cap-2's Life Group leaders as a subset.

In Table 9.11's 'Years in the Church' rows, looking at the cases individually is more useful than trying to compare provincial churches with capital city churches. Prov-2's mean years in the church for all teachers was 6.1 compared to the other three cases, which ranged from 11.4 to 13.3 years. Prov-2's median number of years was 3, with more than half of its teachers (thirteen of twenty-two) having been in the church three years or less. The reason for this dynamic, as compared to the other cases, has already been highlighted in the tables and discussions above—i.e., teaching children as the prominent form of CE at Prov-2 and the youth being responsible for the teaching.

Table 9.11. Teacher backgrounds in the cases (all teachers)

	Prov-1	Prov-2	Cap-1	Cap-2	Prov's	Cap's	All
Years in the Church							
Mean	11.4	6.1	13.2	13.3	8.8	13.3	11
Median	10	3	12.5	15.5	6.5	14	10.3
Years as a Believer							
Mean	10	8	16.2	17.3	9	16.8	12.9
Median	6.5	5	19	17	5.8	18	11.9
Water Baptism							
Yes	16	20	28	22			
No	2	4	2	0			
Years Teaching							
Mean	4.5	3.4	7.3	4.5	4	5.9	4.9
Median	2.5	2	5	2.3	2.3	3.7	3

The information in the 'Years as a Believer' rows tells a different story from the 'Years in the Church' rows. On average, the teachers in the capital city cases had been believers 7.8 years longer than had the provincial teachers. The median numbers provided a clue as to the reason. Both provincial cases had median numbers lower than the means because they had a lot of younger teachers. The median numbers for the capital city cases were high compared to their mean, which generally followed the ages and generations already discussed in Table 9.8. In Cap-1, twenty-three of its thirty teachers had been believers for at least ten years; and in Cap-2, twenty out of its twenty-two teachers had been believers for at least twelve years.

Information in the 'Water Baptism' rows is included because AGC churches typically thought of water baptism as entry into church membership. Since the AGC was still largely in its first generation, most people were members of the church where they were baptized. Most of the teachers in the four cases had been baptized in water (91.4 percent). The eight who had not been baptized were children's teachers. With two exceptions, these teachers not baptized were either teenagers or relatively new to the church.

Looking now at the 'Years Teaching' rows, Cap-1 had the longest tenured teachers, with a mean of 7.3 years and a median of 5 years. The other three cases had a collective mean of 4.1 years and median of 2.3 years. These low figures were the result of the relatively young ages of teachers in Prov-1 and Prov-2 and the newly implemented strategy of Life Groups at Cap-2. Nine of the fourteen Cap-2 Life Group leaders had been teaching 2.5 years or less.

Table 9.12 presents the backgrounds of children's teachers and Life Group leaders in their churches. Looking at children's teachers, the number of years teachers had been in the capital city churches and had been believers is, respectively, 3.6 years and 7.6 years longer than the provincial cases. However, when it came to number of years teaching, Cap-1's children's teachers had fewer years of experience overall, with ten of the fifteen having been teaching two years or less. This result was due to the fact that it recruits trainee teachers to first work as assistants.

Table 9.12. Teacher backgrounds in the cases (children's teachers, life group leaders)

	Prov-1	Prov-2	Cap-1	Cap-2	Prov's	Cap's	All	Cap-2 LG's
Years in Church								
Mean	6.8	4.2	7.2	11	5.5	9.1	7.3	16.2
Median	6	3	5	8	4.5	6.5	5.5	17

Years as Believer								
Mean	6.8	5.8	10.1	17.6	6.3	13.9	10.1	17.9
Median	5.5	5	10	16	5.3	13	9.1	17.5
Water Baptism								
Yes	6	16	13	7				14
No	2	4	2	0				0
Years Teaching								
Mean	3.5	2.3	2.8	5.9	2.9	4.4	3.7	4.2
Median	3	2	1	3	2.5	2	2.3	2

In this table, Cap-2's teachers stand out in two respects. First, the church's children's classes had the most stability of all the cases in terms of teaching tenure, its teachers having 2.4 to 3.6 more years of experience than the other three cases. Second, compared to all the other data in Tables 9.11 and 9.12, Cap-2's Life Group leaders had very high mean and median years in the church and years as believers. As already seen in Table 9.8, most of the Life Group leaders were from the church's key generation. In general, these Life Group leaders were well-educated, in their 30s, and married. All but one had been believers for at least twelve years.

SPIRITUAL LIFE OF THE TEACHERS

This section considers the influences on the spiritual development and current spiritual lives of the teachers in the four cases. The information presented in the following two sub-sections was collected through the Teacher Questionnaire (see Appendix C).

The first sub-section explores answers to the question, "Thinking from the time you first believed until now, what [plural in Khmer] had the most influence on the growth of your faith?" This open-ended question yielded a wide range of answers. I grouped those answers thematically by case without over-referencing the other cases in order to let the 'flavor' of their answers come through as much as possible. Answers that appeared only once have not been included because I was looking for commonly shared experiences that could compare across cases. Frequencies of the answers are noted. The numbers do not equal the number of teachers because, being open-ended questions, more than one answer was given to questions and because some teachers did not answer all the questions.

The second sub-section considers the spiritual lives of teachers at the time of the study. The question about their personal devotional lives was also open-ended. The rest of the questions, which were closed, explored the teachers' Pentecostal experience regarding the baptism in the Holy Spirit and speaking in tongues and how often they prayed for their students.

Influences on the Spiritual Development of the Teachers

Table 9.13 lists the influences that the teachers felt were most important to their spiritual development. Two answers made a strong showing in all four cases—the Bible and prayer. Respondents wrote about 'reading the Bible,' 'knowing the Word,' 'studying the Bible,' and 'listening to the Word via preaching/teaching.' Although listed separately, the Cap-1's Saturday discipleship class was a Bible study. Personal prayer was the second strongest answer in terms of frequency. (The next sub-section explores the teachers' personal habits regarding Bible reading and prayer.)

Table 9.13. Influences on the spiritual development of teachers

Prov-1		Prov-2	
Prayer	8	Christian life experiences	13
The Bible	7	The Bible	9
• Listening to preaching/teaching (3)		Prayer	8
Corporate praise, worship	4	Answers to prayer	8
Miracles (answers to prayer)	2	• Miracles (4)	
		Examples of other people	3

Cap-1		Cap-2	
The Bible	13	Christian life experiences	10
Prayer	7	The Bible	6
Worship services	6	• Studying the Bible (4)	
Christian life experiences	5	Prayer	6

Answers to prayer	4	Church life, activities	6
Help, encouragement from others	4	Serving in ministry	4
Facing difficulties, persecution	3	Power of the Holy Spirit	3
Home groups	2	Seminars	2
Joining in church activities	2		
Saturday discipleship class	2		

'Christian life experiences' received the highest number of references in Prov-2 and Cap-2 and was also mentioned by several people in Cap-1. The answers grouped under this phrase were testimonial in nature; the respondents wrote about experiencing a transformed life, living out their faith, obeying God's voice, and feeling God's guiding presence. Closely related to this theme was 'Facing difficulties, persecution' mentioned by Cap-1 teachers.

One final theme that came through strongly in three of the cases (Prov-1, Prov-2, Cap-1) was 'Answers to prayer' or 'Experiences of God's actions.' Public testimonies of miracles (*ka-ahscha*) were common in all four cases. Many of those labeled 'miracles' did not involve supernatural events or miraculous healings. I wrestled with this term in my field notes before concluding that people were using the term *ka-ahscha* to talk about ways in which they believed God had answered their prayers or intervened on their behalf. Thus, the 'Answers to prayer' listed by the respondents include physical healing, God's help with family problems, freedom from fear of spirits, blessings from God, etc.

Current Spiritual Life of the Teachers

Table 9.14 presents the responses to questions about the case-study teachers' spiritual lives. The first question, which dealt with personal prayer and Bible reading, addressed their devotional life. The large majority responded that they engaged in prayer and Bible reading at least five times per week. Adding in those who reported that they did so three to four times per week takes in almost all the teachers. Six teachers in the provincial churches indicated minimal or no regular devotional habits.

Table 9.14. Elements in the spiritual life of teachers

	Prov-1	%	Prov-2	%	Cap-1	%	Cap-2	%
Personal prayer and Bible reading								
• Five times per week to every day	9		20		22		18	
• Three or four times a week	2		1		6		2	
• Once or twice a week	2		3					
• Not a regular habit	1						1	
The baptism in the Holy Spirit								
• Yes	18	100	6	25	16	53.3	18	81.8
• No	0		18		14		4	
Speaking in tongues as an ongoing experience								
• Daily, almost every day	10		3		9		6	
• At least during worship services	5		2		4		9	
• Not regularly, once in a while	3		1		3		3	
Prayer for students outside of class time								
• Once or twice a week	5		3		7		15	
• Not regularly, once in a while	4		10		5			
• Never			2					

The fourth question, which was about praying for their students outside of class time, can be combined with the first question. A solid group of respondents said that they did so daily or several times a week, with a similar-sized group also doing so once or twice a week. Therefore, we can conclude that the teachers in this study did value—and practiced—praying for their students. As Elmer Towns has said,

"The most effective ministry of a Sunday school teacher is accomplished on his or her knees in prayer."[388]

The responses to the first and fourth questions show that prayer for students was seemingly part of the devotional prayer life of most every teacher. I drew this conclusion because they reported having a robust devotional habit but did not idealize prayer for students (i.e., daily). A few of the teachers shared that they also prayed for their students when they teach. Considering that children's teachers in Prov-1, Cap-1, and Cap-2 taught once or twice a month, praying for students on a less frequent basis is implied.

The second question addressed the baptism in the Holy Spirit with the initial physical evidence of speaking in other tongues (*peasa chamlaik ahscha*), using the same wording as the statement of faith of the Assemblies of God of Cambodia.[389] All the respondents from Prov-1 and most of those from Cap-2 reported having received this experience; and just over half of those at Cap-1 had received it.

Only one quarter of respondents at Prov-2 said they had received the baptism in the Holy Spirit following the official doctrine of the AGC. The revelation of this provoked a loud and passionate response from the focus group who told me that, a few weeks after my time with them, they began to pray for more of their teachers to receive Holy Spirit baptism. As a result, many were dramatically filled during the first service. They continued to pray for the rest over the next two weeks until everyone had received this experience. So, although the responses from the Teacher Questionnaire are listed in Table 9.14, the focus group insisted that the number is now 100 percent.

The third question about speaking in tongues as an ongoing experience directly complemented the second question and also related to the first question as to the teachers' personal devotional lives. Classical Pentecostals like the AGC believe that the gift of speaking in tongues which accompanies Spirit baptism should function as a 'prayer language' and be an ongoing experience. The answers of the teachers assert that most of those who said they had been baptized in the Spirit also spoke in tongues at least during worship services each week, with the largest portion saying that they spoke in tongues daily or almost every day.

---

[388]Towns, *Sunday School Teacher*, 50.
[389]*Statement of Faith of the Assemblies of God of Cambodia*, Khmer language, rev. ed. (Phnom Penh, Cambodia: Assemblies of God of Cambodia, 2011).

CHAPTER 10
Cross-Case Analysis and Findings: Non-Formal CE Teachers (cont.)—Perspectives of the Educational Context and Presentation of Findings

Chapter 9 discussed how non-formal CE teachers were selected and equipped, ideal teacher models, teacher demographics, and the teachers' spiritual life. Chapter 10 continues the discussion on non-formal CE teachers in the four cases by considering their perspectives on their teaching. I begin by examining teacher-student relationships and 'network closure' (teacher relationships with families of students). Then I work through a series of four questions. (1) What do teachers like about teaching? (2) What do they find difficult about teaching? (3) What are the areas in which they want to grow? (4) How has teaching impacted them personally? This first section concludes with a summary and presentation of Finding 5 through Finding 11. The next section considers the teachers' and church leaders' perceptions about the educational context, which leads to Finding 12. The entire chapter then concludes with a summary of the cross-case analysis covered in Chapters 8 through 10, followed by a presentation of the twelve findings that are used to construct the descriptive model in Chapter 11.

PERSPECTIVES OF THE TEACHERS

The sub-sections under this section on non-formal CE teachers dig deeper into the perspectives of the teachers themselves. I wanted to know about their relationships with their students and the students' families. I also wanted to know what the teachers thought/felt about teaching and how teaching had impacted them personally and spiritually. Being relatively untrained volunteers, many of them with whom I interacted during this research had not thought about the above questions or reflected critically on their teaching.

The responses I explore in the sub-sections come from the Teacher Questionnaire (see Appendix C), with the exception of the first sub-section ('Teacher-Student Relationships'), which were taken from closed questions. The remaining sub-sections consider the teachers' responses to the four open-ended questions on the last page of the questionnaire. I have followed the same principles for grouping and presenting responses as I did in the previous sub-section, 'Spiritual Life of the Teachers.'

Teacher-Student Relationships

Table 10.1 presents the responses of teachers in each of the cases to closed questions about their relationships with their students. Their answers provide insight into how they understood their roles as teachers in their churches, which, in turn, provide a point of reference for the chapter's next main section, 'Reflecting on the Educational Context.'

Table 10.1. Relationships between teachers and students

	Prov-1	Prov-2	Cap-1	Cap-2
How many of your students do you know by name?				
• All of them	6	9	9	10
• Most of them	8	10	12	10
• Less than half of them		5		
• A few of them		5	1	1
How many families of your students do you know?				
• All of them	1	2	1	3
• Most of them	7	11	10	11
• Less than half of them	4	2	4	3
• A few of them	1	8	7	4
• None	1	1		
Do you visit your students in their homes?				
• Yes	9	18	12	13
• No	5	6	9	8
If yes, how often?				
○ Every week	2	1		4
○ At least once a month	4	4	4	2
○ A few times a year			4	3
○ Not regularly, once in a while	3	13	4	4

Teacher-student relationships are a key dynamic in non-formal CE, and knowing students by name (first question in Table 10.1) is central to that dynamic. Anne Boylan reports that the ratio of teachers to students in the early Sunday school movement in the United States was one per six to ten, which allowed for "intimate ties between teachers and pupils."[390] Howard Hendricks says that teachers need to know their students personally both in and out of class, both formally and informally because "Teaching that impacts is not head to head, but heart to heart."[391] Speaking from my own Sunday school experience, I learned as much from the personal piety of my teachers as I did from the lesson content. I remember their character more clearly than I remember their lesson points.

Table 10.1 shows that, generally, the teachers knew most—but not all—of their students by name. The rate was about the same across the cases, except for Prov-2. When I asked the focus group at Prov-2 about the responses from their teachers, they explained that church classes can have visitors every week. This explanation was especially true with new village cell groups and with teachers who came from a different village. From this I concluded that knowing all students by name might be difficult to achieve in certain circumstances.

The second and third questions in the table probe 'network closure.' This phrase refers to the network of relationships that provide support, transmit information, provide oversight, and give feedback that can "discourage negative and encourage positive life practices."[392] By these questions, I wanted to explore how much teachers connected to students outside of class times.

With regard to the teachers knowing their students' families, the responses ranged from a few to most. This result surprised me because I had assumed that people in provincial churches would have strong network closure. Instead, I learned that relationships between teachers and the families of their students varied for several reasons. One was because the family and teacher attended the same church. A second was because teachers for classes with university students had little opportunity to know the families of those students who came from elsewhere in the country. And a third was because the children's teachers in the provincial

---

[390]Boylan, *Sunday School*, 137, 139.
[391]Hendricks, *Teaching*, 85, 93-94.
[392]Christian Smith and Melinda Lundquist Denton, *Soul Searching: The Religious and Spiritual Lives of American Teenagers* (Oxford: Oxford University Press, 2005), 226-227, 247.

cases, due in part to their relative youth and lower social standing, had lower levels of social connection.

I also asked about home visitation, since such was a common practice among AGC churches. More than half the teachers across all four cases said they visited students in their homes. As to how often, while they prioritized visitation, frequent visits were not the norm, most saying they did so monthly or occasionally.

The question of visitation came up during the focus group at Cap-1. The group's response was that the 'urban culture of hospitality' had shifted as people began to prefer more privacy. One children's teacher regularly prayed with her students for their families that did not attend church. However, when she offered to visit those families to pray for them or help with problems, the children told her, "There is no need to come."[393]

Table 10.2 takes my teachers-students' families probe one step further by asking the teachers of children and youth if they talked to the parents of their students and, if so, what they talked about. The responses showed a clear distinction between the provincial cases and the capital city cases. Almost all the youth and children's teachers in the capital city cases reported talking with the families, compared to roughly half of the provincial teachers having done so.

The first three reasons in the list for talking to families related to the students' behavior, well-being, and spiritual growth; and the next three reasons involved outreach to the families. The final reason was added by three teachers, that being absenteeism, an issue that comes up again below about the problems that teachers face.

---

[393]The expression *"Mun bach mok the"* is a subtle rebuff meaning, "I would rather that you did not come."

Table 10.2. Talking with families of students

	Prov-1	Prov-2	Cap-1	Cap-2	Totals
If you teach children or youth, do you talk with the families of your students?					
• Yes	5	13	13	18	
• No	8	11	3	0	
If yes, what are the reasons?					
○ Student has personal problems (sad, sick, etc.)	3	8	5	12	28
○ Behavioral problems in class	3	3	3	4	13
○ Talk about the spiritual growth of the child	1	1	6	5	13
○ To share the Good News with the family	1	10	4	8	23
○ To encourage the parents/ family in their faith		4	8	8	20
○ To invite the parents/family to church	1	7	3	3	14
○ When a student is absent	1	1		1	3

Prov-1 teachers tended to talk with families of students only when there were problems with the student, whereas teachers at Prov-2, Cap-1, and Cap-2 reported talking to the families for all the reasons listed. Teachers showed the most concern about student personal problems, with behavioral problems and spiritual growth taking a secondary position. Also, they reported sharing the good news and encouraging their faith as the most common reasons for talking with the students' families. Prov-2 teachers stood out in their emphasis on this being their strongest reason for talking with the families. (The focus group at Prov-2 was quite pleased when they saw this result.)

What Teachers Liked About Teaching

Table 10.3 lists what teachers said they liked about teaching in the church. The most common theme across the four cases was teaching activities. Many mentioned discussions or discussion groups. Others said teaching a particular group of people, playing games, asking questions, telling stories, acting out stories, and dancing. Whatever else can be noted about the teachers in this study, they enjoyed the work of teaching.

The second most common theme across the four cases was helping students grow spiritually. The teacher responses included listening to students share their testimonies, encouraging them, praying with them, and facing real life problems with them. The teachers at Prov-1 talked about seeing behavior changes and Christian character development. The takeaway from this theme is one of teachers who enjoyed seeing their teaching bring results in the lives of their students.

Table 10.3. What teachers liked about teaching

Prov-1		Prov-2	
Seeing students grow spiritually, know God	9	Worship	11
Class activities	5	Teaching activities	11
• Games, dancing, discussion		Interacting with students	8
Seeing students learn, acquire skills	3	The Bible	7

Cap-1		Cap-2	
The Bible	11	Teaching activities	8
Teaching activities	8	• Discussions (4)	
Encouraging students in their faith	8	The Bible	4
Praying with students	4	Teaching children	4
		Seeing students grow spiritually	3
		Worship, music	2

The third theme that stood out in Table 10.3 was the Bible. Teachers mentioned the Bible in all the cases except Prov-1. Those at Cap-1 listed the Bible more often than anything else, whereas it received much less attention at Prov-2 and Cap-2. This result is interesting because of the strong influence of the Bible on the teachers' spiritual development (see Table 9.13) and the strong habits of devotional prayer and Bible reading that most of the teachers reported. (The Bible appears again as a secondary theme in the tables that follow.)

What Teachers Found Difficult About Teaching

Table 10.4 presents thematically grouped answers of teachers about the difficulties they faced in teaching. By far, the most common difficulty was issues related to the teachers themselves and to the work of teaching. Several across the cases said they struggled to understand lessons or biblical texts. Regarding preparation, some wrote about lacking time and energy, struggling to find examples, and "finding lessons to touch their (the students') hearts." Other teachers said they struggled to help students learn, lacked confidence in teaching, or felt like their classes lacked structure. Keeping in mind how much the teachers said they enjoyed teaching in Table 10.3, these responses revealed struggles with basic teaching skills.

Table 10.4. What teachers found difficult about teaching

Prov-1		Prov-2	
Issues related to teachers, teaching	6	Issues related to teachers, teaching	14
• Helping students learn		• Understand the lesson, biblical text (3)	
• Lack of confidence		• Struggling to explain the lesson (3)	
• Lack of structure in classes		• Teacher education level too low (2)	
• "Finding lessons to touch their hearts"		Classroom management	8
Classroom management, behavioral problems	4	Issues related to students	5
Issues related to students	4	• Students not understanding	
• Children new to church or too young		• Student not interested	
• Children cannot remember the lesson		• Teaching adults	
Absenteeism	4		
Cap-1		**Cap-2**	
Classroom management	8	Issued related to teachers, teaching	7
Preparing lessons	6	• Understanding, explaining lessons (4)	
Teaching skills	6	Absenteeism	3

Absenteeism	3	Helping students grow in faith	2
		Classroom management	2
		Lacking helpers with children	2
		Nothing (actual answer)	2

A second difficulty that appeared in the responses of all four cases was classroom management. Some teachers mentioned this term by name, while others wrote about dealing with behavioral problems. Several mentioned children being *ronyaech-ronyach,* meaning noisy, disorderly, or disruptive. I observed this in the children's classes where maintaining order was one of the main roles of the assistant teachers. Classroom management represented a convergence between teacher issues and student issues. On the one hand, teachers were responsible to manage their classes. On the other, student behavioral problems were commonly viewed as the students' responsibility, as we shall see in the discussion on educational context.

Absenteeism was a concern for teachers at Prov-1, Cap-1, and Cap-2. The teachers at Prov-2 did not mention it, likely because they were less structured with their village cell groups and were not required to take attendance. The other three cases had more stable children's classes. All the teachers found this issue difficult to address. Three of them in Table 10.2 mentioned talking to parents about students who were absent.

Teachers in the provincial cases talked about issues with their students. Although the number of responses in this theme was not large, nevertheless the issues that they did mention were of interest. The teachers at Prov-1 talked about students being too new, too young, or unable to remember the lesson the following week. Prov-2 teachers wrote about students attending but not being interested, students not understanding the Bible, and having difficulty teaching adults. The point here is that the teachers tended to view these problems as beyond their control, thus belonging to the students. The distinction is subtle, but this thinking shapes teachers' understanding of their role and impacts their effectiveness. This dichotomy between teacher and student roles will be an important issue in the discussion of perceptions about the national education system below.

Areas in Which Teachers Wanted to Grow

Table 10.5 lists the areas in which teachers said they wanted to grow. The top area across all four cases was pedagogical skill. This result related to the top answers in Tables 10.3 and 10.4—that is, teachers enjoyed the work of teaching but struggled with basic teaching skills. Additionally, several teachers in Prov-1 and Cap-1 said they wanted to grow in mutual development with other teachers. Those at Prov-1 planned together, worked collaboratively, and engaged in ongoing self-evaluation; while Cap-1 paired new teachers with experienced ones and conducted regular in-house training sessions. Six teachers at Cap-2 stated that they wanted more training, two of them expressing interest in creative teaching methods. In summary, the teachers across the cases had a strong desire to develop their teaching skills.

Table 10.5. Areas in which teachers wanted to grow

Prov-1		Prov-2	
Pedagogical skills	12	Personal spiritual growth	13
Mutual development with other teachers	4	• Stronger faith (4)	
Personal spiritual growth	3	• "I want to live so that my life teaches" (3)	
		• More courage (2), perseverance	
		Pedagogical skills	6
		Spiritual growth of students	5
		Evangelism	3
		Bible knowledge	3
		Classroom management	2
		Relationship with students	2
Cap-1		**Cap-2**	
Teaching methods	7	Pedagogical skills	15
Bible knowledge	6	• Want more training (4)	
Classroom management	2	• Creative teaching methods (2)	
Mutual development with other teachers	2	Personal spiritual growth	5
Serve God more	2	Bible Knowledge	2
		Knowledge (unspecified)	2

The second area of desired growth was the teachers' spiritual lives. The information already discussed above seemingly would lead to the conclusion that the teachers in this study were either solid or growing in their faith. However, many expressed a desire to become stronger in their faith, know God more, serve God more, have more courage, and be able to persevere. Three teachers at Prov-2 expressed their desire this way—"I want to live so that my life teaches."

Two areas of desired growth came in weaker than the previous trends would suggest—classroom management and Bible knowledge. Only a few teachers in Prov-2 and Cap-1 mentioned classroom management, which was interesting considering the prominence of this issue in the lists of difficulties. Additionally, only a few teachers in Prov-2 and Cap-2 mentioned Bible knowledge. The Bible had figured prominently in the Cap-1 teachers' responses throughout (see Tables 9.14, 10.1, and 10.4). Remaining consistent and standing out from the other cases, Cap-1 teachers listed Bible knowledge as the second highest area of desired growth.

Impacts of Teaching on Teachers

The teachers' responses regarding the impacts of teaching on themselves revealed that it has been a major influence on their spiritual development. They wrote a lot in response to this question, some as many as six points. Table 10.6 records their answers thematically.

Table 10.6. Impacts of teaching on teachers

Prov-1		Prov-2	
Growth in faith	10	Personal spiritual growth	25
• Trusting God, prayer, church activity, devotional life, closer to God		• Stronger faith (7); know God better (5); obey God more (4)	
Growth as a teacher	8	Growth in character	14
• Understanding children, preparing lessons		• Love (4); helping others (3); self-control, responsibility, courage, joy	

Growth in character	6	Bible knowledge	6
• Perseverance, patience, helping others, living as an example		Knowledge and skills	5
		Relationships with people	2
Growth in Bible knowledge	2	Have received many blessings	2
Cap-1		**Cap-2**	
Growth in character	7	Growth in spiritual life	21
• Desire to live as an example (2)		• Closer to God (8)	
• Love, joy, peace, patience, generosity,		• Trusting God more (3)	
Forgiveness		Teaching	8
Stronger faith	6	The Bible	8
Bible knowledge	5	• Knowledge, reading, understanding	
• Know God more through the Bible (3)		Christian living	7
Growth in ministry (evangelism, children)	3	• Living out faith as an example (3)	
Prayer life	2	• Sacrifice, service, sharing faith,	
Living according to God's will	2	sharing in the problems of others	
		Christian character	6
		• Self-confidence, purity, self-control	
		courage, knowing self better	
		Knowledge (unspecified)	3

The strongest theme across all four cases was 'personal spiritual growth,' with Prov-2 and Cap-2 teachers writing about it far more than the other two cases. Teachers mentioned having stronger faith, knowing God better, and growing in their prayer lives. Two teachers at Prov-1 offered the following comments:

A teacher and youth leader: When we teach them, we teach ourselves. When we help others, God helps us through helping others. We are encouraged as we encourage others. **A youth leader:** As teachers, we study the lesson before we teach. We come closer to the Lord as we prepare. So, teaching causes us to seek God's presence more.

The second area of growth prominent amongst all the cases was 'Christian character,' a term used here to refer to attitudes as opposed to practical living. Teachers wrote about growing in perseverance, patience, love, joy, peace, generosity, forgiveness, self-control, courage, and responsibility. Closely related to Christian character was 'Christian living.' Teachers wrote about living according to God's will, serving, sacrificing, sharing their faith, and sharing in the problems of others. Three respondents at Cap-2 and two at Cap-1 said that teaching motivated them to live out their faith as an example to others.

The theme, 'Bible knowledge,' appeared in all four cases in Table 10.6. It was low in Prov-1 but in the middle in Prov-2, Cap-1, and Cap-2. Three Cap-1 teachers said that they know God more through knowing the Bible.

Lastly, 'growth in teaching' was explicitly mentioned by teachers in Prov-1 and Cap-2 with eight responses each. The Prov-2 teachers who mentioned 'knowledge and skills' may also have been referring to teaching. The teachers wrote about preparing lessons, understanding lessons, helping students understand, and teaching children. One children's teacher at Prov-1 perhaps said it best:

> "Before we teach children, we have to think about how to teach them so that they will understand. Before we teach them, we have to study the Word so that we understand more clearly than before. The better we understand the Word, the better we will teach children."

Conclusions and Findings About Non-Formal CE Teachers

In Chapters 9 and 10, we have examined the processes for selecting and equipping teachers, ideal teacher models, teacher demographics, the teachers' spiritual lives, and their perspectives on teaching. These chapters covered much information that has painted a fuller picture of the approaches to non-formal CE of the four cases in this study. Many of the results suggested fruitful directions for additional research, especially in the areas of teacher demographics and perspectives. This concluding sub-section focuses on the findings from the two chapters that contribute to the construction of the descriptive model in Chapter 11.

Findings 5, 6, and 7 delineate the processes by which teachers were selected in the cases, the values that drove those processes, and the general approaches to equipping teachers. Those findings are stated as follows:

Finding 5: The top leadership of each of the cases in this study was directly responsible to appoint non-formal CE teachers.

Finding 6: Regarding teacher selection, the cases in this study valued genuine personal faith, faithfulness to the church, submission to leadership, and evidence of a gift/love for teaching. Secondary considerations included teaching experience, education levels, and Bible knowledge.

Finding 7: The cases in this study trained children's teachers informally by having new teachers work with experienced teachers and semi-formally by sending teachers to seminars.

Much like Simpson's description of small-church dynamics, the process of teacher selection was conducted by deeply vested leadership that was highly engaged in church life and had a deep sense of responsibility to keep the church faithful to its original vision.[394] The characteristics the church leaders valued in teachers were closely aligned with Bechtle's qualifications for CE workers, especially that of having personal faith and willingness to work under church leadership's direction ("be a team player").[395] None of the cases provided pre-service training, but they all had proactive approaches to in-service training.

Findings 8 and 8a describe the characteristics and values that the teachers and the leaders embraced and/or rejected for non-formal CE teachers. These values reflected each church's culture of learning and a reaction to the educational context (see next section, "Reflecting on the Educational Context"). The values embraced were expressions of what the teachers and leaders believed education should entail and how teachers and students should relate to each other.

Finding 8: The teachers and leaders in the cases valued teacher models that emphasized teacher competency and responsibility, student growth and success, and caring relationships between teachers and students.

---

[394]Simpson, "Christian Education," 159-166.
[395]Bechtle, "The Roles, 238.

Finding 8a: Teacher models were rejected that emphasized knowledge transmission without attention to student development and that depicted unrealistic teacher involvement in the lives of students.

Finding 9 emerges from the cross-case analysis of teacher demographics. The limited educational and economic opportunities in the provincial settings meant that most teachers in Prov-1 and Prov-2 were single, less than thirty years of age, and still in school. Additionally, the provincial cases made children's classes a function of their youth ministries (Finding 10). This approach provided youth a ready-made opportunity for meaningful service and created a norm of service in their church cultures, even though many of these youth would probably leave both that ministry and the community as they progress into the next stage of life. In contrast, the educational and economic opportunities of the capital city provided a higher degree of stability. Consequently, Cap-1 and Cap-2 had teachers from across the generations represented in their congregations and only a few youth teaching children's classes. The mean age of teachers in the capital city cases was 11.5 years higher than that of the provincial cases.

Finding 9: Educational and economic opportunities affected the availability and longevity of non-formal CE teachers.

Finding 10: Children's classes were a function of the youth ministries in the provincial cases.

Lastly, Finding 11 states that the education levels of teachers in the four cases were high compared to national statistics on secondary-education completion. Considering the lack of educational requirements for non-formal CE teachers, this finding highlights the value that these churches and their leaders placed on formal education. Cambodian society was hungry for the benefits and security that education promised. However, listening to public testimonies of most teachers plus the personal dreams of the young teachers, I inferred that their educational attainment was also driven by spiritual motives—i.e., a desire to fulfill what they believed was God's plan for their lives.

Finding 11: The education level of all teachers across the cases was high compared to national statistics. At least 70 percent had completed or were in the process of completing secondary education.

REFLECTING ON THE EDUCATIONAL CONTEXT

This section examines the educational context from the perspectives of the leaders and teachers in the focus groups. My approach was to invite the participants to look back at the five teacher models in the Teacher Questionnaire and state which one they felt to be the most common for primary-school teachers. I then asked them to explain why. As appropriate for each group, I asked the same question about secondary and tertiary teachers. Lastly, I asked them to describe how their approach to CE differed from what they perceived about the national education system. The point of this exercise was to listen to the characteristics and practices they described, not to associate specific teacher models with Cambodia's national education system.

Validity of the views expressed in the focus groups rested on three facts. First, despite their obvious passion, the participants gave thoughtful, even-handed critiques of teachers in the national school system. Second, the characterizations of national system teachers were consistent across the cases. Third, many spoke from personal experience—some having children and grandchildren in the school system; some still in high school or university themselves; a few church leaders having worked closely with local primary schools; and three participants having been qualified teachers, including a retired high school teacher, a school principal, and a pastor who had been a teacher before planting his church.

Non-formal CE in local churches interacts with the formal education context in a variety of ways. The formal education system provides teachers with foundational education, provides models for teacher roles and teacher-student relationships, and creates norms that churches can either follow or reject in their approach to non-formal CE. As a historical example, Sunday school conventions in the early 1800s in America published Johann Pestalozzi's theories about the nature of children.[396] More recently, Howard Hendricks in his book, *Teaching to Change Lives: Seven Proven Ways to Make Your Teaching Come Alive*,[397] utilized John Milton Gregory's *The Seven Laws of Teaching*[398] to train Sunday school teachers. At a more technical level, Marlene LeFever used Bernice McCarthy's hemispheric model of learning theory to construct a Sunday school teaching paradigm based on four learning styles.[399]

---

[396] Boylan, *Sunday School*, 124.
[397] Hendricks, *Teaching*.
[398] Gregory, *The Seven Laws*.
[399] LeFever, *Learning Styles*, 211-216.

These three American examples show one way that non-formal CE can interact with formal education—i.e., by learning from advances in social science research and educational theory. Perhaps not surprisingly, the perspectives of the focus groups did not follow this pattern. Instead, they consciously rejected the values and practices they saw in the local schools.

While there were similarities between non-formal CE in Cambodia and the early Sunday school movements, the educational context was quite different. In America, the movement in the early 1800s complemented the emerging common-school system.[400] In England in the late 1700s and early 1800s, Sunday schools contributed to needed social reform and educational expansion.[401] Both the U.S. and England were predominantly Christian nations that welcomed educational contributions by the Church. In Cambodia, however, non-formal CE is the domain of a minority religion and is surrounded by a national education infrastructure that rapidly developed over the previous three decades, with assistance from international, market-oriented agencies like the World Development Bank.[402]

In the following sub-sections, the first one reports the views of the focus groups regarding teachers in the national education system; the second then considers how the four cases approach non-formal CE in comparison to the national educational system; and the third presents and unpacks Findings 12 and 12a.

Perspectives About Teachers in the National Education System

The Prov-1 focus group chose the Equipper as the model that best fit elementary school teachers in the national system.[403] When asked the reasons for their selection, they described elementary teachers as only concerned with knowledge, not with nurture. This lack of concern about the emotional well-being of the students, they said, was because the teachers assumed emotional well-being to be the responsibility of the parents. That perspective, which differed from the intention of

---

[400]Boylan, *Sunday School*, 29
[401]Willis, *200 Years*, 33-34.
[402]David M. Ayres, *Anatomy of a Crisis: Education, Development, and the State in Cambodia, 1953-1998*, Southeast Asia edition (Chiang Mai, Thailand: Silkworm Books, 2003), 162-163.
[403]Ironically, they also chose the Equipper as the best model for teaching in the church. In so doing, they were using the model in a fluid way to express their views of teachers in each context.

the Equipper model, showed they think of national-system teachers as emotionally distant from the children in their classes.

The Prov-2 focus group was unanimous and emphatic in ascribing the Tea Pot as the most common model for elementary school teachers. From the group members' experience, the teachers did whatever they wanted to do without concern for the students' well-being. One Prov-2 teacher said, "They are not concerned about the students. Those who can get it, get it. That's it." Teachers, they insisted, were unconcerned about students who did not learn. Moreover, no poor students dared approach teachers, and handicapped students were rejected.

Additionally, the Prov-2 focus group had much to say about school teachers. They talked about teachers meting out immediate punishments for small infractions without asking for an explanation from the student. Such punishments included harsh words, hitting with rods, and making students kneel on spikey jackfruit skins. Although corporal punishment was against the law, the teachers acted with impunity because school authorities often did not enforce the law. Such impunity, the focus group asserted, even extended to molestation. If a situation goes too far, families could complain to the principal in the hope that the teacher would self-correct.

The Cap-1 focus group unequivocally pointed to the Gardener as the teacher model most common in elementary schools. Rather than the romantic view of nurturing innocent children that is historically associated with this model, they said teachers taught as if it is a job and left the children to grow on their own. One very knowledgeable participant explained, "Teachers teach, and students get what they can. It is up to the ability of the students, not the skills or responsibility of the teacher." Another Cap-1 teacher complained of how a teacher punished her grandchild for struggling to hold a pencil correctly.

Cap-2's focus group expressed similar views, likewise suggesting that the Tea Pot model best fit elementary school teachers. One Life Group leader explained it this way: "Teaching is their job. They do it for a salary. When they are done, they go home, and they do not worry about how the lives of their students turn out."

The picture that emerged from these views was one of authoritarian classrooms in which teachers did the job of teaching at students as if those students were things instead of people. They tended to view teaching as a profession by which they earned money, not as a calling to make a difference in their students' lives or to make society a better place. Although not a tool of oppression in the political sense, the teacher attitudes that the focus-group participants described resonate with the 'banking education' denounced by Paulo Freire that de-humanizes students by turning them "into 'receptacles' to be 'filled' by the teacher."[404]

When I extended the question to junior high and high school teachers, the focus groups all asserted that the same models applied. However, they were more cynical about secondary teachers, saying that they were stricter and more concerned about money. The Prov-2 focus group said secondary teachers were often late for (even absent from) their classes, yet they would require students (as many as sixty) to attend private classes at the teachers' homes at a cost of 1,500 riel (about 38 cents) per hour of instruction. Oft-times, those who did not attend the private classes were not allowed to pass the test, even if they made a good grade. One Cap-1 participant said, "They are always making students buy things from them. If they do not buy, they don't give them attention." Another person in the same group summarized the attitude of secondary teachers as being "not concerned with depth of understanding, just writing the correct answers."

I also asked the focus groups whether the national-system teachers knew their students by name and interacted with their families. The responses were mixed. Some said that teachers know many or most of their students by name, the Cap-1 group saying that knowing all their students' names is part of their job. However, the consensus across the groups was that the teachers did not form relationships with students outside of class, that they were only *chit snut* (relationally close) with students who give them money.

Also varying was teacher interaction with families of students. Cap-1's focus group said that the teachers talked to parents occasionally, such as when students were absent a lot or their schoolwork was poor. Prov-1 said that teachers never talked to parents of students. The Cap-2 group said that teachers only meet with parents when there was a problem; and when they did so, they 'summoned' *(koh hav)* the parents to meet them.

In summary, the picture of teachers in the national system painted by the focus groups was one of harshness, authoritarianism, and dehumanization. Only a few participants expressed positive experiences with teachers (specifically Christian teachers) who genuinely cared about the emotional well-being of their students. However, two professional teachers at Cap-1 explained that, while having good principles and goals on official forms and on posters at the school, the teachers did not practice them. This view matches the report by Tandon and Fukao whose

---

[404]Freire, *Pedagogy*, 72.

research revealed that, despite the adoption of standards at the ministry level, only about half of teachers were aware of them and only about half of school directors "indicated that the standards play a substantial role in the school's work."[405]

One church leader at Prov-1 summarized the experiences and perspectives expressed by all the groups this way:

> "School teachers have received good training, but they do not put it into practice and have little intention of getting involved in the students' lives. They are more concerned with their jobs. They talk about money a lot, like salaries and getting money from this person or that."

Approaches to Non-Formal CE in Comparison to the National Education System

The discussion above leads to this question, which I put to the focus groups—How did they approach teaching in the church in comparison to the national education system? The answer to this question has already begun to emerge in their views of ideal teacher models and in their characterizations of teachers in the national system. As Findings 8 and 8a state, they wanted CE teachers to be competent, responsible, and personally concerned about their students, and they rejected impersonal knowledge transmission as being unacceptable for teaching in the church.

This present sub-section looks at how their ideals interacted with or reacted to what they saw in the national education system. In summary, the cases intentionally approached non-formal CE differently from the local school system in three ways.

First, the relationship between teachers and students was much closer in the churches. Their CE teachers encouraged students, visited them in their homes, asked about them when they were absent, and brought them help when needed. The teachers prayed with students for their families and reached out to their families because they wanted to share the good news with them. One passionate Cap-1 teacher bore her heart with these words—"Teachers in the church are motivated by love, not benefit. They are not worried about the time they spend or weariness."

---

[405]Tandon and Fukao, *Educating the Next Generation*, 6, http://dx.doi.10.1596/ 978-1-4648-0417-5 (accessed June 9, 2015).

Second, the four cases handled discipline differently from the teachers in the national system. The Prov-2 teachers expressed the view on this point with great clarity, explaining that they used rules to help and encourage students, never corporal punishment. This policy directly paralleled the prohibition of corporal punishment by Sunday school leaders in early 19th century America, in contrast to the harsh and swift punishments that were the norm in common schools. The publications of that time insisted that persuasion and kindness alone were the only tools of discipline for Sunday school teachers.[406]

Third, all the focus groups insisted that non-formal CE was holistic compared to the national education system, although each group expressed this idea in different ways. Prov-1 said their teachers were concerned with the whole lives of the students, including family problems outside of church life. However, they further said their teachers also cared about the 'externals' as well as the 'internals.' They insisted that schools were only concerned with the externals, referring to knowledge and skills that can be demonstrated and can lead to success; whereas 'internal' referred to a person's spiritual life, relationship with God, and character development.

Cap-1 spoke about their holistic approach in terms of moral development, which they said was not a concern of the national system. The pastor of Prov-2 expressed his church's holistic approach to CE in a systematic way, that being, concern about growth in five areas of life—physical, emotional, "wisdom/thinking,"[407] social, and spiritual.

Cap-2's pastor described the holistic ideals of non-formal CE conceptually. He worked with Bloom's three domains of learning (i.e., cognitive, affective, behavioral) in much the same way as Richards and Bredfeldt.[408] Using the terms head, heart, and hands, he said the national-system school focuses on head and hands by giving knowledge, skills, and ability but "is not concerned with the heart, not holistic. The heart is a priority to the church." Speaking of theology that is lived out, he further said, "The church also gives knowledge and skills, but we are more concerned about how they live and their character." Noting that the church was good at addressing the heart, he expressed a desire for an even more holistic approach to CE, believing that the Church ought

---

[406]Boylan, *Sunday School*, 48.
[407]They used the words *brachnya* and *ka-ket*, which mean 'wisdom' and 'thinking.' The term 'intellectual' or 'cognitive' could be used here, but I do not think it captures what they had in mind.
[408]Richards and Bredfeldt, *Creative Bible Teaching*, 135-138.

to address the head and the hands as much as the heart and do so with excellence that even exceeds that of the world.

'Reflecting on Educational Context' Conclusions and Findings

This section has looked at the formal education context in Cambodia through the experiences and voices of the focus groups. Their perspectives are summarized in Findings 12 and 12a, which I unpack in the paragraphs that follow.

Finding 12: The focus groups rejected the norms for teacher attitudes and teacher-student relationships that they perceived in the national school system as unacceptable for teaching in the church.

Finding 12a: They rejected aspects of the national school system that they perceived as harsh, authoritarian, and de-humanizing in favor of a holistic approach to non-formal CE that is characterized by warm, encouraging relationships between teachers and students.

Finding 12 states that the focus groups rejected the attitudes and practices they experienced in the national education system. In other contexts, formal education can guide approaches to non-formal CE or set norms to which non-formal CE is culturally expected to conform. In contexts like the United States, for example, some of those norms have legal ramifications, such as running background checks on teachers and creating secure areas for children. However, CE in contexts like Cambodia interacts with formal education in a different way. In this research, church leaders and teachers saw the norms in the national system as contrary to their values. So they consciously developed a set of values and practices that differed from that system.

Finding 12a lists three aspects of the national system that the focus groups rejected. First, the teachers were perceived as harsh and uncaring toward their students. Second, I have used the term 'authoritarian' to describe the absolute and capricious power teachers reportedly had in their classrooms. Students had to learn how to survive in this environment from the first grade on. Third, 'de-humanizing' was as much a result of the first two aspects as it was an aspect of the learning environment. The focus groups described teachers as objectifying students by treating them as sources of income and by neglecting or rejecting students they deemed as unable to learn. This lack of concern for students as people was itself a powerful form of education. Instead of being encouraged to strive to reach their potential and discover their place in this world, students had to learn to submit to arbitrary power in the classroom in order to survive.

Finding 12a lists two values the focus groups embraced in non-formal CE contrary to their experiences with formal education. First, they felt that non-formal CE should be holistic. Teaching in the church addressed more than just knowledge and observable skills. They felt that CE teachers must also be interested in their students' spiritual lives and in the development of Christian character. In their view, a holistic approach to CE went beyond the spiritual to encompass physical, emotional, and social aspects of life as well.

Second, this holistic approach naturally led to teacher-student relationships that were 'warm' and 'encouraging.' I chose these two terms because they were common Cambodian expressions. The word *kok-kdav* ('warm') in relationships spoke of affection and acceptance. The word *ka-lurk-thuk-chet* ('encouragement') was a common expression that could refer to any action or gift intended to make a person feel good about something good or bad. In the context of non-formal CE, *ka-lurk-thuk-chet* meant that teachers created a learning environment in which students felt safe, were nurtured in their faith, were urged to develop their devotional lives, and were emboldened to live out their faith.

FINDINGS AND SUMMARY OF CHAPTERS 8 THROUGH 10

Chapters 8 through 10 have presented a cross-case analysis of the data from the four cases. The analysis yielded twelve findings (see Table 10.7) that cover four aspects of non-formal CE among AGC churches—organizational models, roles of non-formal CE, non-formal CE teachers, and the educational context. Chapter 11 will present a descriptive model of approaches to non-formal CE among AGC churches constructed from the findings that expresses the interactions among these four aspects.

The 12 findings listed in Table 10.7 were distilled through a process that involved several steps and variations, depending on the type of data. First, raw data were recorded and organized. Second, the raw objective data were further organized into matrices, perspectival data being chunked thematically then organized into matrices by case. Third, themes were identified and a detail-rich list of twenty-three preliminary findings created. Fourth, those preliminary findings were further distilled into the twelve findings in Table 10.7. These twelve provided the bases for construction of the descriptive model presented in Chapter 11.

Table 10.7. Twelve findings of the research

Organizational Models and Non-Formal CE
Finding 1: The congregations in this study functioned like small churches in which non-formal CE pervaded organizational models and dominated church activities.
Roles of Non-Formal CE
Finding 2: The non-formal CE of the cases in this study had a strong internal focus that emphasized Bible knowledge, discipleship, and personal faith through nurture.
Finding 3: The cases in this study used education as one of their primary means of social engagement.
Finding 4: The provincial cases in this study had a stronger level of social engagement through non-formal CE than the capital city cases.
Non-Formal CE Teachers
Finding 5: The top leadership of the cases in this study was directly responsible to appoint non-formal CE teachers.
Finding 6: Regarding teacher selection, the cases in this study valued genuine personal faith, faithfulness to the church, submission to leadership, and evidence of a gift/love for teaching. Secondary considerations included teaching experience, education levels, and Bible knowledge.
Finding 7: The cases in this study trained children's teachers informally by having new teachers work with experienced teachers and semi-formally by sending teachers to seminars.
Finding 8: The teachers and leaders in the cases valued teacher models that emphasized teacher competency and responsibility, student growth and success, and caring relationships between teachers and students.
Finding 8a: They rejected teacher models that emphasized knowledge transmission without attention to student development and that depicted unrealistic teacher involvement in the lives of students.

Finding 9: Educational and economic opportunities affected the availability and longevity of non-formal CE teachers.
Finding 10: Children's ministry was a function of the youth ministries in the provincial cases.
Finding 11: The education level of all teachers across the cases was high compared to national statistics. At least 70 percent of teachers had completed or were in the process of completing secondary education.

Reflecting on the Educational Context
Finding 12: The focus groups rejected the norms for teacher attitudes and teacher-student relationships that they perceived in the national school system as unacceptable for teaching in the church.
Finding 12a: They rejected aspects of the national school system that they perceived as harsh, authoritarian, and de-humanizing in favor of a holistic approach to non-formal CE that is characterized by warm, encouraging relationships between teachers and students.

Chapter 8 analyzed the organizational models of the cases with special attention to the overall role of teaching. The analysis led to the finding that the congregations in this study had more in common with small-church dynamics than with Western organizational approaches that addressed the departmentalization of CE. Rather, CE pervaded the organizational models of the cases and dominated church activities.

Chapter 8 also looked at the roles of non-formal CE in the cases. The data included a comparison of the classes taught in the churches, perceptions about the internal/external roles of those classes, and teacher perceptions about the functions of their classes. The analyses led to these three findings. (1) The non-formal CE in these cases had a strong internal focus that emphasized Bible knowledge, discipleship, and personal faith through nurture; crisis conversions were not part of the picture that emerged. (2) All the cases engaged their communities, with education being one of the leading means of engagement. (3) The provincial cases had a higher degree of social engagement through education than did the capital city cases, with Prov-2 having a strikingly high level of civic participation.

Chapters 9 and 10 looked at the teachers in the four cases. The areas of examination were: selection and equipping of teachers, ideal teacher models, teacher demographics, teachers' spiritual lives, and teachers' perspectives about their experiences in CE teaching. The data in these chapters suggested several directions for future research and useful interventions. In the end, seven findings emerged that could be used to construct the descriptive model in Chapter 11. Those findings described who appoints teachers, primary and secondary values that leaders wanted in teachers, and approaches to training children's teachers. The findings from the valuations of teacher models indicated that teachers and leaders wanted teachers to be competent and responsible, concerned about student growth, and caring in their relationships with students.

The demographic data in Chapter 9 highlighted the differences in educational and economic opportunities between provincial locations and capital city locations. These differences affected the mean ages of teachers, their marital statuses, and their long-term potential for teaching. Provincial churches worked with this dynamic by linking their youth ministries and their children's classes, providing young people with a ready-made place of service as they matured in their faith.

The data in Chapter 9 also revealed that the education level of the teachers in these four cases was high compared to national statistics for secondary education completion. At least 70 percent of teachers had completed or were in the process of completing secondary education. This educational attainment was an expression of the value these churches placed on formal education.

Chapter 10 considered how the leaders and teachers in the cases perceived the educational context and how their approach to non-formal CE reflected or reacted to that context. All the cases expressed strikingly similar views. The leaders and teachers largely rejected the attitudes and teacher-student relationships they had experienced in the national education system as unacceptable for teaching in the church. National-system local teachers, especially at the primary level, were characterized as harsh, authoritarian, and de-humanizing. In reaction, these churches cultivated teaching approaches that were holistic and characterized by warm, encouraging teacher-student relationships.

CHAPTER 11
A Model of Approaches to Non-Formal CE Among AGC Churches

This brief chapter presents a descriptive model of approaches to non-formal CE constructed from the findings of this study. The study's four cases included four AGC churches—two in provincial locations and two in the capital city. These cases were not representative of AGC churches because many congregations had minimal or no non-formal CE at the time of this study. Rather, the cases were chosen because they had engaged in sustained efforts at non-formal CE over many years and represented two different socioeconomic situations in Cambodia.

The findings and descriptive model presented here are intended to be transferable, not generalizable. Transferability "refers to the fit or match between the research context and other contexts as judged by the reader."[409] As such, the findings speak from a specific socioeconomic context and Christian tradition. This research used theoretical replication across the cases to ensure consistency in data that would provide a basis for cross-case analysis and drawing transferable conclusions.[410] Following the standards described by Bloomberg and Volpe, the transferability was strengthened by detailed contextual information that reflected the social world of the cases (credibility) and by clear data collection procedures that could be audited (dependability).[411]

The first section of this chapter describes the four main levels of the model in general terms. In this section, I provide a rationale for the arrangement of this multilevel model. The second section presents a full descriptive model constructed from the findings that were drawn from the cross-case analysis in Chapter 10. This second section considers the interaction between the aspects of the model in detail.

---

[409]Bloomberg and Volpe, *Completing Your Qualitative Dissertation*, 113.
[410]Yin, *Case Study Research*, 54.
[411]Bloomberg and Volpe, *Qualitative Dissertation*, 112-113.

THE FOUR LEVELS OF THE MODEL

The modeling approach in this chapter is one way of presenting the findings of 'emergent theory.' Jacaard and Jacoby describe emergent theory as theory that emerges from data with the anthropological goals of "description, understanding, and explanation."[412] As such, emergent theorists work with propositions and supporting arguments.[413] Since this research proposes to be transferable, Chapter 10 presented conclusions as *findings* specific to the cases as opposed to generalizable *propositions*. This chapter builds an integrated model from those findings.

Jacaard and Jacoby suggest using multilevel modeling when theorists think in terms of "explanatory variables at different levels, focusing on cases where level 1 units are nested within level 2 units."[414] Thus, the descriptive model presented here uses this multilevel approach by placing the model's four main aspects in nesting relationships with each other. One difference with Jacaard and Jacoby is that this research describes and explores relationships between aspects as opposed to describing causal links between variables.

Figure 11.1 presents the four levels of the model as concentric circles 'nested' within one another. As noted in the introduction to Chapter 8, the conceptual framework used to collect data ordered these four levels from the most conceptually general to the most case-specific (see Chapter 2). However, the findings that emerged from the data pointed to a configuration in which the levels were nested within one another based on their interactions.

---

[412] James Jaccard and Jacob Jacoby, *Theory Construction and Model-Building Skills* (New York: The Guilford Press, 2010), 281-282.
[413] Ibid., 277.
[414] Ibid., 320.

Figure 11.1. The four levels of the model

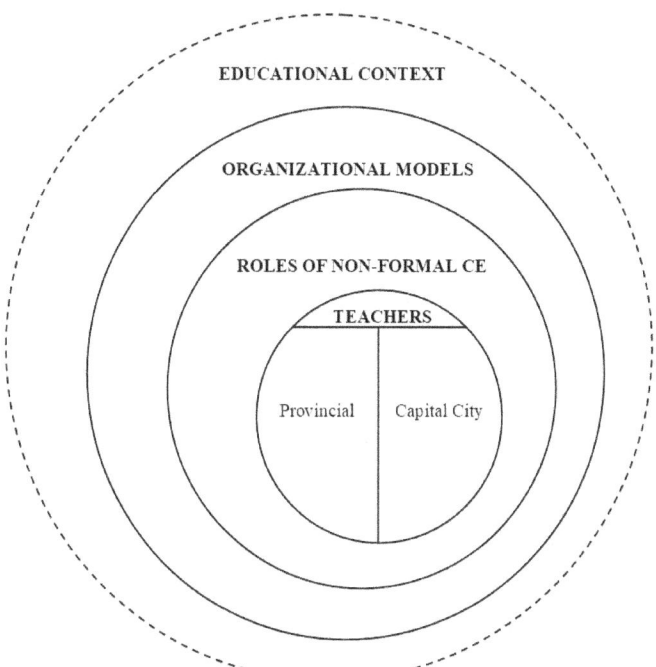

The next section works through the four levels beginning with Organizational Models because this level drives the entire model. The organization of each case embodied the values of the church and its leadership in terms of roles, authority, and responsibility. The Roles of Non-Formal CE level nests within the Organizational Models level because it conceptually represents the foci (internal and external) and the functions of their approaches to non-formal CE. Those values were concretely expressed in the arrangement of classes and in the roles teachers were expected to fill.

Teachers are the core of this model and the main force of non-formal CE in each case. They interacted with all three of the other levels. Teachers were identified, appointed, and equipped from the Organizational Models level. They interacted with the Roles of Non-Formal CE level through the functions of the classes they taught and the position of their classes in the church's overall approach to non-formal CE. Lastly, they interacted with the Educational Context level through their formal education attainment and experiences.

The Educational Context has been drawn as the outermost level of this model because it represents a key socioeconomic element that affects a church's approach to non-formal CE. I have drawn this level with a dashed line because it is not as clearly bounded as the other three. The main educational context in view in this research was the government school system at the primary and secondary levels.

Before moving on to the second section and a full discussion of the model, I would like to address contextual elements that are not included in this model. I focused on the national education system at the primary and secondary levels because that was a key element in the historical development of non-formal CE in the literature (i.e., Sunday school in the United States[415] and in England[416]). My research demonstrated that a similar dynamic was at work in these cases but with a different result (see next section). The research participants were keenly aware of this dynamic, especially with regard to children's classes.

The Educational Context level is one aspect that may need to be adjusted for this descriptive model to be transferable. I focused on formal primary and secondary education because it was in the minds of participants, although non-formal CE could interact with other types of educational and social contexts. Following are some examples.

- The tradition or denomination of the church may dictate or exemplify non-formal CE norms.
- The educational context could include Christian primary and secondary schools that act as benchmarks for non-formal CE for children and youth.
- There could be adult education programs that model adult learning approaches.
- If Christianity is a minority religion, the majority religion may have an educational approach that resonates with contextual expressions of Christianity.[417]

---

[415]Boylan, *Sunday School*, 29.
[416]Willis, *200 Years*, 33-34.
[417]I did not pursue this line of inquiry because the cases showed no interest in modeling Buddhist forms of education. Education in the *Wats* (temples) was primarily for monks, not general religious adherents. Furthermore, Wat schools provided rudimentary literacy instruction up until the 1950s, when King Norodom Sihanouk attempted to modernize the educational system. *Wat* schools were no longer part of mainstream education in Cambodia. Ayres, *Anatomy of a Crisis*, 16, 24, 31-32.

- The political culture could provide a pattern for approaches to non-formal CE, especially with adults.[418]

A MODEL OF APPROACHES TO NON-FORMAL CE AMONG AGC CHURCHES

Figure 11.2 presents a full descriptive model of approaches to non-formal CE constructed from the findings laid out in Chapters 8 through 10. (See Table 10.7 in Chapter 10 for a complete list.) The following four sub-sections work through the details of the model level by level in this order—organizational models, roles of non-formal CE, teachers, and educational contexts.

Organizational Models and Non-Formal CE

The first finding of this research noted that the four cases did not have CE departments. Rather, they operated like small churches with high levels of integration between programs and deeply vested leadership that was involved in all areas of church life. Non-formal CE was one of the pervasive elements of church life and accounted for a large portion of annual and weekly activities.

Finding 1: The congregations in this study functioned like small churches in which non-formal CE pervaded organizational models and dominated church activities.

The Organizational Models level drives this descriptive model. In Figure 11.2, three arrows extend out from the Organizational Models box. The arrow going toward the Roles of Non-Formal CE box demonstrates how the leadership through the organizational structure determined the church's purpose ('Mission statement'), which was then worked out through the organization of classes.

---

[418]Politics dominated social life in Cambodia. One direction for future research would be to examine how political forms of communication, indoctrination, and information dissemination are reflected in church life and CE.

Figure 11.2. A model of approaches to non-formal CE among AGC churches

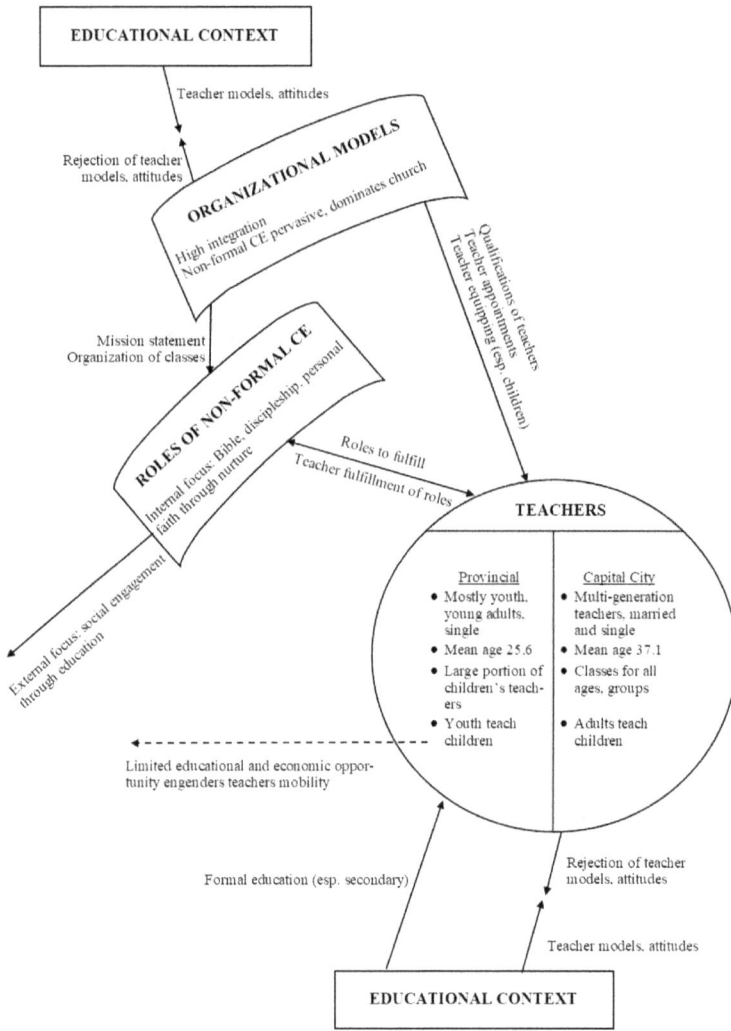

The arrow directed toward the Teachers circle shows how the organizational structure expressed its values through the qualifications, appointment, and equipping of teachers. The qualifications of teachers expressed ideals about Christian life and ministry that the church wanted to perpetuate. The process of appointment reaffirmed those values and empowered teachers to carry out their ministry under the authority of church leadership. The approach taken to equipping teachers was motivated by leadership's desire to see teachers become effective in their ministries and to strengthen the level of teaching in their church. Findings 5, 6, and 7 summarize this connection between organizational models and teachers.

Finding 5: The top leadership of the cases in this study were directly responsible to appoint non-formal CE teachers.

Finding 6: Regarding teacher selection, the cases in this study valued genuine personal faith, faithfulness to the church, submission to leadership, and evidence of a gift/love for teaching. Secondary considerations included teaching experience, education levels, and Bible knowledge.

Finding 7: The cases in this study trained children's teachers informally by having new teachers work with experienced teachers and semi-formally by sending teachers to seminars.

The four cases in this study were all proactive in this relationship between organizational model and teachers. They developed their approaches by learning from outside sources, self-evaluation, and making mistakes. Considering the transferability of this descriptive model, churches that are unclear about qualifications, *ad hoc* in appointing teachers, and negligent in training do not negate the validity of the model. Rather, they express a different set of values from those of these cases.

Lastly, one arrow points from the Organizational Models box toward a returning arrow from the Educational Context box. The leadership of the churches in this study had a negative perception of the teacher models and attitudes in government primary and secondary schools. They intentionally rejected those models in favor of a different set of values. I explore this point in the last sub-section with Findings 12 and 12a.

Roles of Non-Formal CE

Findings 2, 3, and 4 are expressed through the Roles of Non-Formal CE box. The continuum of roles examined by this study ranged from internal (focused entirely on people within the church) to mixed (focused on people outside the church for their benefit and with a view to bringing them into the church) to external (focused on people outside the church for their benefit without regard to affiliation with the church). The focus of non-formal CE in the cases in this study was primary internal. Typical for Pentecostal congregations, the Bible was the authority and primary source of lessons. Discipleship then flowed from that Bible-focus through application to daily living. This emphasis on practical faith was critically important to both the leaders and teachers in this study.

Finding 2: The non-formal CE of the cases in this study had a strong internal focus that emphasized Bible knowledge, discipleship, and personal faith through nurture.

Personal faith through nurture as a primary role of non-formal CE was one of this study's most critical findings. The emphasis on personal faith meant that individuals could not simply become members by application or physical birth into a Christian family. One overarching role of non-formal CE in the cases was to urge each person to come to their own experience of faith.

The emphasis on personal faith through nurture as opposed to crisis conversions was a clear difference with the early Sunday school movement and with my own experience as a Pentecostal. Somehow, without altar calls in Sunday services and teachers inviting students to *tvay kluon* ("give themselves" to Jesus) in class, people nonetheless were coming to personal faith. Their experience of personal faith was validated through public testimony, faithful participation in church life, and water baptism.

The non-formal CE of the cases had external foci as well, with education being one of their key means of engaging the surrounding community. They accomplished this role through formal education in the form of pre-schools, Christian grade schools, and youth outreach offering supplemental education. They also accomplished it through lessons on health, hygiene, civic morals, family dynamics, and agricultural development. Some of these efforts were mixed (for the benefit and evangelism of the community), while others were purely for the benefit of the community in the name of Jesus. All the churches engaged in some kind of external CE efforts; but the provincial churches had a stronger level of social engagement than the capital city churches, especially through their village cell groups.

Finding 3: The cases in this study used education as one of their primary means of social engagement.

Finding 4: The provincial cases in this study had a stronger level of social engagement through non-formal CE than the capital city cases.

Non-Formal CE Teachers

Findings 5, 6, and 7 have already been included above as a point of interaction between teachers and organizational models. Passing over Findings 8 and 8a for the moment, I now turn to the circle labeled Teachers in Figure 11.2. That circle includes four general differences between teachers in provincial and capital city cases; the dynamics undergirding these differences are expressed in Findings 9 and 10.

Finding 9: Educational and economic opportunities affected the availability and longevity of non-formal CE teachers.

Finding 10: Children's ministry was a function of the youth ministries in the provincial cases.

The arrow pointing away from the provincial teachers is dashed because it indicates general conditions that affected the availability and longevity of teachers—namely, educational and economic opportunities. Limited opportunities meant that youth must leave the community for higher education and/or employment. At the same time, the youth brought an energy and enjoyment of teaching children that seemingly was lacking in the older generations. Feeling their way through this dynamic, both provincial churches made teaching children's classes one of the main functions of their youth ministries. As a result, children's classes comprised a significant portion of their non-formal CE activity. Adult classes received much less attention, being designed more to provide fellowship or respond to felt needs. By contrast, the capital city churches had teachers from across the generations and regular classes for all ages and groups. They also had fewer opportunities for youth to begin serving through teaching.

Reflecting on the Educational Context

Figure 11.1 depicts the educational context as encircling the other three nested levels of this model. Figure 11.2 shows that the organizational models and teachers interacted with the educational context in two different ways. The arrow coming up from the Educational Context box toward Teachers circle shows that the educational context provided teachers with their formal education. Using secondary education completion as a benchmark, Finding 11 notes that the teachers' overall education level in all the cases was relatively high.

Finding 11: The education level of all teachers across the cases was high compared to national statistics. At least 70 percent of teachers had completed or were in the process of completing secondary education.

Findings 12 and 12a are expressed in two locations in Figure 11.2. The opposing arrows between the Educational Context and the Organizational Models boxes at the top and the Teachers circle at the bottom show that the leaders and teachers had negative perspectives of what they considered to be common teacher models and attitudes in the government education system at the primary and secondary levels. Their rejection of those norms was intentional and thoughtful.

> ***Finding 12:*** The focus groups rejected the norms for teacher attitudes and teacher-student relationships that they perceived in the national school system as unacceptable for teaching in the church.
>
> ***Finding 12a:*** They rejected aspects of the national school system that they perceived as harsh, authoritarian, and de-humanizing in favor of a holistic approach to non-formal CE that is characterized by warm, encouraging relationships between teachers and students.

Lastly, Findings 8 and 8a were formulated from the perspectives of the teachers and the focus groups regarding ideal teacher models. Perspectives of the educational context were the final section of the focus group protocol. In contrast, the teacher models were explored with research participants without direct reference to educational context. Even so, they express values that run contrary to the common formal educational experiences of the people in these churches (Finding 12a). I have placed them at the end of this explanation of the model because they draw the entire model together around the teachers.

> ***Finding 8:*** The teachers and leaders in the cases valued teacher models that emphasized teacher competency and responsibility, student growth and success, and caring relationships between teachers and students.
>
> ***Finding 8a:*** They rejected teacher models that emphasized knowledge transmission without attention to student development and that depicted unrealistic teacher involvement in the lives of students.

Teachers are the main force of non-formal CE in any context. They carry out the church's mission in tangible ways and embody the values of Christian life and thought that their church wants to cultivate and pass on. The cases in this study valued teachers who felt teaching to be an important responsibility that required competency and knowledge. In other words, teachers had to have something to share with their students. They rejected mechanical transmission of knowledge and skills as being inadequate for teaching in the church because it engaged the head and the hands while leaving the heart (spiritual and moral character) untouched. Although often imperfectly realized, their ideal CE teachers loved to teach, loved their students, and felt the weight of responsibility to share the Word of God in such a way that students' lives were transformed, bringing them to maturity in the faith, ready to serve according to God's plan for them.

CHAPTER 12
Conclusion and Recommendations

Although the Church in Cambodia has experienced remarkable numerical and organizational growth since the early 1990s, many local congregations have yet to develop sustained approaches to non-formal Christian Education and basic discipleship. If Cambodian churches are going to develop effective and culturally appropriate approaches to the ministry of teaching, the conditions behind this dynamic need to be understood. This research took a cutting-edge step towards identifying and understanding those conditions by studying four churches that have engaged in sustained efforts at non-formal CE.

The central question addressed by this research was—What approaches to non-formal CE have been developed by AGC churches? It sought to address that question with a multiple-case study that worked through six procedural sub-questions. Those sub-questions were designed to explore four aspects of a conceptual framework of non-formal CE that was constructed from the literature review. The four levels of the conceptual framework, organized from most general to most specific to a local congregation, were educational context, roles of non-formal CE, organizational models, and teachers.

This study was interested in describing, exploring, and analyzing approaches to non-formal CE across socioeconomic contexts. The four cases included two churches in provincial locations and two in the capital city. All four were first-generation AGC churches, and all four have engaged in sustained efforts at non-formal CE from the earliest stages of their existence. Chapters 6 and 7 presented each of the cases with an emphasis on their historical development and their distinctive approaches. Chapters 8 through 10 detailed a cross-case analysis of the data and a series of 12 findings that were used to construct the descriptive model that was presented in Chapter 11.

This concluding chapter has four sections. The first discusses the contributions of this study to research on the AGC and to non-formal CE in Cambodia. The second summarizes the findings of the research. The third makes recommendations for the AGC from those findings, both the findings and the recommendations being potentially transferrable to churches at similar levels of development and in similar socioeconomic contexts. The fourth section suggests directions for further research. The chapter concludes with some of my final thoughts as the researcher.

CONTRIBUTIONS OF THE RESEARCH

This study makes contributions in four areas. First, it adds to the growing body of research on the Church in Cambodia. At this stage, a few efforts have been made to study the Cambodian Church in terms of its growth and leadership formation.[419] This effort contributes to those works from the Assemblies of God, specifically addressing an area of neglect in the research on Christianity in Cambodia as a whole—nonformal CE in local churches.

Second, this research contributes to our understanding of nonformal CE among AGC churches. The impetus for this work was a deep concern on the part of church leaders about a lack of discipleship in local churches. The remarkable growth of the Church in Cambodia since its rebirth in the early 1990s has not been accompanied by solid teaching in local churches. Anecdotally, most AGC churches (and a large portion of churches in other fellowships) did not have systematic teaching as part of their church life. Thus, this research sought to learn from four churches in two different socioeconomic contexts that had a measure of success in this vital aspect of church life. As such, these cases did not represent the norm among AGC churches. Rather, they pointed to possible solutions for a critical gap in the development of many local churches in the AGC and in similar socioeconomic situations.

Third, the study offers empirical findings on CE. Jim Wilhoit's warning in 1991 still needs to be heard today—"Christian education is in crisis. It is not healthy and vital; as a discipline, it is bankrupt."[420] He urged Christian educators to engage the social sciences in a serious way by conducting rigorous empirical research.[421] This multiple-case study

---

[419]For example, Hyde, "A Missiological and Critical Study;" Joshua J. Lovelace, *From Seedtime to Harvest: The History of the Assemblies of God of Cambodia*, Pentecost Around the World 5 (Baguio City, Philippines: Asia Pacific Theological Seminary Press, 2019); Gil Sung Suh, "Exploring a Contextualized Leadership Development Model Built on Spiritual Formation for Emerging Christian Leaders in Urban Cambodia" (DIS diss., Fuller Theological Seminary, School of Intercultural Studies, 2017).

[420]Wilhoit, *Christian Education*, 9.

[421]Ibid., 122-129.

represents one effort to do just that from the context of a first-generation church in Asia.

Fourth, this research offers a critical response to the general body of CE literature. Most of the standard literature on CE in English comes from the West. Although these resources deserve credit for working with current educational philosophy and striving to present principles that work across socioeconomic situations and church traditions, nevertheless, their usefulness can be limited for contexts like those found in Cambodia. While being informed by Western CE literature, this research offers a critique in return; and it also suggests additional areas of emphasis for CE in Cambodia. The next two sections provide points of critique and offer suggestions for non-formal CE among AGC churches.

MAIN FINDINGS OF THE RESEARCH

The final section of Chapter 10 presented twelve findings from this multiple-case study (see Table 10.7). The cross-case analysis and findings were organized around the four levels of the conceptual framework (Chapters 2 through 4), which were reordered to reflect the way in which the aspects of non-formal CE interacted with one another. Chapter 11 presented a descriptive model and described the interactions among its main components. This section summarizes the study's main findings following the four levels of the model—organizational models and non-formal CE, roles of non-formal CE, non-formal CE teachers, and the educational context.

Findings Related to Organizational Models and Non-Formal CE

This study was interested in the overall role of teaching in the four cases. How did teaching fit into the church's organizational structure? How did teaching fit into church life? What role did top-level church leaders have in teaching? The Church in the West (i.e., America) in the 20th century developed CE departments led by CE pastors. Over time, CE became one program among many in the church. Consequently, the literature in this research addressed CE organizational structures with the goal of *re-integrating* CE with the rest of church life.

The literature on CE organization mentioned above did not resonate with the cases in this study. None of them had CE departments or treated CE as a program among optional programs offered to church members. Instead, Finding 1 stated that non-formal CE pervaded their church organizational models and played a dominant role in church activities. These dynamics fit Mark Simpson's description of the inner workings of small churches.[422] Over time, the four churches in this study will likely grow in size and sophistication but may not develop the problems addressed in the literature. Instead, they may craft more integrated organizational models that do not separate CE into a distinct department. Regardless of what these four do in the future, this finding is still relevant to other AGC churches that are following them in development.

Findings Related to Roles of Non-Formal CE

Whereas the organizational models of the cases seemed to drive each church's CE activity, an examination of roles sheds light on the direction and purposes of their approaches to non-formal CE. This research found that the CE of the cases was primarily directed toward people who were already part of the church. They emphasized Bible knowledge, discipleship, and personal faith through nurture. The first two points speak of emphases, not quality. The third point is one of the most vital for understanding how people come to faith in Cambodia—namely, the churches sought to help people come to personal faith through nurture as opposed to crisis conversions.

The research found that the four cases had a significant external focus in their approaches to non-formal CE. The data demonstrated that teaching was one of the primary ways that they engaged their communities. Teaching in the community was Bible focused; but it also included practical topics like hygiene, family issues, civic morals (e.g., showing respect to elders), and agricultural development. Three of the cases engaged their communities through formal education in addition to non-formal CE. The results also clearly show that the provincial churches had a stronger level of social engagement through CE than did the capital city cases.

Noticeably, the standard Western literature tends to focus on CE that is directed toward people who are already in the church. However, studies like those of Miller and Yamamori on global Pentecostalism[423] and of Tejedo on Pentecostal social engagement in the Philippines[424] demonstrate that Pentecostal churches see their teaching culture as an effective means of addressing social issues and filling gaps in education

---

[422]Mark Edward Simpson, "Christian Education in the Small Church," in *Introducing Christian Education: Foundations for the Twenty-first Century*, ed. Michael J. Anthony (Grand Rapids: Baker Academic, 2001), 159-166.
[423]Miller and Yamamori, *Global Pentecostalism*.
[424]Tejedo, *The Church*.

and social services. These findings affirm that AGC churches have the potential to contribute to their communities through CE as well.

Findings Related to Non-Formal CE Teachers

The data regarding teachers generated seven of the twelve findings of this research (see Chapters 5 and 6). That data covered the selection and equipping of teachers, ideal teacher models, teacher demographics, the teachers' spiritual life, and the teachers' perspectives about their experiences in teaching. When it came to teacher selection, the cases prioritized personal faith, faithfulness to the church, submission to leadership, and a love/gift for teaching. The top leadership was directly responsible to appoint teachers, which fits with the organizational dynamics described above.

The research also found that the cases were proactive about teacher training, especially for children's teachers. All of them made use of occasional seminars to train their teachers, and all trained children's teachers informally by having new ones work with experienced ones.

One aspect of the research asked teachers and church leaders to evaluate teacher models. Data from across the cases demonstrated that they valued teacher competency and responsibility, a focus on student growth and success, and caring relationships between teachers and students. They rejected teacher models that emphasized mechanical transmission of knowledge and that depicted unrealistic teacher involvement in the lives of students. On this last point, they felt that it was too much to expect teachers to be intimately involved in the lives of their students.

The study also found that educational and economic opportunities impacted availability and longevity of teachers. This finding was clearly supported by the demographic data, which highlighted some key differences between provincial locations and capital city locations. These differences affected teacher mean ages, marital statuses, and long-term potential for teaching. In summary, provincial teachers were mostly single youth and young adults who were still in school. Many of them leave the community to continue their education or pursue employment. In contrast, capital city teachers were multi-generational and included people who were married, single, divorced, and widowed. Most of the provincial CE activity was directed toward children, whereas the CE activities of the capital city churches covered all ages and groups. The mean age of provincial churches was 11.5 years lower than that of the capital city churches (25.6 years and 37.1 years, respectively).

The provincial churches worked with these dynamics by making the children's classes a function of their youth ministries.

Educational levels of the teachers were also of interest in this study. The data revealed that, across all four cases, teachers' education levels were high compared to national statistics for secondary education completion. At least 70 percent had completed or were in the process of completing secondary education, compared to just 6 percent nationwide.[425] This educational attainment was an expression of the value these study churches placed on formal education.

Findings Related to Educational Context

The literature on CE typically draws on the social sciences for educational theory. Since most non-formal teachers are untrained volunteers, well-developed educational systems provide useful benchmarks for teacher-student relationships and teaching methodologies. This research found that the cases rejected as unacceptable for teaching in the church the norms for teacher attitudes and teacher-student relationships that they perceived to be common in the Cambodian national school system. They described teachers in primary and secondary schools as harsh, impersonal in transmitting information and skills, and having little concern for their students' emotional well-being or future success. In contrast, they valued a holistic approach to non-formal CE that is characterized by warm, encouraging relationships between teachers and students.

RECOMMENDATIONS FOR NON-FORMAL CE IN THE AGC

Based on the findings of this research, I would like to offer eight recommendations for non-formal CE among AGC churches. They are listed in Table 12.1 and discussed in the paragraphs that follow. Some of them reflect positive findings from the data, while others speak to areas that could be strengthened. All of them, however, point to areas of transferability for churches with similar dynamics or in similar contexts.

---

[425]National Institute of Statistics, *Cambodia Socio-Economic Survey 2016* (Phnom Penh, Cambodia: Ministry of Planning, October 2017), 48, https://www.nis.gov.kh/index.php/en (accessed November 26, 2018).

Table 12.1. Recommendations for non-formal CE in the AGC

1. CE does not have to be a department in the church.
2. Teaching is a good way to engage the community.
3. Prioritize the personal faith of teachers in the selection process.
4. Make teacher development an ongoing priority.
5. Provide training for all teachers in the church, not just children's teachers.
6. Contextually appropriate curriculum is important.
7. Youth can teach children.
8. Learn from the educational context.

1. ***CE does not have to be a department in the church.*** The literature deals with the departmentalization of CE in the local church because that was a natural progression for churches in the West. As they became more sophisticated, they offered increasingly specialized program choices which had to be maintained by people with increasingly specialized skills. Instead of offering classes like choices for customers, AGC churches can cultivate a culture of learning that embraces the whole church. Cap-2's theme for 2018 expresses this attitude well—"Every believer must be a student of the Word."

2. ***Teaching is a good way to engage the community.*** Cheryl Bridges Johns' description of Pentecostal churches as a "teaching community"[426] fits the data of this research. Teaching is natural to AGC churches. My field notes are full of reflections on how the churches taught through songs, testimonies, exhortations, sermons, ceremonies, and classes. There are many ways that AGC churches can use their love of teaching to help their communities, from literacy to educational support to civic morals.

3. ***Prioritize the personal faith of teachers in the selection process.*** I was surprised that the cases prioritized genuine

---

[426] Johns, *Pentecostal Formation*, 124.

personal faith over biblical literacy in the selection of teachers. This choice was more than a pragmatic one made by a first-generation church. Indeed, it was the opposite of looking for 'warm bodies' to teach. They knew that vibrant, personal faith and a love for teaching would naturally be accompanied by a desire to know the Bible more; and they knew that the teachers would share that faith and interest in the Scriptures with their students. Teachers cannot pass on what they do not possess. Personal faith is of vital importance.

4. ***Make teacher development an ongoing priority.*** Most teachers in the cases had been teaching for less than three years. If this is true for other churches, then AGC churches can expect a lot of teacher turnover. Therefore, these churches need to provide some level of ongoing training and look for training opportunities (e.g., seminars, workshops) on a regular basis. One excellent approach used by the study cases is to send teachers for training for a specific curriculum. Some of the best teachers I observed gained their skills from curriculum workshops. Assigning new teachers to work with experienced teachers is good *if* the experienced teachers are skillful. The corollary to the statement in the previous paragraph is that teachers will pass on what they possess—i.e., poor teaching skills and incorrect doctrine can be passed on as well.

5. ***Provide training for all teachers in the church, not just children's teachers.*** When we talk about teacher training, the discussion easily gravitates towards children's teachers to the neglect of youth and adult teachers. The teachers of these latter two groups are typically untrained volunteers as well. Thus, training for all teachers should focus on an accessible philosophy of the ministry of teaching, basic teaching skills appropriate to the group they teach, the teachers' spiritual life (spiritual disciplines), and biblical literacy.

6. ***Contextually appropriate curriculum is important.*** Many teachers in this study had difficulty understanding, preparing, and explaining lessons. Perhaps some of them should not be teaching, but others just needed curriculum that was more context-appropriate. The teachers observed in this study who had curriculum with which they felt comfortable were more confident in their teaching and more effective in connecting

their students to the Bible. In contrast, the teachers I observed who created their own lessons, taught from material not designed for CE classes, or taught the stories from a children's Bible tended to be unclear on the main point of the lessons and were less effective at connecting the biblical text to daily life.

Notice that I have chosen the words 'contextually appropriate,' not 'contextualized.' Contextualized curriculum implies using cultural forms, such as artwork and story-telling techniques. What I am recommending is something more mundane. Contextually appropriate curriculum is easy for teachers to understand as they prepare and natural to use as they engage their students. While it may feel strange at first for untrained volunteers, they will find the curriculum enjoyable, and their own faith grows as they use it.

7. *Youth can teach children.* With proper supervision, youth can be very effective as children's teachers. Many of the young teachers in this study seemed to have passion, energy, and mental agility that was not evident in the older generations. Many said they loved teaching children and had experienced a lot of growth in their faith as they prepared their lessons, prayed for their students, and tried to "live so that my life teaches." The provincial churches in this study made teaching children one of the main functions of their youth ministries. The stability of the city churches made it more difficult to connect the youth ministry and the children's classes in this way; but the youth can still make a good contribution to children's classes and grow in their faith as they do it.

8. *Learn from the educational context.* The churches in this study benefited from the educational context by evaluating what they perceived to be negative practices. On the other hand, the educational milieu may provide good pedagogical principles and models for teacher-student relationships that are true to biblical ideals, make sense culturally, and fit the church's style. AGC churches can learn from good models in all levels of formal education, in adult education programs, and in the educational approaches of other Christian traditions.

DIRECTIONS FOR FURTHER RESEARCH

One of the challenges of exploratory research is choosing what lines of inquiry to pursue and what to hold in suspension for another time. This particular study generated many tantalizing questions in my mind. In this section, I want to share six of those directions for future research.

1. *Non-formal CE among other groups in Cambodia.* The four AGC churches in this study are Pentecostal, a worldwide movement that is nationalistic and congregational in orientation. It is nationalistic in the sense that the Assemblies of God in each country constitutes a sovereign entity. It is congregational in the sense that each congregation (at least in Cambodia and the United States) has the right and is expected to formulate its own approach to CE. What would a study like this reveal about other groups in Cambodia? The possible cases would include independent fellowships led by a strong Cambodian, churches that are part of trans-national denominations (e.g., the Methodist Church in Cambodia), and churches that have a strong identification with the culture or tradition of the founding missionary or organization.

2. *CE in the organizational models of larger churches in Cambodia and throughout Asia.* The churches in this study, while among the largest AGC churches, are nevertheless small compared to many other churches in Asia. It would be valuable to see how the data from this study would compare to the few churches in Cambodia that have reached 500 members, as well as other large Pentecostal churches in Asia in comparable socioeconomic situations. What is the role of CE in their overall organizational structures? Did they develop CE departments like Western churches began to do in the 20th century?

3. *Conditions that hinder churches from making teaching part of regular church life.* This direction for further research comes to the real-life problem that prompted this particular study—Why have so many churches failed to engage in sustained efforts at CE or even basic discipleship despite conditions that should have facilitated CE development? The descriptive model constructed from the findings here can be used as a grid for research into the cultural or socioeconomic

dynamics that are hindering churches from developing a consistent, systematic approach to CE or discipleship. Understanding those dynamics can lead to creation of training and resources to help local churches develop effective, contextual approaches to non-formal CE.

4. *Conversion as a process.* One clear impression of this research is that people in the cases were coming to personal faith in Christ through a process rather than a crisis. The emphasis on nurture that leads to personal faith demonstrated that the leaders and teachers seemed to understand this instinctively. As AGC churches mature into second and third generations, they may become less aware of the process that brought them to faith. Thus, studying this process among church members could help the AGC in the future and provide insight for similar socioeconomic contexts. It would also add an Asian voice to a larger discussion of conversion.

5. *Testimonies as a form of teaching.* I was fascinated by the prominent role of testimonies in the four cases. The formal religion in Cambodia is Buddhism and its practice is animistic, which is fueled by 'testimonies.' For instance, when people hear that the lick of a certain cow cures diseases or that a certain fortune teller is more accurate than others, they believe and act on that belief because Cambodians are pragmatic about religion. Testimonies in the church say that Christian faith works and that God answers prayer. These are a powerful means of informal education. I also noticed that they provided a way for the older generations to speak. The function of testimonies in AGC churches is fertile ground for research.

6. *How teachers model spirituality.* Some of the teachers in the classes I observed were very effective at modeling spirituality for their students. I saw how they shared their love for the Bible, taught their students to pray, and invited them to connect the truths of Scripture to daily life. In the West, primary and secondary school teachers are expected to be

models for their students in their dress and demeanor.[427] The same is true for CE, whether teachers do so intentionally or not. Research into the ways in which AGC teachers model spirituality could add an Asian perspective on this vital aspect of CE.

FINAL THOUGHTS

Teaching is one of the most basic functions of the church. As a Pentecostal denomination, the Assemblies of God has a high view of Scripture and a high expectation that God still speaks through his Word today. As 'people of the Book,' Pentecostals read the Bible, listen to the Bible, sing passages from the Bible, study the Bible, and call the Bible their daily spiritual food. I have met Christians in Cambodia who testified that God miraculously enabled them to read better after they became believers. Since most Cambodians do not have a regular habit of reading, these new believers began to read the Bible as they responded to a natural, spiritual hunger for its truths—and their reading skills naturally improved.

I do not mean to take away from their testimonies; but rather I am returning to the impetus for this research. AGC churches are Bible-centered, and they are full of first-generation Christians who are naturally interested in the Bible. I began this journey asking how the church growth I have witnessed among the AGC could be accompanied by what appears to be feeble growth in the ministry of teaching. I still do not know the answer to that question, but now I know some paths of inquiry by which I can discover conditions that are hindering the growth of this essential aspect of church life.

I owe a great debt to the four churches that participated in this research. Like a friendly teacher, they welcomed me into their classrooms and taught me many things. They have cultivated a culture of teaching to strengthen the faith of their people and to help their communities. I hope that other churches in our fellowship can learn that culture of teaching from them as well.

---

[427]Harry K. Wong and Rosemary T. Wong, *The First Days of School: How to be an Effective Teacher* (Mountain View, CA: Harry K. Wong Publications, 2009), 50-58.

REFERENCES CITED

Anthony, Michael J., ed. *Evangelical Dictionary of Christian Education*. Grand Rapids: Baker Academic, 2001.

_____, ed. *Foundations of Ministry: An Introduction to Christian Education for a New Generation*. Grand Rapids: Baker Books, 1992.

_____, ed. *Introducing Christian Education: Foundations for the Twenty-first Century*. Grand Rapids: Baker Academic, 2001.

_____, and Warren S. Benson. *Exploring the History and Philosophy of Christian Education: Principles for the 21st Century*. Grand Rapids: Kregel, 2003.

Ayres, David M. *Anatomy of a Crisis: Education, Development, and the State in Cambodia, 1953–1998*. Southeast Asian edition. Chiang Mai, Thailand: Silkworm Books, 2003.

Bechtle, Michael A., "Organizational Structures for Christian Education." In *Foundations of Ministry: An Introduction to Christian Education for a New Generation*, edited by Michael J. Anthony, 213-228. Grand Rapids: Baker Books, 1992.

_____. "The Roles and Responsibilities of Christian Education Personnel." In *Foundations of Ministry: An Introduction to Christian Education for a New Generation*, edited by Michael J. Anthony, 229-241. Grand Rapids: Baker Books, 1992.

Benveniste, Luis, Jeffery Marshall, and M. Caridad Araujo. *Teaching in Cambodia*. Washington, DC: World Bank, 2008. datatopics.worldbank.org/hnp/files/ edstats/ KHMwp08.pdf (accessed October 29, 2015).

Bible Society in Cambodia. http://biblecambodia.org (accessed December 4, 2015).

Blackwood, Vernon L. "Freire, Paulo." In *Evangelical Dictionary of Christian Education*, edited by Michael J. Anthony, 302-303. Grand Rapids: Baker Academic, 2001.

Bloomberg, Linda Dale and Marie Volpe. *Completing Your Qualitative Dissertation: A Road Map from Beginning to End*, 2nd ed. Los Angeles: SAGE Publications, 2012.

Boylan, Anne M. *Sunday School: The Formation of an American Institution, 1790-1880*. New Haven, CT: Yale University Press, 1988.

Bushnell, Horace. *Christian Nurture*. New York: Scribner, Armstrong & Co., 1876. Christian Classics Ethereal Library. https://www.ccel.org/ccel/ bushnell/nurture.html (accessed January 28, 2017).

Cannister, Mark W. "Organizational Models of Christian Education." In *Introducing Christian Education: Foundations for the Twenty-first Century*, edited by Michael J. Anthony, 149-158. Grand Rapids: Baker Academic, 2001.

Catholic Cambodia, "Church's History." http://catholiccambodia.org/eng/community-history (accessed December 4, 2014).

Central Intelligence Agency. "Cambodia." The World Factbook. https://www.cia.gov/library/publications/the-world-factbook/geos/cb.html (accessed December 13, 2016).

Chandler, David. *A History of Cambodia*, 4th ed. Southeast Asian edition. Chiang Mai, Thailand: Silkworm Books, 2008.

Choun, Robert J. "Bushnell, Horace." In *Evangelical Dictionary of Christian Education*, edited by Michael J. Anthony, 101-102. Grand Rapids: Baker Academic, 2001.

Christian Broadcasting Network. *Seavpov vises: merean kromchumnum* [Superbook: church edition], Khmer version. Phnom Penh, Cambodia: Christian Broadcasting Network, 2014.

Clements, Darin R. "The Church Reborn out of the Killings Fields: A Preliminary Sketch of the Pentecostal/Charismatic Movement in Cambodia." Paper presented at the Theological Symposium of the Asia Pacific Theological Association, Yangon, Myanmar, July 26-27, 2016.

Clements, Darin R., Ken Huff, and Nyotxay, "The Development of Pentecostalism in Cambodia and Laos." In *Asia Pacific Pentecostalism*, edited by Denise A. Austin, Jacqueline Grey, and Paul Lewis, 129-149. The Netherlands: Brill, 2019.

Cormack, Don. *Killing Fields, Living Fields: An Unfinished Portrait of the Cambodian Church—The Church that Would Not Die*. Crowborough, England: OMF International, 1997.

Creswell, John W. *Educational Research: Planning, Conducting, and Evaluating Quantitative and Qualitative Research*, 4th ed. Boston: Pearson Education, 2014.

De Guzman, Sylvia. *Cambodia: Summary Report: The Impact of Informal School Fees*. Asia-South Pacific Bureau of Adult Education, 2007. ERIC database, a/n ED533596 (accessed June 9, 2015).

Del Rosario, Sur, Glenn Howard Lucas, and Lawrence Romero. *Khachumrunh dowy chetana, pheak thi muoy: khaskoal angh preah khrist* [Intentional Moves, part 1: Know Christ], rev. Khmer ed. Phnom Penh, Cambodia: Cambodia School of Missions, n.d.

———. *Khachumrunh dowy chetana, pheak thi pi: khathomthoat khnong angh preah khrist* [Intentional Moves, part 2: Grow in Christ], rev. Khmer ed. Phnom Penh, Cambodia: Cambodia School of Missions, n.d.

———. *Khachumrunh dowy chetana, pheak thi bai: khabamrar angh preah khrist* [Intentional Moves, part 3: Serve Christ], rev. Khmer ed. Phnom Penh, Cambodia: Cambodia School of Missions, n.d.

Dettoni, John M. "What Is Spiritual Formation?" In *The Christian Educator's Handbook on Spiritual Formation,* edited by Kenneth O. Gangel and James C. Wilhoit, 11-20. Grand Rapids: Baker Books, 1994.

Dorsey, Carolyn. "Information Regarding the Founding of the Assemblies of God Work in Cambodia." Unpublished manuscript, May 2005.

Dy, Sideth S. "Strategies and Policies for Basic Education in Cambodia: Historical Perspectives." *International Education Journal* 5, no. 1 (2004): 90-97. http://www.iefcomparative.org (accessed April 30, 2015).

Estep, James R., Jr., Michael J. Anthony, and Gregg R. Allison. *A Theology for Christian Education*. Nashville: B & H Publishing, 2008.

Estrebilla, Rowena S., Phun Thurain, and Voeun Rotha. *Khmeng somnop* [Beloved Child]. Takeo Province, Cambodia: Partners Against Poverty (Western Australia), 2016.

Fetterman, David M. *Ethnography: Step-by-Step*, 3rd ed. Applied Social Research Methods Series, vol. 17, edited by Leonard Bickman and Debra J. Rog. Los Angeles: SAGE Publications, 2010.

Freire, Paulo. *Pedagogy of the Oppressed*, 30th anniversary ed. Translated by Myra Bergman Ramos. Introduction by Donaldo Macedo. New York: Continuum, 2005.

Garland, Kenneth R. "Organizing Christian Education in the Small Church." In *Foundations of Ministry: An Introduction to Christian Education for a New Generation*, edited by Michael J. Anthony, 242-254. Grand Rapids: Baker Books, 1992.

Gregory, John Milton. *The Seven Laws of Teaching*. Boston: Congregational Sunday-School and Publishing Society, 1886. Printed by ReadaClassic.com, San Bernardino, CA, 12 December 2015.

Hastings, Lachlan. "Vanquished in the 70s, Catholic Church Still on the Mend." *The Phnom Penh Post*, March 25, 2005. http://www.

phnompenh post.com/ national/vanquished-70s-catholic-still-mend (accessed January 2, 2017).

Hendricks, Howard. *Teaching to Change Lives: Seven Proven Ways to Make Your Teaching Come Alive*. Colorado Springs: Multnomah Books, 1987.

Hoey, Brian A. "A Simple Introduction to the Practice of Ethnography and Guide to Ethnographic Fieldnotes." *Marshall University Digital Scholar*, June 2014. http://works.bepress.com/brian_hoey/12 (accessed December 2, 2017).

Houger, Barbara Rose. "Instructors' Pedagogies as the Frame of Influence for East Asian Assemblies of God Bible Schools." PhD diss., Biola University, 2011.

Hyde, Steven. "History of the Church in Cambodia." Unpublished work. Phnom Penh, Cambodia, November 2014.

_____. "A Missiological and Critical Study of Cambodia's Historical, Cultural, and Sociopolitical Characteristics to Identify the Factors of Rapid Church Growth and Propose its Future Prognosis." PhD diss., Bethany International University, Singapore, 2015.

_____. "Portrait of the Body of Christ in Cambodia." Phnom Penh, Cambodia: Words of Life Ministries, 2012.

Jaccard, James and Jacob Jacoby. *Theory Construction and Model-Building Skills*. New York: The Guilford Press, 2010.

Johns, Cheryl Bridges. *Pentecostal Formation: A Pedagogy among the Oppressed*. Eugene, OR: Whipf and Stock, 1998.

Joshua Project. "Cambodia." http://joshuaproject.net/countries/ CB (accessed January 7, 2017).

Keng, Chansopheak. "Household Determinants of School Progression among Rural Children in Cambodia." *International Education Journal* 5, no. 4 (2004): 552-561. http://www.iefcomparative.org (accessed April 19, 2015).

Kennedy, William B. "Conversation with Paulo Freire." *Religious Education* 79, no. 4 (Fall 1984): 511-522. EBSCOhost, ATLA Religion Database (accessed September 7, 2016).

Kim, Heeja. "Korean Christian Education: Past, Present, and Future." In "International Perspectives on Christian Education." Supplemental issue, *Christian Education Journal* 10, S3 (Fall 2013): S219-S232. http://journals.biola.edu/ns/cej/ (accessed June 25, 2015).

Knight, Peter T. *Small-scale Research: Pragmatic Inquiry in Social Science and the Caring Professions*. London: SAGE Publications, 2002.

Lawson, Michael S., and Robert J. Choun, Jr. *Directing Christian Education: The Changing Role of the Christian Education Specialist.* Chicago: Moody Press, 1992.

LeCompte, Margaret D., and Jean J. Schensul. *Designing and Conducting Ethnographic Research: An Introduction,* 2nd ed. Ethnographer's Toolkit, book 1, edited by Jean J. Schensul and Margaret D. LeCompte. Lanham, MD: AltaMira Press, 2010.

LeFever, Marlene. *Learning Styles: Reaching Everyone God Gave You.* Colorado Springs: David C Cook, 2004.

Lie, Tan Giok. "The Context and Challenges of the Church's Educational Ministry in Indonesia." In "International Perspectives on Christian Education." Supplemental issue, *Christian Education Journal* 10, S3 (Fall 2013): S233-S241. http://journals.biola.edu/ns/cej/ (accessed June 25, 2015).

Lingenfelter, Judith, and Sherwood G. Lingenfelter. *Teaching Cross-Culturally: An Incarnational Model for Learning and Teaching.* Grand Rapids: Baker Academic, 2003.

Lovelace, Joshua J. *From Seedtime to Harvest: The History of the Assemblies of God in Cambodia.* Pentecost Around the World 5. Baguio City, Philippines: Asia Pacific Theological Seminary Press, 2019.

Maher, Brian. "Cambodian Church History." Cambodian Christian. http://www.cambodian christian.com/church_history (accessed April 30, 2014).

Maher, Brian, and Seila Uon. *Cry of the Gecko: History of the Christian Mission in Cambodia.* Centralia, WA: Gorham Printing, 2012.

Mam, Barnabas. *Church behind the Wire.* Chicago: Moody Publishers, 2012.

Miles, Matthew B., and A. Michael Huberman. *Qualitative Data Analysis,* 2nd ed. Thousand Oaks, CA: SAGE, 1994.

Miller, Donald E. and Tetsunao Yamamori. *Global Pentecostalism: The New Face of Christian Social Engagement.* Berkeley: University of California Press, 2007.

Ministry of Economy and Finance. "Public Holidays in Cambodia for the Year 2015." http://www.mef.gov.kh/public-holiday.html (accessed August 5, 2015).

Mitchell, Russ. "The Top 20 Countries where Christianity is Growing the Fastest." Disciple All Nations. August 25, 2013. https://discipleallnations.word press.com/2013/08/25/the-top-20-countries-where-christianity-is-growing-the-fastest/ (accessed January 27, 2017).

National Institute of Statistics. *Cambodia Socio-Economic Survey 2016*. Phnom Penh, Cambodia: Ministry of Planning, October 2017. https://www.nis.gov.kh/index.php/en/ (accessed November 26, 2018).

Newton, Gary C. "Nonformal Education." In *Evangelical Dictionary of Christian Education*. Edited by Michael J. Anthony, 505-506. Grand Rapids: Baker Academic, 2001.

———. "Sunday School, Early Origins." In *Evangelical Dictionary of Christian Education*. Edited by Michael J. Anthony, 672-673. Grand Rapids: Baker Academic, 2001.

Philippines General Council of the Assemblies of God, The. *Intentional Moves Training Manual*. ICI Ministries: The Philippines, 2015. http://www.iciphilippines.org/wp-content/uploads/2015/01/IM-manual-Empowered-Local-Churches.pdf (accessed June 6, 2018).

Ponchaud, François. *The Cathedral in the Rice Paddy: The 450 Year Long History of the Church in Cambodia,* 2nd ed. Phnom Penh, Cambodia: Catholic Catechetical Center Cambodia (CCCC), 2012.

Prasertsri, Supote. *Rebirth of the Learning Tradition: A Case Study on the Achievements of Education for All in Cambodia*. Paris: United Nations Educational, Scientific, and Cultural Organization, 1996. ERIC database, a/n ED433269 (accessed June 9, 2015).

Reed, James E., and Ronnie Prevost. *A History of Christian Education*. Nashville: Broadman and Holman, 1993.

Richards, Lawrence O., and Gary J. Bredfeldt. *Creative Bible Teaching*, 2nd ed. Chicago: Moody Press, 1998.

Rubottom, Verda. *First Steps for Effective Teaching: A Guide for Christian Educators*. N.p.: Xulon Press, 2012.

Samaritan's Purse. *Domnar chivit da l'ah bomphot* [The Greatest Journey], Khmer version. Phnom Penh, Cambodia: Samaritan's Purse, 2017.

Simpson, Mark Edward. "Christian Education in the Small Church." In *Introducing Christian Education: Foundations for the Twenty-first Century*, edited by Michael J. Anthony, 159-166. Grand Rapids: Baker Academic, 2001.

Smith, Christian, and Melinda Lundquist Denton. *Soul Searching: The Religious and Spiritual Lives of American Teenagers*. Oxford: Oxford University Press, 2005.

Snowman, Jack, Rick McCown, and Robert Biehler. *Psychology Applied to Teaching*, 12th ed. Boston: Houghton Mifflin, 2009.

Stake, Robert E. "Case Studies." In *Handbook of Qualitative Research*, 2nd ed., edited by Norman K. Denzin and Yvonna S. Lincoln, 435-454. Thousand Oaks, CA: SAGE Publications, 2000.

Statement of Faith of the Assemblies of God of Cambodia, Khmer language, rev. Phnom Penh, Cambodia: Assemblies of God of Cambodia, 2011.

Stonehouse, Catherine, and Scottie May. *Listening to Children on the Spiritual Journey: Guidance for Those Who Teach and Nurture*. Grand Rapids: Baker Academic, 2010.

Suh, Gil Sung. "Exploring a Contextualized Leadership Development Model Built on Spiritual Formation for Emerging Christian Leaders in Urban Cambodia." DIS diss., Fuller Theological Seminary, School of Intercultural Studies, 2017.

Tandon, Prateek and Tsuyoshi Fukao. *Educating the Next Generation: Improving Teacher Quality in Cambodia*. Directions in Development: Human Development. Washington, D.C.: World Bank, 2015. http://dx.doi.10.1596/978-1-4648-0417-5 (accessed June 9, 2015).

Tejedo, Joel A. *The Church in the Public Square: Engaging our Christian Witness in the Community*. Baguio City, Philippines: Sambayahanihan Publishers, 2016.

Towns, Elmer L. *What Every Sunday School Teacher Should Know: 24 Secrets that Can Help You Change Lives.* Ventura, CA: Gospel Light, 2001.

Turabian, Kate L. *A Manual for Writers of Term Papers, Theses, and Dissertations*, 8th ed. Chicago: University of Chicago Press, 2007.

Tyler, Ralph W. *Basic Principles of Curriculum and Instruction.* Chicago: University of Chicago, 1949.

Uon, Seila. "Seila Uon's Story," *Mission in Cambodia*. https://www.youtube.com/watch?v=T92qw_LWU04 (accessed August 7, 2017).

Wilhoit, James C. *Christian Education and the Search for Meaning*. 2nd ed. Grand Rapids: Baker Book House, 1991.

Williams, Dennis E. "Christian Education." In *Evangelical Dictionary of Christian Education*. Edited by Michael J. Anthony, 132-134. Grand Rapids: Baker Academic, 2001.

Willis, Wesley R. *200 Years—and Still Counting! Past, Present, and Future of the Sunday School*. Wheaton, IL: SP Publications, 1979.

Wong, Harry K., and Rosemary T. Wong. *The First Days of School: How to be an Effective Teacher*. Mountain View, CA: Harry K. Wong Publications, 2009.

Yin, Robert K. *Case Study Research: Design and Methods*, 4th ed. Applied Social Research Methods Series, vol. 5, edited by Leonard Bickman and Debra J. Rog. Los Angeles: SAGE Publications, 2009.

Yount, William R. *Created to Learn: A Christian Teacher's Introduction to Educational Psychology*, 2nd ed. Nashville: B&H Academic, 2010.

⸻. "Learning Theory for Christian Teachers." In *Introducing Christian Education: Foundations for the Twenty-first Century*, edited by Michael J. Anthony, 101-110. Grand Rapids: Baker Academic, 2001.

APPENDIX A

CASE BACKGROUND QUESTIONNAIRE

Church name and location: _____
Pastor's Name: _____
Date: _____

Thank you for spending your valuable the time to fill out this questionnaire. Please answer as many questions as you can. If you do not have the answers to some questions, please let me know who can provide the information. I will set a time to talk with you about this questionnaire and to ask additional questions. God bless you.

1. Origins of the congregation
   a. What year was your church founded?
   b. Who founded your church? If a missionary was involved, what was their nationality and agency?
   c. What was one major political or historical event the year your church was founded?
   d. What other churches were founded about the same time as your church?
   e. Was your church planted by a mother church? If so, which church?
   f. Was your church planted as part of or along with another kind of work or ministry? If so, what was that work or ministry? (i.e., community development work, health center, school project, etc.)
   g. Do you have an historical record of the founding of your church? If so, what kind of records do you have? (i.e., written records, photographs, etc.)

2. Development of your church
   a. Has your church changed pastors from the founding pastor? If so, please give the year, names of the pastors, and reasons for the changes.
   b. What was the original vision of the church? Has it changed from that original vision? If so, what is the new vision? What were the reasons for the change?
   c. Please describe major stages or changes in your church since its founding.

3. Facilities
   a. Where did your church meet at first, that is, before having a building?
   b. Does your church rent or own the facilities? If owned, is it owned by an individual, the congregation, or another entity?
   c. If the property was purchased, when was it purchased and what was the source of the funds?
   d. Who built the original buildings and what was the source of the funds?
   e. What is the current size of the church property?
   f. Please describe additional major construction projects after the initial construction with the years and the source of funding for each.
   g. Please write a summary description of your facilities in terms of buildings and rooms.
   h. Which rooms do you use for CE? What spaces are only or mostly used for CE?
   i. Does your church have air conditioners? If so, which rooms and buildings have air conditioners?

4. Congregation statistics
   a. What type of records of attendance and membership does the church have?
   b. What is the regular attendance for Sunday services? Please give the breakdown of adults and children if you have it.
   c. Does your church have formal membership? If so, how many members does your church have?

5. Church finances
   a. What is the monthly budget/expenses of the church?
      i. Less than $50
      ii. $50-$100
      iii. $101-$200
      iv. $301-$500
      v. $501-$1,000
      vi. More than $1,000
   b. What portion of the monthly budget/expenses is used for CE? (Do not include utilities.)
      i. If you have a preschool or other formal education programs, please list that separately.

6. Personal information about the pastor
   a. Age
   b. Gender
   c. Are you originally from a city or a village?
   d. How many brothers and sisters do you have?
   e. What were the professions, jobs, or work of your father and your mother? Or, what was your family's main source of income?
   f. How long have you been married?
   g. What is the vocation, job, or work of your spouse?
   h. How many children do you have? Please list the age and education level of each one.
   i. How many of your children are married?
   j. How many grandchildren do you have?
   k. Please describe your education
      i. Elementary school
      ii. Secondary school
      iii. University
      iv. Ministerial training
      v. Professional training
      vi. Other training
   l. What vocational experience do you have outside of pastoral ministry?
   m. How much time do you spend in pastoral work each week? (Choose one answer.)
      i. Full-time
      ii. Part-time with additional job or source of income
         - What is your other work? How many hours a week are you involved in that work?
      iii. Fulfills pastoral work in spare time
         - What is your main work or source of income?
   n. What support do you receive from your church?
      i. Full-time
      ii. Part-time
      iii. Some (more than gas money, but not enough to live on)
      iv. Minimal (i.e., gas money)
      v. None

7. Philosophy of the church
   a. What is your church's purpose statement or vision statement? If you do not have one, please describe your church's core philosophy?

b. Does your church have a constitution? If so, please provide me with a copy.
c. Does your church have formal plans and goals (i.e., a five-year plan)? If so, please describe your plan or make a copy for me.
d. How would you characterize the personality of your church?
e. How does your church's approach to CE express the vision statement or the core philosophy written above?

APPENDIX B

APPROACH TO CE QUESTIONNAIRE

Church name and location: _____
Pastor's name: _____
Name of person answering if different from the pastor:
_____

Date: _____

Thank you for spending your valuable time to fill out this questionnaire. Please answer as many questions as you can. If you do not have the answers to some questions, please let me know who can provide the information. I will set a time to talk with you about this questionnaire and to ask additional questions. God bless you.

Organizational Structure

1. Please describe the organizational structure of your church. What are the positions and responsibilities? If you already have charts or documents, please provide me with a copy.
2. Which people are the key leaders in your organizational structure?
3. How long has this organizational structure been in place? What was the main influence in developing this organizational structure?
4. Did you use a different organizational structure before? If so, what is different? Why did you make those changes?
5. What is the process for people to come into positions in your organizational structure? Who makes the appointments or decisions?
6. What are the qualifications for leaders in your church? If you have documents that list the qualifications, please provide me with a copy.
7. Are there family relationships between individuals in your organizational structure? If so, please describe who is related to whom.
8. How does CE fit into your organizational structure? Or, do you have a separate organizational structure for CE?
9. If you have a separate organizational structure for CE, please describe it for me with positions and responsibilities. If you already have charts or documents, please provide me with a copy.
10. Please make a list of the CE classes in your church.
    a. What is the reason for organizing classes in this way?

b. Please fill out the information about each class at the end of this questionnaire.
11. How long have you been using this approach to organizing classes/groups of students?
12. Is this approach different from before? If so, how is this approach different from what you were doing before? Why did you make those changes?
13. Do you keep records of class attendance and some personal student information? If so, how do you keep that information? What do you do with that information?

Philosophy and Roles of CE

1. What is the main purpose of CE in your church? If you have a written statement, please provide me with a copy.
2. Thinking in general, which sentence is the best description of the role of teaching/CE in your church? Please explain why you chose that sentence.
   a. Teaching is a key characteristic of our church. Almost everything we do is related to teaching.
   b. Teaching is one of several ministries of our church. It is one part of our whole vision.
   c. We have classes for everyone who wants to study, but we do not expect everyone to be involved.
   d. We do not have regular classes. We offer classes depending on when we have teachers.
   e. Other: _____
3. Do you have classes for new believers? If so, please describe the classes and the lessons they study.
4. Do you have classes for water baptism or membership? If so, please describe the classes and the lessons.
5. Do you require workers and leaders to go through certain classes as part of their qualifications? If so, please explain.
6. Do you have classes to equip people for specific ministries? If so, please explain.
7. Does your CE include any kind of general education or supplemental education to meet the needs of people in your church or community? If so, what classes or programs do you have? (Think of education that functions as ministry, as in, no fees are paid.)
8. If you do have classes for the community, how do you use the Bible in these classes? (Choose all that fit your program.)

i. They do not use the Bible at all.
ii. They add a few Bible verses for encouragement.
iii. They use both Bible lessons and non-Bible lessons.
iv. They use the Bible as the main book to teach about other things.
v. They mainly teach Bible lessons to help the community.
vi. Other _____
9. Do you have other educational programs in your church that do not fit the questions above? If so, please describe them. (i.e., formal education, preschool, various classes with fees)

Teachers

1. Do you have written qualifications for teachers? If so, please provide me with a copy. If not, please describe the qualifications that you think are important for a CE teacher.
2. What is the process for selecting teachers? Who makes the decisions?
3. Do you have training for CE teachers? If so, please describe it.
    a. Do you have help from outside to train your teachers? If so, please describe it.
4. Does your church do things to show appreciation to your teachers? If so, what do you do? How often?
5. What is your general approach to curriculum? (I will ask for specific information for each class in a different place.)
    a. Do the teachers use prepared lessons or make their own lessons?
    b. If teachers make their own lessons, is there some guidance for them or do they have freedom to choose? Please explain your answer.
    c. If you use prepared lessons, what curriculum do you use? Please explain why you use that curriculum.
    d. Who makes the decisions regarding curriculum? Please describe your process for choosing curriculum.
6. Do you have church policy to protect children from abuse by teachers and to protect teachers from accusations by parents of children? If it is a written policy, please provide me with a copy. If it is not written, please describe your policy to prevent abuse and to address these kinds of problems, should they arise.

[separate page in Khmer]
Information for Each Class

Please provide the following information about each class/group in your CE.
1. Name of Class/Group
2. Ages/Grades
3. Class Times
4. Location
5. Teacher/s' (gender)
6. Curriculum/lesson (i.e., prepared, created by teachers)
7. Total number of students
   a. Male
   b. Female
8. How many of the students in this class attend worship services regularly?
9. What are the purposes of this class? (mark all that are true for this class)
   a. To make disciples
   b. To increase Bible knowledge
   c. To make sure the people in the church have received salvation
   d. To create opportunities for fellowship and strengthen relationships
   e. To provide care for one another
   f. To prepare people for ministry
   g. To build relationships with the community around our church
   h. To help the community around our church
   i. To evangelize the community around the church
   j. Other _____

APPENDIX C
TEACHER QUESTIONNAIRE

Name: _____ Telephone:_____
Church: _____
Class/Group you currently teach: _____
Date: _____

Thank you for participating in my research into Christian education in your church. I will keep all your answers private. Please be sure to write your name in case I have additional questions about your answers. Thank you, and may God bless you in your ministry of teaching.

Personal Information

1. Age:
2. Gender:
3. Marital Status:
    a. Single
    b. Engaged
    c. Married (how many years)
    d. Divorced
    e. Widowed
4. How many children do you have? What are their ages? Do you have grandchildren?
5. What is your education level? What diplomas have you received?
6. What is your job, vocation, or source of income?
7. How long have you been part of this church?
8. How long have you been a believer in Jesus?
9. Have you been baptized in water? If so, when?
10. Have you been baptized in the Holy Spirit with the evidence of speaking in tongues? Yes/No
    Do you continue to speak in tongues as part of prayer and worship?
    a. Regularly (every day, almost every day)
    b. Once or twice a week
    c. Only during worship at church
    d. Not regularly, once in a while
    e. No
11. In one week, how often do you have times of personal prayer and Bible reading?

12. Thinking from the time you first believed until now, what [plural in Khmer] had the most influence on the growth of your faith?

Teaching in the Church

1. How long have you been teaching in the church?
2. How did you begin teaching in the church? Who encouraged you to begin teaching?
3. How often do you pray for your students outside of class time?
    a. Daily
    b. Several times each week
    c. Once or twice a week
    d. Not regularly, once in a while
    e. Never
4. Do you give students opportunities to receive salvation in class?
   Yes _____ No _____
   If so, how often?
    a. Every class
    b. Once or twice a month
    c. Not regularly, once in a while
    d. Other _____
5. How many of your students do you know by name?
    a. All of them
    b. Most of them
    c. Less than half of them
    d. A few of them
    e. None
6. How many families of students do you know?
    a. All of them
    b. Most of them
    c. Less than half of them
    d. One or two of them
    e. None
7. Do you visit your students in their homes? Yes _____ No _____
   If so, how often?
    a. Every week
    b. At least once a month
    c. A few times a year
    d. Not regularly, once in a while

Appendix C   255

8. If you teach children or youth, do you talk with the parents/family of your students? Yes_____ No_____
   If so, when or why do you talk with them? (You can choose more than one.)
   a. When the student has behavioral problems in the class
   b. When I see the student has a personal problem (i.e., crying, sad, sick)
   c. To talk about the spiritual growth of their children
   d. To share the good news with the parents/family
   e. To invite the parents/family to church
   f. To encourage the parents/family in their faith
9. Have you received training for teaching in the church? If so, please describe it.

Roles of Teachers

Please read each sentence below that describes the roles of teachers. Then mark the box according how well you think it fits teaching in the church. Your answers are not correct or incorrect. I want to know your opinion.

	Weak	Good	Very Good
1. As a gardener takes care of plants, teachers nurture students to reach their potential as they naturally grow.			
2. As a tea pot pours liquid into a cup, teachers provide students with important knowledge and abilities.			
3. Teachers equip students with the knowledge and understanding they need for successful lives.			
4. Teachers lead students to experience truths that will transform their lives.			
5. Teachers and students are on the same journey in which they are learning from each other.			

Short Interview Questions

1. What do you like most about teaching in your church?
2. What is the most difficult part for you about teaching in your church?
3. Describe one area in which you want to grow as a teacher in your church.
4. Has your ministry of teaching in the church had an impact on your own spiritual growth? If so, please describe that impact.

APPENDIX D

CLASSROOM OBSERVATION PROTOCOL

Official class time: _____
Name/s of teacher/s (gender): _____
Note: The spaces for writing have been removed.

General Observations

1. Description of the teaching environment
   a. Room
   b. Lighting
   c. Air flow
   d. Cleanliness (swept) and orderliness (chairs and materials arranged)
2. Teacher's arrival time
3. Teacher's physical appearance (grooming)
4. Teacher's activities before class
5. Arrival times of students
6. Number of students present (by the end of the class)
   a. Female
   b. Male
7. How were the students groomed? Was there evidence of care (hygiene)?
8. Actual start and finish times
9. Teacher's activities after class (cleaning up, interacting with students, etc.)
10. Time of teacher's departure from the teaching environment
11. Topic or main point of the lesson and key Scripture text/s
12. List the main elements of the class (greeting, introduction, conclusion, etc.) or obtain a copy of the lesson plan.
13. If there was more than one teacher, what were their roles? How did they appear to work together (i.e., leader and assistants, tandem, etc.)? (This will be clarified in the follow up interview.)

General Descriptors

Strong—a key item for this class/teacher; exemplary
Very Good—skill in this item; very effective
Good—adequate; effective

Weak—minimal; ineffective or not very effective; only in passing or briefly touched on
N/P—not present but could relevant to this class
N/A—not applicable to this class

Lesson Content and Delivery

1.	Captured the interest of the students, directed them to the lesson	
2.	Topic or main point stated clearly (beginning of the lesson)	
3.	Lesson outline (if applicable)	
4.	Handling of the text (clear, adequate, correct interpretation)	
5.	Use of illustrations (verbal, stories, objects, pictures, etc.)	
6.	Applications of the text/lesson to daily life	
7.	Use of activities to reinforce the lesson (songs, games, crafts, discussions, etc.)	
8.	Continuity of lesson content (main point reinforced throughout, stayed on topic)	
9.	Flow of lesson elements (evidence of teacher preparation)	

Engagement between Teacher/s and Students

1.	Cultural expressions of respect (greetings, teacher/student or familial terms of address)	
2.	The teacher/s spoke clearly with enough volume for all to hear.	
3.	The teacher/s were enthusiastic about the class and the lesson.	
4.	The teacher/s were emotionally warm and showed personal interest in the students.	
5.	The teacher/s maintained control of the class proactively and positively. a. Gave clear and easy-to-follow instructions b. Did not have favorite students	

	c. Dealt effectively with disruptive students and unwanted behavior d. Did not use empty threats ("No snack today unless…")	
6.	Students responded positively and quickly to directions from the teacher/s.	
7.	Students demonstrated interest through body language and participation.	

Spiritual Atmosphere

1.	The teacher/s set a good spiritual tone through their example and demeanor.	
2.	List of prayer times and prayer leaders (teacher or students)	
3.	The teacher/s demonstrated respect for Scripture (holding the Bible, reading from the Bible, Bible-focused class)	
4.	Songs were used appropriately to praise and worship God.	

Follow up questions
Date, time, and location of interview:

1. If there was more than one teacher, please describe the roles of each person.
2. How much time did you take to prepare this lesson?
3. Did you create this lesson or use a prepared lesson? If you used a prepared lesson, what material did you use?
4. If you created the lesson, where did you get the idea?
5. If you used a prepared lesson, did you find it easy or difficult to use? In what ways was it easy or difficult to use?
6. If you used a prepared lesson, did you make changes to the original? If you made changes, describe the changes and your reasons for making changes.
7. How did you prepare yourself spiritually to teach today?
8. What problems did you encounter today in class? How did you manage each situation?

APPENDIX E

FOCUS GROUP PROTOCOL

Purpose

The purpose of this focus group is to meet with a selected group of knowledgeable leaders and teachers from the case to confirm the information and impressions of the researcher, and to gain additional perceptual information.

General

1. Time frame: one hour
2. Location: a room that is quiet enough to record the conversation with minimal interruptions
3. Handouts: Findings and questions for discussion
4. Recording: two recorders to ensure all voices are captured
5. Photographic/video record of participants
6. Ideal participants: five to six people
    a. Pastor
    b. 2 pillar leaders, not necessarily teachers
    c. 2-3 teachers, not key leaders
    d. It is possible for people to fill more than one role
    e. Mixed gender (not all male or all female)
    f. Note: The pastor has the authority to invite people to participate.

Greetings and Introductions

1. Greeting and introduction
    a. "Thank you all for coming to this focus group today. Thank you especially to Pastor _____ for allowing me to learn from your church's approach to CE. Thank you all for allowing me to visit your classes and join in with your church during my research."
    b. "I am going to present some of my findings from your church today. I have two purposes for this focus group:"
        i. "I want to check my information and my impressions about your church in the areas of organizational structure, teachers, and roles of your CE."

ii. "I want to ask for your views of teacher roles and your approach to CE compared to the national education system."
   c. "Please know that I am not evaluating your church or looking for 'correct' answers. I want to learn from your approach to CE and your rationale for that approach."
   d. "I will be recording our conversation on two devices so that I can listen to it later and record your responses accurately."
2. Identification of the participants
   a. Each participant states their name and role for the recording.

Presentation and Discussion of Findings

1. Organizational Model
   a. Basic chart (reproduction of their chart)
   b. Identification of "pillar leaders"
   c. Chart with genders
   d. What does this model say about your church? What do you think when you see this chart?
2. Teacher Questionnaire
   a. Demographics
   b. Answers to questions about personal experience and attitudes towards teaching
3. Class Information
   a. List of classes with basic information and demographics
4. Roles of CE
   a. Present the priority of teaching in each of the parts of the organizational model
   b. Ask participants to place each class on a spectrum of internal—mixed—external focus
      i. Internal:
         • Evangelism/conversion: people already in the church, people joining the church
         • Nurture: discipleship
      ii. External: community needs, less concern with conversion
      iii. Mixed: somewhere in the middle, can lean internally or externally

Appendix E 263

Discussion for Additional Perceptual Information

1. The five teacher models (group pile sort)
   a. Which of the five models is weakest for teaching in the church? Why?
   b. Which of the five models is strongest for teaching in the church? Why?
   c. Present the findings (strongest and weakest) from Teacher Questionnaire for this case.
      i. Rated strongest to weakest without the numerical values
2. Educational context
   a. How does teaching in your CE compare to teaching in the national education system? (Answer questions 1-5 for children's classes.)
      i. Which of the teacher models above are common in elementary schools (i.e., government schools)?
      ii. How would you describe relationships between teachers and students in elementary schools?
      iii. Do teachers know their students by name?
      iv. Do teachers meet with parents? If so, how often? What do they meet to discuss?
         - Refer to responses from Teacher Questionnaire for questions 6-9 (knowing students' names, knowing families, visiting, talking to parents).
      v. Compare the purpose of teaching in your church with the purpose of teaching in the national educational system.
      vi. Reflect on the above questions for junior high and high school teachers.
      vii. Reflect on the above questions for university teachers.

Zeal with KNOWLEDGE
The First Sixty Years of FEAST / APTS

WILLIAM W. MENZIES
JOHN F. CARTER
DAVE JOHNSON

New Expanded Edition

available at www.aptspress.org

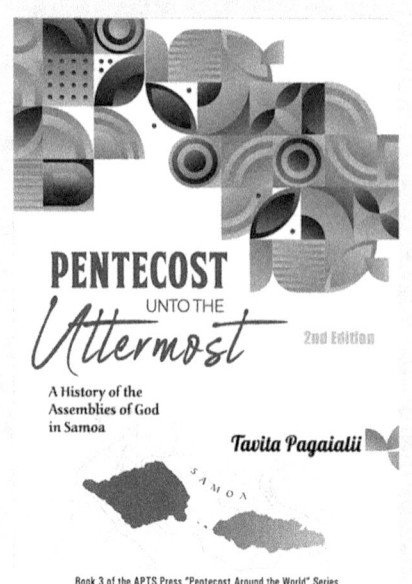

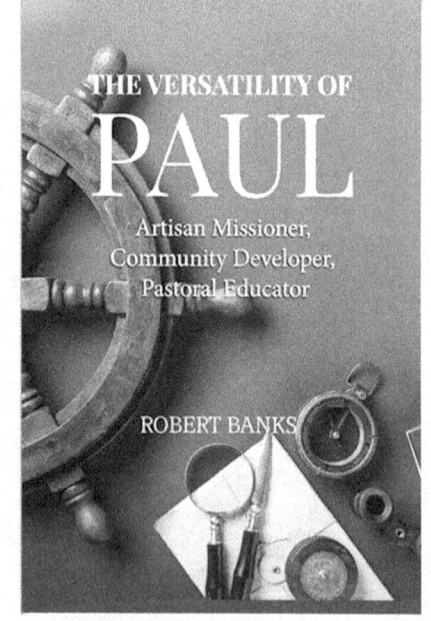

available at www.aptspress.org

available at www.aptspress.org

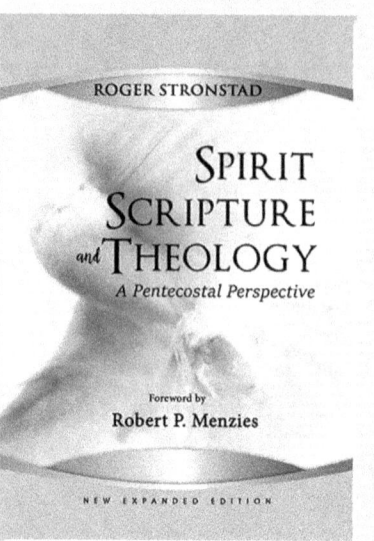

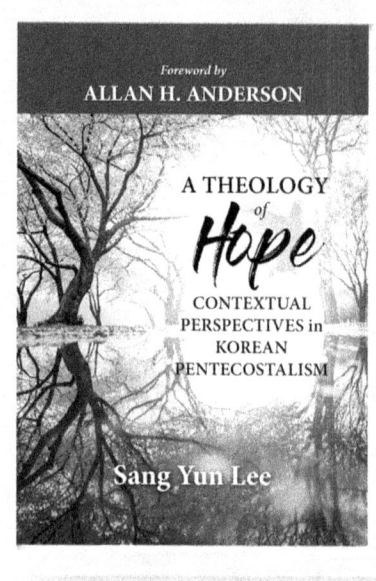

available at www.aptspress.org

APTS
Asia Pacific Theological Seminary

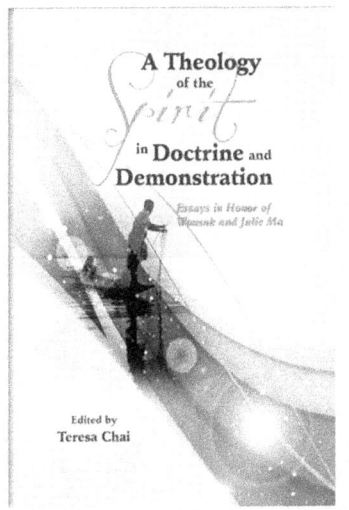

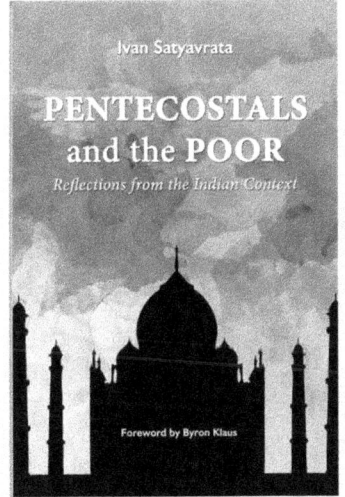

available at www.aptspress.org

available at www.aptspress.org

www.ingramcontent.com/pod-product-compliance
Lightning Source LLC
Chambersburg PA
CBHW071244230426
43668CB00011B/1582